The Essentials of Greek and Roman Law

The Essentials of Greek and Roman Law

Russ VerSteeg

CAROLINA ACADEMIC PRESS

Durham, North Carolina

Library of Congress Cataloging-in-Publication Data

VerSteeg, Russ.
The essentials of Greek and Roman law / Russ VerSteeg.
    p. cm.
Includes index.
ISBN 978-1-59460-556-7 (alk. paper)
1. Roman law. 2. Law, Greek. I. Title.

KJA172.V47 2009
340.5'38--dc22

                                        2009006433

CAROLINA ACADEMIC PRESS
700 Kent Street
Durham, North Carolina 27701
Telephone (919) 489-7486
Fax (919) 493-5668
www.cap-press.com

Printed in the United States of America

CONTENTS

PREFACE

Countless books detail the development of Roman law and explain the laws of the ancient Romans. Similarly, many scholars have traced the law of ancient Athens. I wrote THE ESSENTIALS OF GREEK AND ROMAN LAW with students and educated lay readers in mind. The chapters dealing with ancient Greece focus primarily on the law of ancient Athens in the 5th and 4th centuries B.C.E. But material relating to other Greek colonies and city states also plays a significant role in the development of ancient Greek law. The Roman law chapters explore both law and legal institutions and emphasize the growth and expansion of legal principles. Roman law still serves as the foundation for the civil laws of many nations today. And given the importance of globalization, Roman law is likely to continue to influence the modern world for the foreseeable future.

Each unit begins with a "Background and Beginnings" chapter that establishes the historical context in which law developed and introduces relevant principles of jurisprudence (*i.e.*, legal philosophy). The second chapter in each unit covers procedural aspects of the law, such as court structure, judges, trial procedure, evidence, and legislation. The remaining chapters examine substantive legal topics such as property, contracts, family law, criminal law, and the like. The text also maintains a focus on the connections and influences of social, cultural, economic, philosophical, and political forces as they have affected law and its development.

In addition, I have included several sections that are intended to add another dimension. These sections, entitled "Law in Literature," use works of ancient literature to explore aspects of law as seen through the eyes of poets, dramatists, orators, and historians. In theory, modern readers can learn a great deal about law through literature because literature often lacks the "official filter" of many traditional legal sources. Of course each individual author brings his own biases about law and the legal system to his writing. But as long as we acknowledge the potential for such bias, these sections can offer completely different perspectives and insights.

Several years ago I wrote LAW IN THE ANCIENT WORLD. That book surveyed law in ancient Mesopotamia, Egypt, Greece and Rome. I used the chapters on Greek and Roman law in that book as a starting point for writing THE ESSENTIALS OF GREEK AND ROMAN LAW. But I significantly rewrote, restructured, and/or revised virtually everything.

I would like to thank my daughter, Whitney Barclay VerSteeg, who read and provided useful criticism on the manuscript. Thanks also to Dean John O'Brien and the Board of Trustees of New England Law Boston who supported my work with an Honorable James R. Lawton Summer Stipend during the summer of 2008.

Russ VerSteeg
August 2009

The Essentials of Greek and Roman Law

CHAPTER 1

Background and Beginnings of Athenian Law

§ 1.01 Introduction

Scholars who specialize in ancient Greek law often observe that Greek law has failed to significantly influence the law of later societies. They have, in short, apologized for Greek law; concluding that "ancient Greek law has had a negligible influence on posterity."[1] Nevertheless, as MacDowell remarks in his influential book, *The Law In Classical Athens*, "[T]he attempt to understand the subject is worth making. Law is the formal expression of a people's beliefs about right and wrong conduct, and no people in the world has had more interesting and original beliefs about conduct than the ancient Greeks."[2] Besides, the Romans, who are world-famous for their influence on subsequent legal development, read and studied Greek philosophers who wrote about law. Thus, the ancient Greeks had a profound effect on legal progress and evolution, albeit in an indirect manner.

Much of what we know about the particulars of ancient Athenian law itself comes from over one hundred forensic speeches of the late 5th and early 4th centuries B.C. These speeches were written with the intention that they would be presented orally in court. In terms of our understanding of legal philosophy, we can turn to the abstract discussions of law in the writings of Greek philosophers. Especially relevant are Plato (*Laws, Republic*), Aristotle (*Nicomichean Ethics*), and Theophrastus, Aristotle's pupil, (*Laws*). But before we turn our attention to the laws of Classical Athens during its Golden Age in the 5th and 4th Centuries B.C., we shall first examine its antecedents in the 8th through 6th centuries B.C.

---

1. S.C. Todd, The Shape of Athenian Law 4 (1993) [hereinafter "Todd, Shape"]. *See also Id.* at 3 ("Law is one of the very few areas of social practice in which the ancient Greeks have had no significant influence on subsequent Societies.").

2. Douglas MacDowell, The Law In Classical Athens 8 (1977).

§ 1.02 The Earliest Greek Law

Our earliest evidence for law in ancient Greece comes from the poetry of Homer and Hesiod.[3] In Homer's *Iliad* and *Odyssey*, it is not unusual for individuals to resolve their conflicts simply by fighting. Quite often in the Homeric poems, persons seek vengeance as a means to redress wrongs, and that pattern of violent self-help was formative in early Greek law. Despite legendary traditions (which held that early Greek lawgivers were guided by gods), there is no historical evidence that early Greek law was founded on religious rules or divine commandment to restrain or remedy violence.[4]

In classical mythology, *Dikē* was a virgin daughter of Zeus. Early in Greek literature, writers began using the word "*dikē*" to refer to an orderly means of dispute resolution. Both Homer and the 8th Century B.C. poet, Hesiod, frequently referred to "*dikē*." Homer and Hesiod used the word *dikē* to refer to "law," "judgment," or in a more abstract sense "justice." Hesiod said that "*dikē* is a distinctive feature of human societies...."[5] According to Sealey in his book *The Justice Of The Greeks*, "the goal of *dikē* or of law is to resolve disputes without violence."[6]

In Homer we do see evidence that archaic Greek society was beginning to explore an orderly means of dispute resolution. There are a number of instances, for example, in the *Iliad* where quarrelling individuals appeal to an impartial outsider in order to resolve their differences. On several occasions, a king acts as arbiter. There are, of course, a number of reasons why a king is a logical person to resolve disputes. First, a king is likely to be older and therefore have considerable experience. Second, as a rule, kings are thought to have received divine inspiration. Third, kings hold authority by consent of the aristocracy whom they rule. In addition, a king ordinarily has the power, the brute force, to enforce his judgments.

---

3. Although Professor Gagarin himself frequently uses Homer and Hesiod as evidence for early Greek law, he cautions: "[W]e do find a few explicit rules of behavior ... [in Homer and Hesiod]. But these rules concern a broad range of human behavior, and none of them is singled out as having a special status, not even those rules that we might be tempted to call laws." MICHAEL GAGARIN, EARLY GREEK LAW 11 (1986) [hereinafter "GAGARIN, EARLY GREEK LAW"].

4. *See* GAGARIN, EARLY GREEK LAW 15–16 ("A common view of law ... is that the earliest law ... is strongly religious, only becoming fully secular in its later historical development. Whatever validity this view might have with respect to other societies, ... religious factors are of little significance in the earliest stages of Greek law.") (footnote omitted).

5. GAGARIN, EARLY GREEK LAW 49.

6. RAPHAEL SEALEY, THE JUSTICE OF THE GREEKS 102 (1994) [hereinafter "SEALEY, JUSTICE"].

Hesiod's poetry makes a strong plea for justice, and argues that "without an effective legal process the social order will disintegrate."[7] In his work entitled *The Theogony*, Hesiod noted that kings succeed when they give "straight judgments," provide "restitution," and speak with "soft words." In his poem called *The Works and Days*, Hesiod described the ordinary judicial procedure as one where individuals take their disputes to a king who then renders his decision.

In addition to kings giving judgments in Homer's *Iliad* and *Odyssey*, both epics depict instances where groups of elders—rather than an individual king—make judicial decisions. In those situations, the elders make their judgments in public; therefore public opinion presumably influenced the decision of the judges. One remarkable example of this procedure appears in Book 18 of Homer's *Iliad* when the god Hephaestus forges a new set of armor for the Greek hero Achilles. Among the many scenes that he fashions on the face of Achilles' shield, he engraves a trial scene; apparently at a tense moment in the midst of litigation.

> The people were assembled in the marketplace, where a quarrel had arisen, and two men were disputing over the blood price for a man who had been killed. One man promised full restitution in a public statement, but the other refused and would accept nothing. Both made for an arbitrator, to have a decision, and the people were speaking up on either side, to help both men. But the heralds kept the people in hand, as meanwhile the elders were in session on benches of polished stone in the sacred circle and held in their voices. The two men rushed before these, and took turns speaking their cases, and between them lay on the ground two talents of gold, to be given to that judge who in this case spoke the straightest opinion.[8]

This scene depicts a formal public dispute resolution mechanism at work. Sealey contends that the two litigants are actually arguing about different things: one argues that he has paid the price while the other maintains that he will not accept the payment. Thus, the dispute is really about whether the payment by the defendant is effective to make the plaintiff's argument irrelevant.[9] Apparently, then, the defendant has been accused of homicide but there is some argument about whether the payment, the "*poine*," either has been paid, or is,

---

7. GAGARIN, EARLY GREEK LAW 50. For a general discussion of Hesiod's views on justice and the legal implications of his poetry, *see Id.* at 46–50.

8. Homer, *Iliad*, bk 18, 497–508, at 388 *in Iliad of Homer* (R. Lattimore trans. 1976).

9. *See* SEALEY, JUSTICE 104.

for some other reason, not acceptable. According to the text, the two talents of gold had been set aside for a judge whom the people chose as having pronounced the most acceptable resolution to the dispute. It seems that each of several judges would have his chance to render an opinion, but that the public's opinion influenced the outcome. Thus, we can see, even as early as Homer, that Greek culture established a decidedly democratic approach to law.[10]

Gagarin offer this view of the Greek protoliterate judicial system:

> A judge who satisfied both litigants most of the time would gain a reputation for "justice," and once such a judge became well known, all those who basically accepted the social order and wished to have their disputes with their neighbors settled peacefully would naturally resort to this judge.[11]

In both Homer and Hesiod, using the procedure for dispute resolution was voluntary. Each litigant had to agree to submit his case to an arbitrator. It is not until later that dispute resolution evolved into a mandatory process. In addition to being voluntary, the procedure took place in a public forum, involved a judge or group of judges who tried to fashion a compromised settlement acceptable to both parties, and often involved the swearing of oaths. Furthermore, the formal, public dispute resolution procedure was in place long before any substantive laws regarding conduct were established.

§ 1.03 The First "Lawgivers" & Written Laws

A. Introduction

The first written laws began to appear in the Greek world in the mid-7th century B.C., and, by the close of the next century, many Greek cities had followed suit. Zaleucus is the Greek who, according to tradition, first wrote laws in 662 B.C. His laws were for a Greek colony in southern Italy. He was supposedly a shepherd who learned his laws (*nomoi*) from the goddess, Athena. Some scholars have suggested that Mesopotamian laws influenced Zaleucus' laws, but the evidence is inconclusive. He is known for simplifying contracts, for creating several procedural laws, and for providing stiff penalties for anyone

---

10. It is probably unwise to assume that all early Greek communities used an orderly procedure for dispute resolution like the one described on the Shield of Achilles. We must, rather, admit that this is merely one poet's representation. *See* Todd, Shape 33–35.

11. Gagarin, Early Greek Law 22.

who tried to change his laws. Legend has it that if someone wanted to suggest a change to his laws, that individual had to present his proposal with a noose around his neck. Thus, if the proffered amendment was rejected, the person making the proposal would be hanged immediately. This law illustrates the significance of legal procedure. In fact, it is important to emphasize that procedural laws predominate during this era when the Greeks first began writing laws. Gagarin accentuates this point: "By far the largest area of innovation ... was legal procedure, which ... was the area of greatest concern to the early lawgivers."[12]

The city of Dreros on the island of Crete in the 7th century also had written laws. And as the 6th century dawned, many other large Greek cities had begun to embrace written laws as well. Athens, Mytilene, Cyrene, and Greek colonies in southern Italy and Sicily enacted written laws. There was a distinct pattern for the cities that adopted written laws during this period. According to Gagarin:

> [I]n a time of civil strife a city would call for a special person, not currently a member of the ruling class (who would presumably be too partisan) and in some cases a foreigner, to write a set of laws for the city.[13]

In addition to Zaleucus, literary tradition has preserved the names of several other early Greek lawgivers; for example: Minos and Rhadamanthys of Crete (probably fictitious); Charondas of Katane; Philolaos of Corinth (who wrote laws for Thebes); Diokles of Syracuse; and, Demonax of Mantinea. Charondas supposedly prohibited sales made on credit; requiring that only cash payments would be permitted for sales transactions. He demanded that citizens serve as jurors and may have enacted a law of *lex talionis* (retribution).

The Gortyn Code from southern Crete represents an exceptional early attempt to codify ancient Greek law. This code was inscribed in twelve rather large columns that comprise part of a wall. There are over 500 lines of text dealing with various legal subjects such as marriage and family, inheritance, debtors, and procedure. Other shorter 6th century legal inscriptions have been

---

12. *Id.* at 78.

13. *Id.* at 60. *See also Id.* at 137 ("[T]he appointment of a lawgiver was an act of negotiation and compromise—the result of a long period of struggle in which all factions in the city came to understand that if a law code was to have public authority, it could not be enacted by a single group."). *See also* SEALEY, JUSTICE 25 ("A Greek city suffering internal strife sometimes invited a man or men from another city to come and draw up rules.").

found on Chios (*c.* 575–550 B.C.), at Argos, Thessaly, and Eretria (*c.* 550–525 B.C.). In addition to the most prevalent type of law, namely, legal procedure (often restricting the powers of magistrates), these inscriptions also show a great deal of concern for matters relating to family, property, and inheritance.

Sparta and Athens, the two city states that eventually came to dominate the Greek mainland during the Classical period of the 5th Century B.C., had distinctly different experiences at this critical time when written laws were sweeping through Greece. In Sparta, tradition maintained that Lycourgos was the lawgiver who, among other things, forbade the use of gold and silver coinage. Ironically, according to tradition, Lycourgos also prohibited written laws. One of the reasons that he did not want laws to be written was to afford flexibility for change in the future. In Athens, on the other hand, two famous lawgivers, Draco and Solon, initiated a strong tradition of written law. Their importance merits separate treatment.

B. Draco

According to tradition, Draco promulgated the first written laws in Athens in 621 B.C. Draco's laws were important and influential. If for no other reason, they were important because they were in writing. The ancient biographer Plutarch relates that death was the penalty for nearly every one of the offenses proscribed by Draco. But this reputation for severity probably arose because Draco provided for lethal self-help (not execution) for various offenses. However, our evidence today is actually weak regarding the particulars of Draco's laws. Although his laws were concerned with other offenses as well, one principal subject with which Draco's laws dealt was homicide. Even as late as the 4th century B.C., the Athenians attributed their laws relating to homicide to Draco, who had written them two centuries earlier. Draco's homicide law contained both substantive and procedural elements. Gagarin summarizes Draco's homicide law by saying that it "establishes exile as the penalty for homicide and then deals largely with procedural matters: the trial, the obtaining of pardon, and the protection of the killer from the threat of retaliation by self-help."[14] Draco recognized the procedures called *apagogē* and *endeixis*, which permitted the arrest of certain criminals as a substitute for unrestrained self-help.[15] Draco's laws helped to achieve two primary social objectives: 1) to curb violent conduct, particularly revenge; and, 2) to establish a judicial procedure that was mandatory rather than voluntary.

---

14. GAGARIN, EARLY GREEK LAW 63. For greater detail *see Id.* at 86–89.
15. *See infra* § 2.02.

C. Solon

In 594 B.C., Solon abolished most of Draco's laws but not those relating to homicide. Solon's laws were inscribed on wooden *axones* (four-sided wooden structures that could rotate to facilitate the reading of the laws). Orators of the 4th century B.C. frequently referred to the laws of Solon. These laws were extensive, covering many different substantive topics of law. Broadly speaking, for the sake of convenience, we may categorize his laws as: 1) Procedural; 2) Private; 3) Political; 4) Economic/Commercial; and, 5) Religious.[16] His greatest contribution to Athenian law appears to have been in procedural matters. Solon was responsible for inventing several important institutions of Athenian legal procedure: 1) the public cause of action that later came to be called *graphē* (permitting a third person to bring suit on behalf of another in certain circumstances);[17] 2) the procedure known as *dikē exoulēs* (permitting a creditor to sue on a rendered judgment (or verdict) that forced the defendant to pay a double penalty);[18] 3) *eisangelia* (providing impeachment for tyranny);[19] and, 4) *ephesis* (permitting a right of appeal to the popular courts).[20] In addition to these innovations, like several other early lawgivers, Solon decreed some fixed penalties. For example, he established a 100-drachma punishment for rape (apparently without abrogating the customary rule of self-help). Also relating to procedure, Solon enacted laws appertaining to witnesses and oaths.

Solon was responsible for a number of private family laws relating to matters such as adoption, marriage, dowries, inheritance, and the behavior of women. Under Solon's laws, private individuals were required to survey their real property, and were restricted in the manner in which they could build houses, dig wells, locate a beehive, and plant trees. Laws that regulated political activity concerned affairs such as citizenship, qualification for political office, taxes, and public meals. His laws also controlled many components of economic activity in Athens. In particular, some of Solon's economic laws dealt with mortgages, suretyship, debt slavery, interest rates, and agricultural ex-

---

16. But we cannot be certain just what *his* categories were nor how broad his scope. *See* TODD, SHAPE 55.

17. *See infra* § 2.02.

18. *See* GAGARIN, EARLY GREEK LAW 74. Professor Gagarin notes that *dikē exoulēs* was designed "to remedy one of the greatest weaknesses in Athenian (and other Greek) law, the difficulty of enforcing a verdict...." *Id.* Technically, *dikē exoulēs* did not require that a defendant pay double damages to the plaintiff/prosecutor. Rather, he paid the amount owed to the plaintiff/prosecutor plus the same amount as a fine to the State. *See also infra* § 2.14.

19. *See* GAGARIN, EARLY GREEK LAW 76. *See also infra* § 2.02.

20. *See* GAGARIN, EARLY GREEK LAW 73 (quoting Aristotle).

ports. As regards religion, Solon drafted rules dealing with public festivals and sacrifices.

D. The Impact of Written Laws

The early lawgivers were both recorders and innovators. To a certain extent, they merely codified a community's customs. But in doing so, they must have endeavored to harmonize inconsistencies and clarify ambiguities. In addition, they occasionally originated novel legislation to solve new problems. The mere fact that laws were written affected Greek communities in at least four profound ways: 1) it promoted equality in law; 2) it increased the use of the judicial system because it made legal procedure mandatory instead of voluntary; 3) it diminished the power of individual magistrates, by providing innovations such as term limits and a right of appeal; and, 4) it increased the authority of the *polis* over its citizens and all who lived there.

§ 1.04 The Evolving Vocabulary of "Law"

The Athenians never formulated precise legal definitions with the exactitude that we strive to achieve today in contemporary American law. Todd remarks: "Athenian law never developed a fully technical vocabulary precisely because there was no way for words to be legally defined."[21] In most cases there were no recognized experts to explicate the law. Well informed laymen, though, could recognize and explain technical vocabulary.

In the 4th century B.C., jurors swore an oath at the beginning of every year; not at the outset of each individual trial. Demosthenes gives the substance of the jurors' oath: "I will judge according to the laws and the decrees of Athens, and matters about which there are no laws, I will decide by the justest opinion."[22] The Greek word that was used for "laws" in the jurors' oath, "*nomos*", means "custom, way of life." It is "a term of a norm of action recognized by a society, what is agreed to be the right thing to do."[23] By the early 4th century B.C., the word "*nomos*" was adopted at Athens to mean "statute" or "written

---

21. TODD, SHAPE 205; *also see* SEALEY, JUSTICE 53.

22. MacDOWELL, THE LAW IN CLASSICAL ATHENS 44 (footnote omitted). *See also infra* §2.08.

23. MacDOWELL, THE LAW IN CLASSICAL ATHENS 44. The standard Classical Greek dictionary, *Liddell & Scott*, defines "*nomos*" as "that which is in an habitual practice, usage, custom." H.G. LIDDELL AND R. SCOTT COMPS., A GREEK-ENGLISH LEXICON 1180 (1977).

law." Early lawgivers, Draco in particular, used the word *"thesmos"* for their laws. The *Liddell & Scott* lexicon defines *"thesmos"* as "that which is laid down, law, ordinance."[24] Some scholars have argued that the gradual shift in terminology from *"thesmos"* to *"nomos"* illustrates a shift to a more democratic definition of law (*i.e.,* that which is acknowledged to be customary in society). As Plato argued in *The Laws,* community acceptance supersedes "the power of the ruler."[25]

§ 1.05 The "Reinscription" of Laws

Near the end of the Peloponnesian War, the great war between Athens and Sparta, in about 410 B.C., a special commission called the *Anagrapheis* was appointed to inscribe Solon's laws on stone. Shortly thereafter, the *Anagrapheis* undertook the task to inscribe Draco's homicide law also on stone. Between 410 and 404 B.C., the *Anagrapheis* reinscribed the laws of Solon and Draco, and thus made Athenian law more accessible, at least to the literate. According to Sealey:

> [T]he recorders were merely to transcribe the laws, that is, collect the scattered records with a view to stocking a central archive. Where contradictions were discovered, they were to be resolved by the council and assembly or from 403/2 B.C. for reasons of economy, by the board of lawgivers. Consequently, some measures, such as the law of Draco on homicide, were published anew on stone. But it is concluded there was no general publication of the whole list of laws.[26]

After the chaotic year of 404 B.C., and rule by "The Thirty," a special group, the *Nomothetai* ("law givers"), along with the *Boulē* ("council") established a new beginning of legal order in Athens. Initially the *Nomothetai* were selected from a portion of the jurors for that particular year. MacDowell states that: "no law passed before 403/2 was valid, henceforth unless it was included in the new inscriptions in the years from 410–403; no uninscribed law was to be enforced; no decree could override a law; and no prosecution could be brought henceforth for offences committed before 403/2."[27] From that time forward, the Ionic alphabet was used for all legal inscriptions. At that time (if not earlier), the Athenians established a central records office for keeping copies of

---

24. H.G. Liddell and R. Scott Comps., A Greek-English Lexicon 795 (1977).
25. MacDowell, The Law in Classical Athens 44.
26. Sealey, Justice 47.
27. MacDowell, The Law in Classical Athens 47 (footnote omitted).

the laws. It was also at this same time that a new procedure for enacting laws was established. Henceforth, the *Nomothetai* had to review and vote on every proposed change to a law that the citizen assembly, the *Ekklēsia*, handed down.[28] Furthermore, any new law first had to be proposed in writing and read aloud at three meetings of the *Ekklēsia*, (only at certain times of the year). As the 4th century progressed, both the restriction that laws could only be proposed at certain times of the year and the requirement that they had to be read aloud three times at the *Ekklēsia* fell into disuse.

§ 1.06 Justice & Jurisprudence: The Role of Law

It is well beyond the scope of this book to treat Athenian jurisprudence fully. Briefly, however, a surface-level glimpse into a few of the more salient works of Sophocles, Plato, and Aristotle is instructive. In them we see principles such as natural law, equality, and community as paramount legal influences. In Sophocles' play, *Antigone*, the character Antigone challenges King Creon by burying her brother in contravention of Creon's law. She argues that unwritten, immutable laws of god and heaven take precedence over mortal edicts. By traditional reading, her sympathetic position illustrates an Athenian ideal; namely, that there existed certain natural laws that superseded the positive legislation of humans (man-made laws).

A similar concept is discernable in Plato's (429–348 B.C.) *Republic*, in his metaphor of the shadows in the cave. The people in the cave perceive only one aspect of truth—like a ruler who enacts statutes—whereas the world outside the cave represents complete truth—like Antigone's universal, higher law. It is also in the *Republic* that Plato proposes that law's purpose is to benefit all people in a society not just any one class. According to Plato, law either persuades or compels citizens to unite, and it helps them to share the benefits that each individual is able to give the community. Plato asserts that one important function of law is to establish peace and unanimity in the midst of strife.[29] Plato believed that law was essential for a society to thrive. In the *Laws*, his last dialogue, Plato emphasizes two tenets: 1) that laws must apply equally to all; and, 2) that the voluntary acceptance of citizens to the rule of law is what gives it its

---

28. The Classical Athenian assembly of citizens was called the *Ekklēsia*. It was comprised of all male citizens who were at least 18 years old and older. It met about every nine days. TODD, SHAPE 294.

29. *Plato, Laws* 627–28.

force—not the government's foisting it upon citizens. In terms of equality, Plato insists that no one group can be permitted to acquire too much wealth nor can poverty be tolerated. Plato proposes that proper education should encourage citizens to desire the rule of law. This explains how law's strength will emanate from the voluntary acceptance of the citizens. In the *Laws*, then, Plato stresses that elective consent to law is important. For law to function properly, citizens must rationally believe that the laws are correct. Voluntary acceptance is preferable to coercion. And, for Plato, voluntary acceptance is natural law.

In the *Nichomacean Ethics*, Aristotle (384–322 B.C.) takes the position that an unjust man is one who either breaks the law or one who appropriates for himself more than his fair share. Therefore, for Aristotle, justice is something that should be both lawful and equal. Aristotle believed that natural law controlled ethical and political life. He postulates a distinction between natural law (that retains its validity in all times and places) as opposed to man-made laws (that are merely conventions adopted by communities with individual differences). Thus, although government creates positive law that is subject to change, natural law is universal and immutable. Aristotle also explains that there were two kinds of justice: 1) distributive justice; and, 2) corrective justice. Distributive justice relates to equality. Distributive justice operates to reward individuals for the benefits that they confer upon society. In simple terms, those who are equals receive equal rewards while those who are non-equals receive unequal shares. Corrective justice, on the other hand, relates to lawfulness. Judges exercise corrective justice when they punish criminals, award damages, or impose injunctions to settle disputes. For Aristotle, law is the operation of judgment in deciding right and wrong. Magistrates are the ones responsible for creating and administering law to bring about order for the community.

Thus, in the writings of Sophocles, Plato, and Aristotle, we recognize several different jurisprudential concepts. The distinction between natural law and positive law is prominent, as is the notion of equality. These writers saw law as an instrument to benefit society by supplying peace, equality, and unity.

§ 1.07 Chapter Summary

The law of ancient Greece is interesting in and of itself. In addition, because of its influence on the Romans, it indirectly helped to shape a great deal of later legal thought and development. Our most important sources for the details of ancient Athenian law are the forensic speeches of 4th century orators and, for information concerning abstract principles of the philosophy of law, Plato, Aristotle, and Theophrastus provide our best picture. Some of our earliest evidence for Greek law may be found in the poetry of Homer and Hesiod. They used the word *dikē* to refer to "law", "judgment", and "justice". They also depicted kings serving as judges. In addition, Homer shows a council of elders making judicial decisions. The famous trial scene in book 18 of the *Iliad* suggests that public opinion could play some role in the legal dispute process. Still, what is remarkable is that the Greeks in the protoliterate period seem to have employed a formal legal procedure for resolving differences.

A number of cities in the Greek world began adopting written laws as early as the middle of the 7th century B.C. Among the earliest to adopt written laws were the Athenians, cities in southern Italy, and communities on Crete, Mytilene, and Sicily. Typically, an individual "lawgiver" was responsible for producing a series of laws; and usually procedural laws received the most attention. Of particular importance was the Gortyn Code from southern Crete. In Athens, Draco is notorious for the severity of his laws (especially dealing with homicide), but that is probably because he legitimized potentially lethal self-help. Solon is best known for giving Athens a number of procedural, private, commercial, and religious laws, including *graphē*, *dikē exoulēs*, *eisangelia*, and *ephesis*. As regards substantive law, Solon's laws dealt with matters such as family law, inheritance, property, politics, commercial law, and religion. Written laws promoted equality, encouraged the use of the judicial system, placed additional power in the hands of ordinary citizens, and increased the power of the *polis* over its citizens. Lycourgos of Sparta, on the other hand, purposely chose not to adopt written laws, relying instead on unwritten laws for the sake of preserving flexibility.

Even though the Athenians did not develop an extensive legal vocabulary, they used two words to refer to law in different contexts. Both Draco and Solon used the word *thesmos* ("ordinance") for their laws. *Nomos* initially meant "custom" but gradually evolved to mean "statute" or "written law". At the close of the 5th century B.C., a special commission called the *Anagrapheis* collected the laws of Draco and Solon—the so-called "Reinscription of the laws." After the Reinscription, the *Nomothetai* ("law givers") had to approve every law after the *Ekklēsia* (citizen assembly) had first voted on it.

The works of playwrights and philosophers suggest that the ancient Athenians viewed law as a natural force and that law should promote social justice. Sophocles' character Antigone, for example, steadfastly believed that unwritten, universal natural laws were more important than man-made legislation. Plato argued that citizens must voluntarily accept the rule of law and that law should apply equally to all persons regardless of wealth and social standing. Aristotle recognized a distinction between natural law and man-made law. He also contrasted "distributive justice" (based on notions of equality) and "corrective justice" (based on notions of punishment).

CHAPTER 2

Legal Procedure, Institutions, and Organization

§2.01 Private & Public Arbitration; *Dēme* Judges

As is true in modern American law, ancient Athenians could submit a dispute to independent (*i.e.*, non-judicial) arbitration. Such arbitrations could be legally binding even prior to the Reinscription of the laws (410–403 B.C.). In order to be binding, the parties had to agree in advance: 1) who would serve as arbitrator(s); and, 2) what was the content of the question for the arbitrator(s) to resolve. Like other contracts in Classical Athens, an agreement to arbitrate did not have to be in writing. The only other requirement was that the arbitrator(s) had to take an oath before the arbitration began.

One of the best known examples of private arbitration in ancient Athens comes from Menander's comedy, *Epitrepontes*. A character named Daos finds a baby and gives it to another, Syriskos, to rear. Daos, however, wishes to keep the baby's valuable necklace. Syriskos objects. They waste virtually no time arguing but instead accost a total stranger on the street, Smikrines, and convince him to arbitrate their dispute. In a humorous scene, Smikrines ultimately decides in favor of Syriskos; and although Daos is displeased, he does, nevertheless, acquiesce and accepts the arbitrator's decision. In theory, private arbitration sounds great. But in practice, parties often had difficulty agreeing who should arbitrate. That is why public arbitration also came to be an important part of Athenian law. In the 4th century B.C., most disputes first went to a public arbitrator who sought to mediate a settlement.

At age 59 all male citizens were required to perform the civic duty of serving as public arbitrators. A plaintiff was responsible for paying the arbitrator's fee of one drachma. Arbitrators heard cases in public as the litigants argued their sides and presented evidence. Under Athenian law, a litigant could not produce evidence later at trial unless he had produced it first at the arbitration. Thus, litigants were compelled to take the compulsory public arbitration seriously and therefore assembled whatever evidence they could. On many occasions, an arbitration itself must have consumed several days. When an arbitrator made his decision, he related it forthwith to the four tribe judges who had referred the case to him in the first place. According to MacDowell, "[i]f both disputants accepted the arbitrator's judgement, it was final. But either could appeal against it."[1] One could accept or appeal judgement

By the middle of the 5th century B.C., there were 30 *dēme* judges who rotated throughout Attica. There is insufficient evidence about them to know how they were appointed or anything of substance about their procedures or the disputes that they heard. In about 400 B.C., the number of *dēme* judges was increased to 40. Each of the ten tribes now picked four judges by sortition. "The Forty" (as they came to be called) heard the majority of private cases brought by means of a *dikē* (except cases under the jurisdiction of the *archon* or *thesmothetai*).[2] A plaintiff first took his complaint to the four judges from his own tribe. If the amount in dispute was ten drachmas or less, they could decide the matter by themselves. If the amount in controversy was more than ten drachmas, the tribe judges were required, after 399 B.C., to refer the case to a public arbitrator. And this is the only way that a public arbitrator got a case.

§ 2.02 The Vocabulary of Athenian Legal Procedure

In order to understand Athenian procedure, it is worthwhile to be familiar with several terms. The word used for a law case, or lawsuit, ordinarily is *dikē*. Although technically speaking a private case was called a *dikē idia* and the term for a public case was *dikē demosia*, the word *dikē* evolved to mean basically a private action and the most common procedure for bringing a public action came to be called *graphē*. As has been noted,[3] tradition credits Solon with having introduced the procedure by which a volunteer could instigate a suit on behalf of a third party or regarding matters that affected the community at large. This is the procedure that came to be called *graphē*. Thus, as early as the laws of Solon (594 B.C.), the Athenians recognized certain wrongs that should be pun-

---

1. MacDowell, The Law in Classical Athens 209.
2. For more regarding the *archon* and *thesmothetai*, *see infra* §2.05.
3. *See supra* §1.03[C].

ished in the public interest. In this way, Solon's laws made it possible for an individual, in certain circumstances, to bring a law suit to avenge wrongs committed against a third party. This "volunteer prosecutor" could only act in certain types of cases. Nevertheless, this innovation of Solon's laws became an important component in Athenian law thereafter. A number of scholars have also noted that the "volunteer prosecutor" aspect of Athenian procedure, in Cohen's words, "enhanced the opportunities for individuals to manipulate legal institutions to serve private purposes."[4] In fact, a great deal of Athenian litigation appears to have been the result of the upper classes using the court system as a tool that was integral in advancing their personal enmities and feuds.[5] "[M]uch litigation should be viewed as a form of feuding behavior, and ... it was acknowledged as such by Athenian judges and litigants."[6]

In addition to the general term *graphē*, which literally means "writing," the Athenians had several other specialized terms for different types of public cases which volunteer prosecutors could bring; often called "summary procedures." Different types of cases permitted different procedural avenues. The most prominent of these procedures were as follows. 1) *Apagogē*: The volunteer prosecutor arrests the defendant first and then brings him to the competent official (forcibly if necessary). 2) *Ephegesis*: The volunteer prosecutor leads the magistrate to the defendant for arrest. 3) *Endeixis*: The volunteer prosecutor first explains the charge to the magistrate and is then authorized to make the arrest. 4) *Apographē*: The volunteer prosecutor lists property wrongfully held by the defendant, property that rightfully belongs to the State. 5) *Eisangelia*: First the volunteer prosecutor denounces the defendant to the *Ekklēsia* or *Boulē* or to the Archon—the latter in cases concerning mistreatment of an orphan or "heiress."[7] 6) *Probolē*: A preliminary hearing at the *Ekklēsia* regarding official misconduct. 7) *Dokimasia*: A hearing where a candidate might be disqualified from citizenship, public office, or speaking in the assembly (*Ekklēsia*). 8) *Euthynai*: Review of performance in public office.

As was mentioned, most often private cases were simply called *dikē*. The word *dikē* was used to refer to a case concerning matters that did not relate to the community as a whole but rather only to an individual: "a private ordinary prosecution, as opposed to a *graphē*."[8] In the case of a *dikē*, only the in-

---

4. DAVID COHEN, LAW, VIOLENCE AND COMMUNITY IN CLASSICAL ATHENS 21 (1995) [hereinafter, "COHEN, LAW, VIOLENCE AND COMMUNITY IN CLASSICAL ATHENS"].

5. *See Id.* at 23, 72, 83, 87, 101, 112, 183, 188, 194.

6. *Id.* at 87.

7. *See infra* §§ 5.02, 6.01.

8. TODD, SHAPE 100.

dividual himself who actually had been wronged could act as the plaintiff/prosecutor. Cases involving homicide were *sui generis*, since the victim, himself, was unable to prosecute. Nevertheless, homicide was still considered a *dikē* (*dikē phonou*), and the term *graphē* was not used in homicide cases of this type (though some homicides could be prosecuted by *apagogē* or *endeixis*).

This multiplicity of procedures led to considerable confusion and overlap. For example, theft could be prosecuted by *apagogē*, *ephegesis*, *graphē*, or *dikē*. However, only the established procedures could be used.

In addition to the cases which could be brought by "volunteer prosecutors," some cases could be brought by public prosecutors called *Synēgroi* ("supporting speakers").[9] The *Synēgroi*, as a rule, only brought actions against men who were acting in an official capacity. The *Synēgroi* were ten citizens selected by lot who were paid one drachma per day.

§ 2.03 Litigation Procedure

The ancient Athenians had a reputation for being extremely litigious. In Aristophanes' comedy *The Clouds*, when someone points to a city on a map of Greece and claims that it is Athens, the character, Strepsiades, protests that it cannot be Athens because he does not see courts in session. Although there was a great deal of litigation, it is curious to modern sensibilities that "neither judges nor litigants had any formal legal training and the system as a whole relied almost entirely upon the initiative of private citizens."[10]

Although a few types of legal claims could be filed on any day of the year, many could only be instituted on particular days and only in particular months. Therefore, a would-be plaintiff/prosecutor had first to consult the judicial calendar to make sure that he was filing his suit during the right kind of month and on the right kind of day. Generally speaking,[11] a plaintiff/prosecutor's first formal step was to issue a summons (*prosklesis*) to the defendant, in the pres-

---

9. *See* MacDowell, The Law in Classical Athens 61.

10. Cohen, Law, Violence and Community in Classical Athens 61.

11. Some notable exceptions include cases brought by the following procedures: 1) *Apagogē* (the procedure by which an accuser personally arrested a thief and escorted him to The Eleven); 2) *Ephegesis* (the procedure by which an accuser went directly to The Eleven and notified them of the whereabouts of a thief); and 3) *Endeixis* (the procedure by which an accuser alleged that a disenfranchised man had gone into a prohibited area). *See* MacDowell, The Law in Classical Athens 238.

ence of a witness.[12] This summons alerted the defendant to three crucial facts: 1) the specific date on which the defendant was to appear; 2) the magistrate(s) before whom the defendant was to appear; and, 3) the alleged wrong for which the defendant was to appear.

On the established day, the plaintiff/prosecutor filed his claim in writing and paid a filing fee (*prytaneia*) of 3 or 30 drachmas (depending on the amount in dispute). If the plaintiff/prosecutor prevailed at trial, the defendant had to reimburse him for the *prytaneia*. The magistrate who heard the initial complaint (on that day when it was originally filed) also then scheduled another formal hearing, a pre-trial conference (*anakrisis*). At the *anakrisis* the magistrate read the complaint aloud and asked the defendant to admit or deny the allegations. Both parties vowed that they were telling the truth and the magistrate questioned them. If the defendant wished to raise a procedural challenge to the claim by *paragraphē*, this was the time to do so.[13] The Athenians used this pretrial conference to delineate and clarify the triable issues. At the conclusion of the *anakrisis*, the magistrate then assigned a trial date (unless it was a case before the four tribe judges, in which case the matter went directly to a public arbitrator).[14]

At a trial's beginning, a court clerk announced the case and recited the complaint for all to hear. If one of the parties was absent and had a legitimate excuse (*e.g.*, he was sick, or, he was out of town for some appropriate reason), a friend could appear on his behalf and swear an oath as to the party's justification for his absence. The jury then voted either: 1) to postpone the trial due to the party's excused absence; or, 2) to grant the party in attendance a default judgment. Of course, if one of the parties failed to appear and no one offered an excuse on his behalf, the jury automatically granted the party in attendance a default judgment. A party who was the victim of a default judgment could, however, resuscitate his case if within two months he could demonstrate good cause for his failure to appear on the original trial date.

The Athenians managed to finish almost all of their trials in one day or, very often, less than a full day. After the clerk's reading of the complaint, the plaintiff/prosecutor spoke first, followed then by the defendant. Evidently, in pri-

---

12. Todd notes: "The exception was the threefold procedure of *apagoge, endexis*, and *ephegesis*, where summons (and sometimes also indictment) were replaced by summary arrest." TODD, SHAPE 125 n. 3. *See also* MACDOWELL, THE LAW IN CLASSICAL ATHENS 238.

13. *See infra* § 2.04[B].

14. *See supra* § 2.01. Another exception to this general rule was for homicide cases where the Basileus scheduled three *prodikasia* (pre-trial conferences) for three straight months. *See infra* § 7.02[C].

vate cases (*i.e.,* those brought by *dikē*), the plaintiff and defendant each made a second speech as well. But in public cases (*i.e.,* those brought by *graphē*), the prosecutor and defendant were limited to just one oration per speaker (though several might speak on each side). Athenian law restricted the time allowed for speeches and, thus, court personnel timed them with a water clock (*klepsydra*).[15] The permissible duration of a speech varied depending upon the type of case (*i.e., graphē* or *dikē*) and also depending on whether it was the litigant's first or second speech in the trial.

Each litigant represented himself and pled his own case on his own behalf (*i.e.,* without an advocate).[16] Litigants, however, routinely hired speech writers, called *logographoi,* to construct their written arguments for them. Each *logographos* acted like a ghost writer, attempting to forge a compelling story of facts, laws, logic, reason, and proof. In effect, these were the Athenian trial lawyers (or nearest approximation thereof). Most scholars believe that litigants memorized and recited the speeches written by their *logographoi*—rather than reading them aloud—in an attempt to give an impression of spontaneity, candor, and sincerity. In addition to presenting logical argumentation and proof, Athenians were not above using pure sympathy and emotional appeals. For example in Aristophanes' play *The Wasps,* a juror describes a litigant who "drags his children out in front—all his little girls and boys" who "all grovel in a heap, bleating."[17] The litigant then implores the jury to "hear the cry of my son" and "let my daughter persuade thee."[18] The juror even admits, "And after that, perhaps, I relax my severity a little."[19]

The jury voted without deliberation as soon as the litigants concluded their speeches. Unlike modern American trial procedure, the presiding Athenian magistrate did not provide the jury with a summation nor did he impart jury instructions to advise the jury how they should apply legal rules to the facts of the case. Each juror individually had to decide how to vote. Because the jurors, the *dikastai,* did not articulate the reasons for their decisions, it is doubtful that any given case could really have precedential force for a subsequent case—certainly not in the modern common law sense of precedent. However,

---

15. The *klepsydra* "was allowed to flow during the speech itself and was blocked up for the reading of evidence." Todd, Shape 130. *See also* MacDowell, The Law in Classical Athens 249.

16. Occasionally a litigant also asked a close friend or relative to speak on his behalf as a "supporting speaker." *See* MacDowell, The Law in Classical Athens 250–51.

17. Aristophanes, Wasps 58 (David Barrett trans. 1964).

18. *Id.*

19. *Id.*

in one speech involving an accusation of *hubris*,[20] Demosthenes did encourage his jury to set a precedent.

Although the precise physical mechanics of voting did change during the Classical period, throughout both the 5th and 4th centuries jurors recorded their votes by using small tokens that they dropped into urns. In the 5th century, jurors voted by placing a pebble or shell into one of two urns; one marked for the prosecutor/plaintiff, and the other marked for the defendant/accused. In the 4th century, jurors went to court with two kinds of tokens in their possession: a bronze disk with a solid shaft in the middle and a bronze disk with a hollow shaft in the middle. Jurors voted for a *plaintiff/prosecutor* by placing the bronze disk with the *hollow shaft* in its middle into an urn for registering votes; and voted for a *defendant/accused* by placing the bronze disk with a *solid shaft* in its middle into an urn for registering votes. They dropped their other bronze disk (*i.e.,* the one that they did not intend to count) into a different urn designated as the urn for discarded or invalid votes. When each juror had recorded his vote by placing his token(s) into the appropriate urn(s), the votes were counted and a simple majority decided the case (a tie going to the defendant/accused).

If the plaintiff/prosecutor had prevailed, the jury's last duty was, then, to assess the defendant's/accused's penalty or damages owed to the plaintiff/prosecutor.[21] Ordinarily, the jury simply picked between two alternatives that the litigants each offered in yet another (much shorter) speech: one penalty proposed by the successful plaintiff/prosecutor; and the other penalty submitted by the vanquished defendant/accused. Obviously, it was in the defendant's/accused's best interest not to suggest a penalty that was *too* lenient lest the jury reject it in a perfunctory manner in favor of the plaintiff/prosecutor's (obviously harsher) proposal.

§ 2.04 Pleading & Forms of Action

A. *Diamartyria*

In some cases a litigant could assert his rights simply by having a witness affirm decisive facts before the magistrate. In one instance, a defendant was able to bar a suit for damages simply by having a witness affirm that the case was

---

20. *See infra* § 7.06.

21. "In some types of trial, no decision was required, because it was already fixed by statute; in others, the law permitted a range of penalties...." TODD, SHAPE 133–134.

already settled. This procedure was called *diamartyria*.[22] MacDowell says, "*Diamartyria* was a formal assertion of fact by a witness who was in a position to know it."[23] According to Todd, "It is normally produced on behalf of the defendant, to show reason why the case must be halted; but in one case it is used for the plaintiff, to show why it must continue...."[24]

B. *Paragraphē*

In about the year 400 B.C., the Athenians began to realize that not all challenges to jurisdiction or other procedural flaws could be resolved simply by relying on someone's bare assertion of fact (*diamartyria*). Thus, one of the most important procedural devices in Athenian law came into being: *paragraphē*. *Paragraphē* became the commonest way for a defendant to mount a procedural challenge to a plaintiff's case in the 4th century B.C. "*Paragraphē* probably means 'prosecution in opposition', 'counter-prosecution'; and the procedure was essentially a separate trial in which the original prosecutor was himself prosecuted for bringing a prosecution in a way forbidden by law."[25] "The original case was postponed until the *paragraphē* case was decided; the result of the *paragraphē* trial settled whether the original case should proceed or not."[26] In short, the *paragraphē* was a technical, legal mechanism employed by defendants in an effort to short-circuit a plaintiff's case. In the 4th century, defendants used *paragraphē* to assert what modern American law recognizes as a variety of procedural defenses. For example, it was used to assert the same as the following modern procedural challenges: 1) *res judicata* (*i.e.*, an assertion that another court has already adjudicated the same issue); 2) statute of limitations (*i.e.*, the period of time within which a claim of the nature at issue should have been brought has already passed); 3) lack of subject matter jurisdiction (*i.e.*, the court is not authorized to adjudicate claims of the nature at issue); and, 4) statute of frauds (*i.e.*, certain types of contracts must be in writ-

---

22. If a defendant tried to claim that the court lacked jurisdiction to decide a case (for example, arguing that the plaintiff was an alien, and, thus, that the polemarch (*See infra* §2.05) should be hearing the case instead of the tribe judges), the plaintiff could produce a witness to counter such an assertion. For example, a witness could claim that the plaintiff was in fact an Athenian citizen.

23. MacDowell, The Law in Classical Athens 212.

24. Todd, Shape 136(citation omitted).

25. MacDowell, The Law in Classical Athens 215. *See also* Todd, Shape 136 ("It is a counter-prosecution, by means of which the original defendant charges his opponent with attempting to bring an illegal prosecution.").

26. MacDowell, The Law in Classical Athens 215.

ing in order to be considered valid). *Paragraphē* was, however, not without financial risk. The unsuccessful party in the *paragraphē* had to pay one-sixth of the amount in dispute.

§ 2.05 Organization & Personnel: Judges, Courts, & Calendars[27]

Although Athens may have been ruled by kings at some early point, by the Classical period she was ruled by nine archons. The Archon Eponymous (who gave his name to the year) controlled property and family matters. Another archon, called the "Archon Basileus," was responsible for laws regarding religion, homicide, and acts of deliberate wounding. A third archon, called the "Archon Polemarchus," was responsible for law dealing with non-Athenians. In addition to these three, there were six *Thesmothetai*. They were in charge of many other types of cases. The Board of Generals, the *Strategoi*, had jurisdiction in military affairs. In addition to these, there were a number of additional officials responsible for many other aspects of Athenian legal life. For example, the officials called the *Agoranomoi* and the *Sitophylakes* settled commercial disputes in the marketplace.

In the 7th and 6th centuries B.C., as written laws and juries became commonplace throughout the Greek world,[28] the subjective power of each individual magistrate decreased. The existence of written laws and the presence of a jury as a decision-making body curtailed the discretion of the magistrates.

In Athens in the 7th century B.C., the aristocratic council called the *Areopagus* held virtually unlimited power; particularly with respect to serious offenses such as intentional homicide, wounding, arson, the destruction of sacred olive trees, and tyranny.

The complexity of Athenian society increased as the Athenian Empire grew during the 5th century B.C. Along with heightened complexity came the need for a more organized legal system. Thus, the Athenians began formulating a judicial calendar. They assigned certain types of cases to be heard during certain months. It is possible that by scheduling cases in this manner, they hoped to make attending trials more convenient for those who were from the member states of their Delian League.[29] A decree from 445 B.C. mentions for the

---

27. *See generally* MACDOWELL, THE LAW IN CLASSICAL ATHENS 25–28, 224–233.

28. *See supra* § 1.03[A].

29. Following the Persian Wars (*c.* 479 B.C.) the Athenians formed the Delian League; an association comprised of Athens, herself, and numerous island states that pooled their

first time a group of magistrates called *nautodikai* ("judges of sailors"). The *nautodikai* handled cases involving Athenians who either lived overseas or sailed as mariners or merchants. During the 5th century, Athens formed a board called the *xenodikai*, judges of foreigners. We know precious little about how the *nautodikai* and *xenodikai* operated in the 5th century. Nevertheless, their mere existence attests to the Athenian desire to construct a more organized legal framework in the wake of their burgeoning empire.

Around 350 B.C. the Athenians abolished both the *xenodikai* and *nautodikai*. Presumably, persons with commercial interests in Athens (both citizens and foreigners) had become exasperated with the sluggishness of the legal machinery. The *thesmothetai* henceforth maintained jurisdiction to hear cases involving merchants and shipmasters, the *dikai emporikai* ("mercantile cases"). A new law permitted litigants to bring *dikai emporikai* on a monthly basis, from the Athenian months called "*Boedromion*" through "*Mounikhion*" (roughly September-April).[30] Thus, sea merchants and other traders could conduct commercial business during good sailing weather and resolve their legal differences during the time of year when it was precarious to venture out to sea anyway. In terms of administrative efficiency, it is significant that the *dikai emporikai* were available to, and applied to, both citizens and non-citizens. The *dikai emporikai* were, however, narrowly defined. These cases could only be initiated if the dispute at issue pertained to an alleged breach of a *written* contract that either: 1) had been concluded in the Athenian Market itself; or, 2) related to a transaction that involved shipping either into or out of the Athenian Market.

The success of categorizing a group of cases and scheduling them to be heard by a certain adjudicative body at specific times was not lost on the ancient Athenian lawmakers. Soon they began establishing other case categories with their own judicial schedules. For example, there was a category comprised of tax-collecting cases, a category comprised of mining cases, and a category for financial/banking cases.

By the late 4th century, the Athenian court system was divided into distinct jurisdictional classifications dependent upon either the subject matter of the dispute or the status of one of the litigants. However, as Todd puts it, "[a]lthough they presided over the court, they [*i.e.*, the presiding magistrates] had no right of jury direction, no right to rule evidence or arguments out of order, and no

---

financial and naval resources in an effort to provide protection and to serve as a deterrent to further Persian aggression. *See* CYRIL ROBINSON, HISTORY OF GREECE 127 (1965).

30. But some legal historians theorize that the months should be transposed; thus meaning that the cases were brought only *during* the summer. *See* TODD, SHAPE 335.

power of summing up."[31] The magistrates and their respective jurisdictional spheres were as follows:

1) **Archon Eponymous.** Cases involving inheritance and other matters among family members. Cases relating to particular religious festivals.
2) **Basileus.** Homicide cases. Cases pertaining to religion.
3) **Polemarch.** Cases relating to metics (*i.e.*, resident aliens).[32]
4) **Thesmothetai.** *Dikai emporikai* (mercantile cases), cases regarding treaties with other states, and a variety of other public cases.
5) **The Eleven.** Cases involving *kakourgoi*,[33] and cases that required a defendant to be incarcerated while awaiting trial.
6) **Agoranomoi.** Cases involving disputes brought in the Agora (the Athenian Market).
7) **Sitophylakes.** Cases concerning grain and grain sellers.
8) **Epimelētai Tou Emporiou.** Cases involving the sale of grain in the wholesale market that was conducted in the Athenian port, the Peiraeus, at the *Emporion*.
9) **Eisagogeis.** Pecuniary cases related to loans and banking.
10) **The Forty.** The majority of private cases brought by means of a *dikē* (except cases under the jurisdiction of the Archon, *Thesmothetai*, or some other specialized court).

§ 2.06 Cases Involving Non-citizens

Originally, the Polemarch probably was responsible for initiating cases involving a non-citizen (*i.e.*, when the non-citizen was either prosecutor or defendant). By the mid-5th century the Polemarch was too busy to handle all cases involving foreigners. Thus, new magistrates called *Xenodikai* were created to handle certain kinds of cases pertaining to foreigners. Later, somewhere around 400 B.C., most public cases relating to aliens were transferred from the Polemarch and the *Xenodikai* to the same courts as public cases involving citizens. By the middle of the 4th century, there were probably few procedural distinctions between a case involving a metic versus a case involving a citizen.[34]

---

31. Todd, Shape 79.
32. *See infra* § 3.02.
33. *See infra* § 7.03.
34. *See infra* Chapter 3 regarding metics and citizens.

§ 2.07 *Graphē Paranomēn*

In order to keep their laws conservative and devoid of rash changes, the Athenians used a procedure called *graphē paranomēn* ("prosecution for illegalities"). This was in use by the late 5th century to block decrees that contradicted or conflicted with established laws. A person found guilty of *graphē paranomēn* three times was punished by *atimia* (*i.e.*, a kind of disenfranchisement).[35]

In the early 4th century, when *laws* were significantly distinct from *decrees*, improper laws could be challenged by a suit "for submitting unsuitable law." Simply stated, when an individual proposed a law, he was subject to the accusation that his proposal conflicted with an existing law. If the proposer was found guilty, his new law was invalidated and he was fined. In the year 382 B.C., one jury even imposed the death penalty. There was, however, a statute of limitations of one year, after which the legislator could no longer be punished, but his law could still be invalidated.

§ 2.08 Juries

In 594 B.C., Solon redirected judicial decision-making authority from the magistrates[36] to the people. The assembly of all Athenian citizens (*i.e.*, all Athenian males over the age of 18) was called the *Ekklēsia*.[37] However, when the *Ekklēsia* was convened for a judicial purpose, it was referred to as the *Heliaia*. Solon's new law permitted a citizen to appeal a magistrate's decision (at least regarding some types of decisions) to the *Heliaia*. The *Heliaia* then could hear the case *de novo* and render a judgment in the matter. However, a citizen's right of appeal was not absolute and was probably only available in certain types of cases. Because Solon gave citizens a right of appeal, the entire judicial process ultimately changed. By the 5th century B.C., magistrates simply held an initial hearing and then arranged for the *Heliaia* to conduct a trial. At that trial, the magistrate presided and then pronounced the jury's verdict. We cannot pinpoint an exact date for this change. It was probably evolutionary during the 6th and 5th centuries B.C. Simply stated, since an appeal became certain, it became pointless for a magistrate to render a decision. This change was firmly in place by the end of the 5th century B.C.

---

35. *See infra* § 3.01.
36. *See supra* §§ 1.03[C] and 2.05.
37. *See infra* § 3.01 regarding citizenship.

Because the *Ekklēsia* was such a large group, it was impractical for it to convene on a regular basis to function as a jury. Therefore, by the middle of the 5th century B.C., Athens began using a representative jury system. In the 450's B.C., Pericles instituted pay for jury service. In order to serve on an Athenian jury, one had to be at least 30 years old and a male citizen. Six thousand jurors were selected by lot every year. They did not, however, sit every day on jury service. In order to be eligible to serve as a juror for the coming year, at the beginning of every year, each *dikastes* was required to swear the "dikastic oath." As it has been preserved for us, the dikastic oath states: "I will vote in accordance with the laws and decrees of the people of Athens and of the council of five hundred, and on matters where there are no laws, I will vote in accordance with the most just opinion."[38] A juror was paid two *obols* per day for his work. In 425 B.C., payment for jury service was increased to three *obols* per day. Some historians have suggested that pay for jury service may have helped representation of the poorer classes. Many who served on juries were old men for whom jury pay was like an old-age pension. The playwright Aristophanes painted a rather comic portrait of jury service in his play, *The Wasps* (422 B.C.). By the 4th century B.C., juries were customarily comprised of 500 jurors. In addition to the normal number of 500, we know of certain special occasions when juries consisted of 1,000, 1,500 and 2,000 jurors.

The system of jury selection was elaborate. When the system began, jurors were selected by lots drawn from containers on the morning of their prospective jury duty. At the beginning of every year, jurors were assigned to a panel designated by a particular letter of the alphabet. All jurors who had the same letter would go to the same court on any given day. Based on evidence in the plays of Aristophanes, it appears that this system was still in place in the 390's and 380's B.C. By the 370's B.C., the system of jury selection was changed to a far more complicated system. The new system involved selection using black and white balls (or cubes) as well as a *pinakion*. A *pinakion* was a wooden or bronze "ticket" that had each juror's name on it and one of the first ten letters of the alphabet, as well. The black and white balls were sorted in an allotment machine called a *klēroterion*. In addition to the use of the balls and the *pinakion*, colored sticks were also used to determine which court (if any) a particular

---

38. SEALEY, JUSTICE 51. According to Todd, "The opening words of the oath promise to give a verdict 'in accordance with the *nomoi* (laws) and the *psephismata* (decrees) of the Athenian *demos* (*i.e.*, the *Ekklēsia* or assembly) and of the *Boulē* (council)." TODD, SHAPE 54. *See also Id.* at 83. Apparently, the jurors had two tasks: 1) to apply laws and decrees; and, 2) to decide what was most just in the absence of laws and decrees. SEALEY, JUSTICE 51–52.

juror might go to on a given day. This elaborate system was necessary to prevent bribery.

The fact that the Athenians chose their jurors by lot is a clear indication of their tremendous faith in democracy. The Athenians devoted substantial resources to this elaborate jury selection system. The confidence that the Athenians placed in their jury system is also illustrated by the fact that there was no appeal from a decision of an Athenian jury.

§ 2.09 Evidence

If a public arbitrator had heard a case first, then the litigants could not offer into evidence anything that they had failed to use as evidence before the arbitrator.[39] There were basically two kinds of evidence that an Athenian might offer to prove his case: 1) evidence of relevant laws; and, 2) evidence of facts. Athenian litigants were responsible for bringing copies of germane laws to the court's attention.[40] A court clerk might have read aloud the actual text of a law furnished by a party. Many statutes are quoted in the speeches of the Attic orators. Parties also presented the facts of their cases by means of witnesses (testimony), documents (*e.g.*, contracts, wills, deeds), and other exhibits (*e.g.*, an article of clothing, a piece of jewelry, a weapon). In the 5th century B.C., witnesses usually testified orally. Then, in about 375 B.C., the law changed to require that a witness's testimony be transcribed ahead of time and then simply read aloud for the jury at trial.[41] The witness was, however, ordinarily present at the trial to attest to the veracity of his written statement. In fact, a litigant could demand, by means of a summons, that a witness appear; and if the witness refused to make a statement to be recorded, the litigant could write his own version of the testimony (*martyria*) and then demand that the reluctant witness either confirm it or else swear an oath that it was untrue.

Either party could challenge the veracity of the opposing side's witness by bringing a *dikē* for false testimony. In fact, it is clear that many witnesses testified falsely themselves. Demosthenes recognized that perjury was common. Witnesses, according to Demosthenes, lied because they were bribed, because

---

39. *See supra* § 2.01.

40. "It was not the task of the court to know or to discover what law or laws applied in particular circumstances; rather it was the litigant's right to bring forward any law(s) which he felt would support his case...." TODD, SHAPE 59 (citation omitted).

41. Sealey states that the date for this change was 389 B.C. SEALEY, JUSTICE 138.

they were friends with the party for whom they were testifying, or because they were personally at odds with the party against whom they were testifying. At certain points in Athenian legal history, it was also possible for anyone to bring a *dikē* for false testimony (*pseudomartyrion*). Nevertheless, a litigant's speech was far more important to his case than the testimony of witnesses. Interestingly, there was no cross-examination nor did "experts" testify to evaluate evidence.

At least three kinds of evidence were *in*admissible in Athenian trials: 1) testimony by the litigant himself; 2) hearsay (*i.e.*, statements by a witness regarding what some third party had said); and, 3) the testimony of certain persons (*i.e.*, women, children, and citizens who had otherwise been disenfranchised). A party himself could not testify on his own behalf. Even though it was he who argued the case in court, he was not permitted to offer his own written testimony of the facts. Like modern American rules of evidence, the Athenians, generally speaking, disallowed hearsay evidence; that is, evidence of statements made out of court that are offered for the purpose of proving the truth of the matter asserted. One notable exception to the exclusion of hearsay was that statements made by slaves (even female slaves!) under torture were admissible. According to Isaios in his speech *On the Estate of Ciron*, although regular witnesses habitually lie, when witnesses testify under torture, they tell the truth. Interestingly, however, even though they might have had pertinent things to say about an incident, Athenian rules of evidence routinely barred the testimony of women,[42] children, and the disenfranchised.

No matter what evidence was offered, we know that on many occasions—perhaps most—litigants and witnesses simply told opposite stories. Consequently, juries often were forced to make decisions based upon the comparative reputations and societal contributions (both prior and anticipated) of the litigants rather than on a dispassionate analysis of facts.

§2.10 Legislation

After the Athenian democracy was established in about 509 B.C. by the reformer Kleisthenes, it was the *Ekklēsia* that enacted laws. During the Classical period, a law was passed in the following manner. A citizen could propose a

---

42. Women were permitted to serve as witnesses under certain circumstances. *See* RAPHAEL SEALEY, WOMEN AND LAW IN CLASSICAL GREECE 43, 151 (1990) [hereinafter "SEALEY, WOMEN AND LAW"].

law to the *Boulē*.[43] If approved by the *Boulē*, the *Boulē* then took the matter to the *Ekklēsia*. If approved by the *Ekklēsia*, it would then become a law. A law enacted in this manner was called a *psephisma*. During much of the 5th century B.C., the words *nomos* and *psephisma* functioned as overlapping terms for "laws." Later, after the Reinscription of the Laws in 403/2 B.C.,[44] the Athenians formally distinguished the two: a *nomos* ("law") was thereafter intended to be universal and permanent; whereas, a *psephisma* ("decree") was intended to have limited effect, or, in other words, to be ephemeral.

New laws were inscribed in either wood or stone and displayed in a public place. Although we know that some public officials kept copies of individual statutes that bore a direct relationship to their own sphere of influence, there is conflicting evidence as to whether there was a central collection of laws prior to the 5th century B.C. It is certain, though, that the Athenians did not impose any kind of comprehensive and/or macroscopic organization on their statutory corpus until late in the 4th century B.C.

By the 5th century B.C., written laws began with an identification of the year date and the procedure by which the law had been enacted. This information was called the "prescript." Following the prescript, the law identified what conduct it prohibited. The language was relatively plain and simple, with no definition of terms. Some laws also established penalties for their violation.

§ 2.11 Sychophancy

Sycophancy was one interesting by-product of the Athenian system that allowed volunteer prosecutors. Since volunteer prosecutors often received a percentage of a convicted defendant's fine, some persons found that it was profitable to make a living suing others in hopes of financial gain. Aristophanes ridiculed these *sycophants*, or legal bounty hunters, in his play *The Acharnians*. A sycophant brought cases hoping either to win a percentage of the judgment or hoping to bribe the accused into settling the case. In order to discourage sycophancy, the Athenians enacted laws providing that, when an unsuccessful prosecutor failed to gain at least 20% of the jury's vote in a public case, he was punished with a 1,000 drachma fine. In some cases, a sycophant could be punished by

To prevent this, disinsentive was applied

---

43. The *Boulē* was a citizen council comprised of 500 members (50 from each of the 10 tribes), appointed by a quota system. The minimum age for *Boulē* membership was 30, just like for jury duty and for other public offices. The *Boulē* determined the agenda for the *Ekklēsia*, and performed other miscellaneous executive duties.

44. *See supra* § 1.05.

disenfranchisement (*atimia*)[45] as well. This 1,000 drachma fine could be assessed when an unsuccessful prosecutor failed either to get 20% of the jury's vote or when he abandoned a case once it had been initiated (apparently to discourage settlement blackmail). By the 4th century B.C., the penalty for sycophancy included both the 1,000 drachma fine as well as loss of the right to bring cases of the same type in the future. Once a year it was possible to bring charges of sycophancy to the *Ekklēsia* by the procedure called *probolē*. At the *probolē*, the *Ekklēsia* held a hearing first and a jury trial followed. It was also possible to prosecute sycophancy by *graphē* or *eisangelia*.[46] At least three different activities were deemed serious enough to warrant prosecution for sycophancy: 1) paying another to prosecute a case; 2) threatening to prosecute another unless paid to forbear (bribery); and, 3) prosecuting a case when one did not actually believe his charges. Although the Athenians tried, apparently they were quite unsuccessful in their efforts to deter sycophancy.

§ 2.12 Remedies, Damages, & Punishments

Some Athenian statutes fixed precise penalties for their violation while, in many other instances, the possibilities for punishment appear to have been virtually limitless. A litigant could suggest "any penalty he thought suitable, however unusual."[47] In most cases, the guilty defendant had to pay a sum or sums of money. For most private cases (brought by *dikē*), a defendant paid damages to the plaintiff/prosecutor; although in some cases he also had to pay a fine to the State. For most public cases (brought by *graphē*), a defendant paid a fine to the State; and in some cases the plaintiff/prosecutor got to keep a percentage as a bounty.

The death penalty was carried out either by: 1) hurling the convicted individual into a pit (*barathron*); 2) exposing the convicted individual by securing his neck, wrists, and ankles to a vertical wooden plank (*apotumpanismos*); or, 3) forcing the convicted individual to drink hemlock. Short of death, the an-

---

45. *See infra* § 3.01.

46. *See supra* § 2.02.

47. MacDowell, The Law in Classical Athens 254. Todd emphasizes that:

Punishment at Athens was designed neither to fit the crime nor to fit the criminal, but rather to reorder the relative position of the two litigants. It is for this reason that Athenian law granted to the would-be prosecutor a wide range of procedures for use in a given case; and also that the latter's choice of procedure (inevitably in some sense a political choice) determined both the penalty faced by the defendant and the risk faced by the prosecutor.

Todd, Shape 163.

cient Athenians could also, depending upon the defendant and the offense committed, impose punishments such as: exile; fine; confinement in stocks; confiscation of property; enslavement; disenfranchisement (*atimia*); and, imprisonment (relatively rare). Although many of these punishments appear brutal to modern readers, Todd explains: "Societies which catch very few criminals tend to punish these very severely, and this may be one of the reasons why Athenian judicial penalties were so savage."[48]

§ 2.13 Appeals & the Finality of Judgments

A jury's decision was, as a rule, final. There were, however, exceptions. For example, if a defendant had been found guilty by a default judgment,[49] he could (provided that he had justification for his absence at trial) secure a new trial within two months.[50] Similarly, where a defendant had been found guilty due to a witness's false testimony, he could then be acquitted. In addition, the family of a victim of *unintentional* homicide could pardon an exile. "Otherwise retrials and appeals against a jury's decision ... were not allowed."[51] Other than the special exceptions applicable to default judgments, perjury, and a family pardon for unintentional homicide, it is difficult to imagine any way to overturn a jury's determination.

§ 2.14 *Dikē Exoulēs*

Because of the difficulty of enforcing judgments, Athenian law provided a means by which a defendant (*i.e.*, a defendant whom a jury had found liable for damages) would have to pay an extra fine to the State if he failed to pay the plaintiff what was due. This was accomplished by a unique procedure called *dikē exoulēs*. Sealey interprets judicial enforcement as involving a party's right to rely on self-help. A successful plaintiff, for example, "had the burden of executing the judgment; that is he resumed his act of self-help."[52] According to Sealey:

---

48. Todd, Shape 79.
49. *See supra* § 2.03.
50. *See Id.*
51. MacDowell, The Law in Classical Athens 258.
52. Sealey, Justice 110.

If in executing the judgment he tried to seize property and was impeded, classical Athens would do no more than offer him the "action against being kept out" (*dikē exoulēs*). If he won this action, the person impeding him was ordered to pay twice the value that had been at issue.[53]

§2.15 Chapter Summary

Even as early as the 5th century B.C., Athenian citizens could agree by contract to have an arbitrator (under oath) resolve private disputes. Parties could agree orally to submit to arbitration so long as they agreed both on who would serve as arbitrator(s) and precisely what issue they expected to be resolved by arbitration. In the 4th century, public arbitration became mandatory for many cases. All male citizens were required to serve as public arbitrators at age 59. Because a litigant was prohibited from introducing evidence into court unless that same evidence had been introduced first in arbitration, Athenians approached public arbitration seriously. The first *dēme* judges appeared in the 5th century B.C. But in the 4th century, each of the ten tribes randomly selected four *dēme* judges each; and these came to be called "the Forty." Thereafter, the Forty heard the majority of private cases brought by *dikē*.

Dikē was the most common term used to describe a private case. Interestingly, even homicide was considered a private matter to be resolved legally by *dikē*. *Graphē*—a procedure attributed to Solon—was the usual term for a public case. A volunteer prosecutor could bring suit by *graphē* in cases where the community's interests were affected. Volunteer prosecutors could also initiate lawsuits using a number of other procedures, such as *apagogē*, *ephegesis*, *endeixis*, *apographē*, *eisangelia*, *probolē*, *dokimasia*, and *euthynai*. Because so many procedural forms existed, there was, indeed, room for considerable overlap. A plaintiff/prosecutor had to choose which procedural mechanism he wished to use to pursue any given claim.

As Aristophanes' play *The Clouds* suggests, the Athenians had a reputation for being exceedingly litigious. In order to initiate a lawsuit, a plaintiff/prosecutor had to issue a summons (*prosklesis*) to the defendant, file a complaint, and pay a fee (*prytaneia*). After a pre-trial conference (*anakrisis*), the matter went to trial. If one of the litigants (usually a defendant) failed to appear at trial without a

---

53. *Id.*

legitimate excuse, the judge could enter a default judgment against him. Ordinarily, however, when both parties were present, a clerk read the complaint and the parties made separate speeches; the plaintiff/prosecutor spoke first. The number of speeches and their lengths varied depending on whether the case was brought by *graphē* or *dikē*. A water clock (*klepsydra*) kept track of the time allotted for each speech. The litigants represented themselves but typically relied on professional speech writers, called *logographoi*, to serve as legal counsel. After the final speeches, the jurors (*dikastes*) voted immediately, without the benefit of anything even remotely similar to the modern jury instructions. Without deliberating, juries voted, using special tokens that they placed into specific urns. Jurors also determined penalties; selecting from alternatives proposed by the plaintiff/prosecutor and defendant.

The Athenians had a special form of pleading—*diamartyria* (*i.e.*, summary judgment on decisive evidence)—that they used, for instance, to contest a court's jurisdiction. In the 4th century B.C., the most common way that an Athenian defendant challenged the procedure used by a plaintiff/prosecutor was by means of the *paragraphē*. The Athenians used *paragraphē* to contest issues that modern American law would characterize as *res judicata*, statute of limitations, subject matter jurisdiction, and the statute of frauds. A variety of groups were responsible for different aspects of legal administration in Athens. The Archons (who handled matters relating to property, family, religion, homicide, and non-citizens), *Thesmothetae*, *Strategoi* (who dealt with internal military disputes), *Agoranomoi* and *Sitophylakes* (who judged commercial issues) and the Council of the *Areopagus* (who adjudicated claims involving arson, sacred olive trees, and intentional homicide), exercised considerable authority. In the middle of the 4th century B.C., Athenians began scheduling their court cases in a systematic manner for administrative efficiency. Certain types of courts heard cases only at specific times. And specific bodies adjudicated cases related to particular subjects; such as the *Nautodikai* (judges of sailors), *Xenodikai* (judges of foreigners), and, later in the 4th century, the *Thesmothetae* heard suits involving *dikai emporikai* (mercantile cases). By the close of the 4th century B.C., the Athenian court system was divided into distinct jurisdictional classifications, dependent upon either the subject matter of the dispute or the status of one of the litigants. Although originally the *Archon Polemarchus* was responsible for cases involving non-citizens, eventually the *Xenodikai* assumed that jurisdiction until the time that such matters were assimilated into the mainstream of public cases involving Athenian citizens. Also, in the late 5th and early 4th centuries, the Athenians developed the conservative devices, *graphē paranomēn* and related devices in an effort to inhibit the passage of laws that contradicted existing law.

The Athenian jury system seems to have its roots in Solon's reforms. Tradition credits Solon for giving the citizen assembly—the *Ekklēsia* (referred to as the *Heliaia* when convened to serve as a jury)—the authority to review decisions of magistrates. Because the *Ekklēsia*/*Heliaia* was such a large group, it was impractical for it to convene on a regular basis to function as a jury. Therefore, by the 5th century, Athens instituted a representative jury system. Jurors were selected randomly by elaborate procedures designed to prevent bribery. A combination of black and white balls, a "ticket" (*pinakion*), alphabetical assignment, and the use of a sorting machine (*kleroterion*) helped to ensure a neutral jury selection. All jurors were male, at least thirty years old, and were paid for their service. In the 4th century B.C., it was customary to impanel 500 jurors to serve in a typical trial. Litigants were responsible for providing relevant statutes to the court as evidence. Litigants also brought witnesses to testify (or—later in the 4th century—written statements prepared by witnesses) and pertinent documents and exhibits to help prove the facts of their case. Ordinarily, either party could challenge the veracity of a witness by bringing a *dikē* for perjury and, at certain points in Athenian legal history, it was possible for anyone to bring a *graphē* for perjury (*pseudomartyrion*). At least three kinds of evidence were inadmissible in Athenian trials: 1) testimony by a litigant; 2) hearsay; and, 3) testimony of women, children, and the disenfranchised.

Statutes first approved by the *Boulē* and then enacted by the *Ekklēsia* were called *psephismata* (*psephisma*, singular). Sometimes the Athenians inscribed them on wood or stone to be publicly displayed, but they had no central collection and organization of statutes until the late 4th century. Typically, a *psephisma* begins with a prescript that identifies the year of enactment and the procedure used to bring about enactment, followed by the prohibited conduct and prescribed punishment.

In order to discourage *sychophancy* (*i.e.,* paying another to prosecute a case, threatening to prosecute unless paid to forbear, or prosecuting without believing the truth of the charges), the Athenians enacted laws that severely punished volunteer prosecutors who failed to gain at least 20% of the jury's votes.

Defendants found guilty/liable ordinarily paid money damages as compensation (or fines). In criminal cases, the guilty also could be punished with death, exile, loss of property, enslavement, disenfranchisement (*atimia*), and imprisonment. Once a jury had decided a case, appeal to higher authority was virtually unknown in the Athenian legal system. As an incentive to encourage compliance with a court's order, Athenian law, through a procedure called *dikē exoulēs*, imposed on those found liable an additional fine paid to the State.

Law in Literature:
Jurors and Juries—Aristophanes' *The Wasps*

Introduction

The Athenian playwright Aristophanes wrote *The Wasps* in the Fifth Century B.C. The play focuses on contemporary Athenian politics and the Athenian court system. It mocks a fifth century politician named Cleon. Cleon and politicians like him were considered demagogues. Some viewed these men as popular leaders who protected the interests of the common man. But Aristophanes paints Cleon as a manipulative and self-centered figure; his main concern being his own wealth and comfort. The play also questions the efficacy of the Athenian court system, asking whether it is truly what it purports to be— a system that preserves justice—or a system manipulated by the demagogues to their own benefit.

I. The Noble Juror

The play begins with Procleon, an old man, trying desperately to escape from the house of Contracleon, his son. By naming both of the main characters after the politician Cleon, Aristophanes manages to keep the focus of the play political at all times. Contracleon has enlisted two of his slaves to prevent Procleon from leaving the house, meeting up with his jurymates, and presenting himself to the Athenian court to serve in his much loved position as a juror.

Athenian jury panels were quite large, between two hundred and five hundred members. Jurors were selected in the morning on a daily basis from a pre-designated group by lot. A jury member received three obols a day as pay, little more than minimum wage. Men over the age of thirty were eligible for jury duty, but Aristophanes characterizes the jury members all as elderly men. This may have been an accurate view of the jury. Although young men would have been able to earn more pay in other ways, elderly men were more limited in their choice of work. Hence, the elderly viewed the three obols as a welcome addition to their pockets. The jurors listened to courtroom speeches, decided guilt and innocence, and sentenced the guilty. The jurors' choice of sentence, however, did not leave much room for creativity. Sentencing involved deciding between two alternatives, one proffered by the prosecutor and another, lighter, sentence argued by the defendant. Jurors voted for guilt or innocence by depositing pebbles into an urn and they dictated the severity of a sentence by scratching a mark of a certain length into a wax tablet. The length of the mark represented the relative severity of the punishment the juror had chosen; the longer the mark the more severe the punishment. Aristophanes alludes to a number of details regarding the jury system at various points throughout the play.

After Procleon has failed in several attempts to escape his captors, a chorus of jurors (the Wasps) arrives on the scene and attempts to free Procleon so that he might join them on the jury panel. Contracleon, Procleon, the two slaves and the chorus members themselves, all refer to the jury members as a "swarm of wasps." Aristophanes employs this visual image to promote the view that the jury is a posse of crotchety old men who are always going to "sting" the defendant, no matter what the facts of the case may be. The comparison to wasps also suggests that the group wielded significant power and instilled fear in the unlucky defendants. The chorus members accuse Contracleon of tyranny and call on the politician Cleon for help. A scuffle ensues between the swarm of wasps, Contracleon, and the slaves. Contracleon then decides to try to reason with his father. Contracleon proposes that they each present their best argument on the issue; whether Procleon's work as a juror benefits himself or the demagogues. Procleon states that the chorus members should judge between the two arguments and agrees to abide by their judgment, stating that he will cease to attend jury duty if he loses the argument. This agreement between Procleon and Contracleon is similar to a private arbitration agreement, a practice encouraged by the Athenians.

II. Debate

A formal *agon* (*i.e.*, a formal dispute between two characters of ancient Greek comedy) follows. Procleon argues that the benefits of being a jury member "make mere wealth seem worthless." Serving as a juror has become the center of Procleon's life. He wears the ragged cape reserved for jurors with pride while his son sees it as a source of embarrassment for the family. Procleon gains a sense of responsibility and power from his daily position on the jury panel. Procleon begins the debate by likening the position of juror to that of a king. He states that a line of men stand outside of the courthouse and when he approaches they beg him for mercy. He claims that as a juror he is feared and respected by all. In addition he mentions all the interesting cases he hears, including deciding the wills of orphaned virgins. Athenian law was lenient concerning the admission of evidence. Procleon points out several instances of witnesses testifying regarding matters that would by modern-day standards be considered attempts to wrongfully influence the jury or inadmissible character evidence.

According to Procleon, as a juror he enjoys the great protection of Cleon as well. Lastly he mentions the benefit of his pay; the three obels a day. Believing that he has succeeded in convincing the jury, Procleon turns the stage over to Contracleon. Contracleon begins his argument by pointing out that the measly three obels a day that Procleon receives for his services is not equal to even ten percent of the state revenue. Contracleon explains that the rest of the money goes to pay for the lavish lifestyles of demagogues like Cleon. Contracleon argues that the low pay keeps the men of Procleon's generation in poverty even though they are the ones who sacrificed to make Athens wealthy by fighting for the state when they were younger. Contracleon tells Procleon that he does not want to see him exploited by the government any longer and urges that instead Procleon should relax in his old age and let his son provide for his every desire.

The chorus renders its verdict in favor of Contracleon at this point and reminds Procleon of his promise to give up the life of a juror. When this seems too painful of a choice for Procleon, Contracleon comes up with an alternative. Instead of going to court each day to judge cases, Procleon can serve as the jury of the household, and receive his pay from Contracleon. Contracleon emphasizes the benefits of presiding at home including sleeping in late and avoiding the bad weather. Procleon is convinced and is ready to start his new position immediately! So Contracleon has convinced his father to leave his position as a juror by urging him to try cases at home.

III. Procleon's New Role

Contracleon attempts to make his father as comfortable as possible as he readies himself to hear his first household case. He brings his father soup in case he gets hungry and a water jug in which to urinate. In the Athenian court, speeches were timed by a water clock. The stop was taken out of a jug and the party was permitted to speak until the jug emptied. Procleon intends to preside over his "court" until his water jug is full!

Procleon faces a case almost immediately. One of the dogs, Labes, is accused of eating a piece of cheese from the kitchen, and litigation ensues, *The Household vs. Labes the Dog*. Procleon demands that the trial begin, shouting "Come on, let's get started. I am dying to fine someone! ... I can't wait to run my fingers through that lovely soft wax!" The trial has yet to begin and Procleon already had his mind made up; Labes is guilty, and he imposes a fine. Aristophanes is clearly poking fun at the role of the jury system in Athens, and the assumption that a person is guilty of the charges brought against him. Procleon loves his wax and feels that he is needed.

The trial of Labes illustrates both the sequence of events of an Athenian trial and also how evidence played a role. Character witnesses are called, including the Big Dish, Grinder, Cheese grater, Griddle, Honey pot, and "any other little pieces with burnished bottoms" that were in the kitchen which was the "scene of the crime." Labes, the defendant, chooses to remain silent, invoking the equivalent of the United States Fifth Amendment. Contracleon, acting as defense counsel, reminds the jury of Labes' previous extreme bravery and "highest pedigree," demonstrating Labes' good character. He notes that Labes chased away "hostile wolves," rounded up "great multitudes" of sheep, guarded the door, and most importantly, notes his lack of a previous criminal history. Contracleon pleads for leniency, appealing to the juror's heartstrings by telling the story of Labes' underprivileged upbringing, his "deprived kennel," his lack of musical abilities, and his current life that requires him to live "off old bones and rotten fish" while another household dog lives the life of a "lapdog." Puppies parade in, playing the role of the tearful family.

Procleon is amazed that he is actually touched by the appearance of Labes' "children" stating, "It's the sickness dreaded by all jurors; I'm actually being persuaded!" Isn't that the point? Procleon is supposed to be persuaded, yet as a juror, he thinks that he mustn't find a person innocent! Aristophanes clearly picked an absurd situation, accusing an animal of theft, and calling kitchen appliances and young puppies to testify. Procleon finds Labes not guilty, but only through Contracleon's trickery. For Contracleon surreptitiously switched the guilty and non-guilty urns when Procleon wasn't looking.

IV. The Transformation

As the play progresses, Contracleon attempts to teach his father proper etiquette. It is interesting to note that in the first part of *The Wasps* Contracleon appears mean spirited, and almost evil, for wanting to keep his father at home away from the courtroom. Yet in the second part of the play, Contracleon becomes the protagonist, working to give his father a better life and assimilate him into society.

Contracleon gives his father a Persian robe, which Procleon thinks is symbolic of his having become a "turncoat." Surely he is breaking his allegiance to his fellow underprivileged jurors if he does not continue his 'oath' of poverty as a juror but instead wears fine clothing. Contracleon continues to push nice, but formal, items and ideas on Procleon. He gives him a fork for eating, Spartan boots, shows him how to walk properly, and explains the appropriate manner for talking when with company. To his chagrin, Procleon first refuses everything, and rages against Contracleon, believing everything is the "enemy" and refusing to adopt a fine manner. Procleon eventually acquiesces, wears the clothing, and half-heartedly attempts to adopt a fine manner.

But Procleon fails to adopt a civil manner and is unable to fit in as a functioning member of society. Procleon's lack of restraint and civility leads to a drunken fight with a young boy, a rough-and-tumble stumble as he leaves a party inebriated, and an attempted fling with a prostitute. A variety of injured parties and witnesses present themselves on Contracleon's doorstep, demanding justice in court for Procleon's wild ways. Procleon's life has reversed itself completely; from a juror who determined a party's guilt to the party found guilty. His outrageous behavior soon leads to lawsuits against him, and in keeping with the tradition of Athenian juries, he is found guilty even before his trial begins. The play ends with Procleon dancing like a hooligan, and demanding a "victory feast." Yet it is unlikely that Procleon will be a victor in the near future. He will undoubtedly be found guilty again and again. It is ironic that Procleon is oblivious to the fact that he could be found guilty as a defendant. His lack of comprehension furthers Aristophanes' humor by highlighting the absurdity of the jurors' mind set.

Conclusion

Was Athenian society in a better position when Procleon was a juror, even if he was biased? In the beginning of *The Wasps*, Procleon is criticized for serving as a juror because of the life of poverty it brought and the commitment it required. At the conclusion of the play, however, the audience realizes those commitments as a juror kept Procleon from becoming a burden on society or a nuisance and, to the contrary, actually made him a productive member of society.

CHAPTER 3

Personal Status

§ 3.01 Citizenship

All legal rights in Classical Athens depended on an individual's citizenship status. Until the mid-5th century B.C., persons whose fathers were Athenian citizens automatically received Athenian citizenship, regardless of their mother's citizenship status. The great Athenian statesman, Pericles, initiated a significant legal change about 451/50 B.C. whereby citizenship depended on *both* parents being Athenian citizens—not just the father.

> Two laws were passed. By the first a foreign man who was convicted of living with an Athenian woman as her husband was to be sold into slavery, his goods confiscated, and one-third of the proceeds given to his accuser; a foreign woman convicted of living with an Athenian man as his wife was liable to the same penalty, and in addition the man had to pay a fine of 1,000 drachmai. By the second law anyone ('any Athenian' must be meant) who was convicted of giving a foreign woman in marriage to an Athenian man representing her as related to him (viz., related in such a way as entitled him to give her in marriage) is to suffer *atimia*, his goods are to be confiscated, and a third of the proceeds to be paid to his accuser.[1]

This new citizenship law, however, did not operate retroactively; therefore it did not nullify the citizenship of persons already born of an Athenian father but a non-Athenian mother. The chaotic circumstances that prevailed during the Peloponnesian War (431–404 B.C.) prevented the Athenians from enforcing Pericles' citizenship law strictly. But after the war, the Reinscription of the laws[2] reaffirmed Pericles' citizenship law and it again became effective in 403 B.C.

---

1. A.R.W. Harrison, The Law of Athens (Vol. I) 26 (1968) [hereinafter "Harrison, The Law of Athens (Vol. I)".

2. *See supra* § 1.05.

Citizenship was originally organized around and based upon the four traditional tribes (*phylae*) of Attica. In his reforms (*c.* 508 B.C.), Kleisthenes reorganized citizenship so that a person's citizenship depended on the small village units called *dēmes*. There were over 150 *dēmes*. After the time of Kleisthenes, *dēme* membership was hereditary. Thus, even when someone relocated to another part of Attica, he retained his *dēme* membership in the *dēme* where his family had been in 508 B.C. All Athenian males whose parents were both citizens could join their *dēme* during their 18th year. In a process called *dokimasia*, the *dēme* members voted whether to accept a boy's membership. Primarily, the *dēme* had to determine—in a culture without marriage certificates or birth certificates—whether the boy was old enough and of appropriate parentage to qualify for membership. After a *dēme* had voted to accept a boy, the *Boulē* reviewed the *dēme*'s determination. If the *Boulē* was of the opinion that the boy was not qualified (and thus that the *dēme*'s decision had been erroneous), the *Boulē* fined the *dēme* members themselves. Since girls were not registered in *dēmes*, apparently, the Athenians had to rely on oral testimony regarding a woman's (*i.e.*, mother's) citizenship. It was possible to challenge the validity of another person's citizenship by *graphē*.[3] The accused was imprisoned to await trial, and the penalty for impersonating a citizen was enslavement to the highest bidder.

Although some legal historians doubt Plutarch's (the Greek biographer of the late 1st and early 2nd century A.D.) veracity on this point, Plutarch states that Solon's laws permitted a foreigner to become a citizen: 1) if he had been exiled from his own country; or, 2) if he relocated his entire family to Athens and established a trade there. If Plutarch's claim is inaccurate, then until about 370 B.C. (by which time the *Ekklēsia* could vote to confer citizenship on a foreigner), Athens had no routinized naturalization process by which a foreigner could become an Athenian citizen. There were, on occasion, extraordinary means by which some foreigners were granted citizenship, but those situations were usually limited to a grant of citizenship to an illustrious foreigner for political reasons or a grant to military volunteers during times of war when the Athenians needed additional soldiers or oarsmen to fill their ranks. According to Harrison, "[t]here is good evidence that Athens had conferred this right on certain cities in Euboia towards the end of the 5th century, and in 401/400...."[4]

Citizenship was a bundle of rights and obligations. Among the rights in the bundle were the following: 1) the right to vote; 2) the right to enter temples;

---

3. *See supra* § 2.02.
4. HARRISON, THE LAW OF ATHENS (Vol. I) 29.

3) the right to enter the Agora; 4) the right to hold public office; 5) the right to marry an Athenian citizen; 6) the right to own property; 7) the right to serve on a jury; 8) the right to speak in the *Ekklēsia*; and, 9) the right to speak in a law court and exercise legal remedies (in one's own person). Among the obligations were military service and payment of taxes. Tradition credits Solon and Draco with establishing a law that even required all citizens to maintain a job or be subject to a 100 drachma fine. But, generally speaking, adult male citizens enjoyed remarkable freedom in Classical Athens. They were not subject to anyone else's control; they could own property and were the masters of their own *oikoi* (households).

All Athenian male citizens and metics[5] ages 18–60 had mandatory military service. Whenever Athens needed her army or navy, the *Strategoi* (the board of ten generals) called on those eligible to serve. There were some valid excuses for avoiding service; such as illness and the performance of some other types of public service. Anyone could prosecute another for evasion of military service (by *graphē*) for the offense called *deilia* (draft dodging). The penalty for draft dodging was *atimia* (the loss of many—but probably not all—of a person's citizenship rights). The *Strategoi* reserved the authority, with broad discretion, to punish active soldiers and sailors for misbehavior in the line of duty.

As a penalty for certain wrongdoings, a citizen could be punished by *atimia*. The complete picture is unclear but *atimia* probably entailed the loss of the right to vote, the right to hold public office, the right to serve on juries, the right to speak in the *Ekklēsia* and courts, and the right to enter the Agora and temples. Thus *atimia* probably did not erase a citizen's rights to own property and to marry; nor did it relieve him of his responsibilities to perform military service and to pay taxes.

§ 3.02 Foreigners & Metics

Foreigners in Athens could neither own property nor marry an Athenian woman. Foreigners were, however, required to pay taxes if they wished to transact mercantile business in the Agora. Interestingly, a foreigner was permitted to speak in Athenian law courts.

If a foreigner resided in Athens for a particular period of time, he could qualify for status as a *metic*. Metics were "resident aliens" who were accepted into the fabric of Athenian society. A slave who had been given his freedom

---

5. *See infra* §3.02.

also became a metic under Athenian law. According to Todd, "Broadly speaking, a metic was liable to all those obligations which would have been imposed on a citizen of equivalent wealth, together with some additional responsibilities."[6] They were obliged to pay a special metic's tax (*metoikion*) and had to serve in the military if called.[7] Metics were also required to maintain a *prostates*, an Athenian citizen to serve as something like a guardian. It is unclear exactly how the *prostates* functioned in reality, but it appears that the *prostates* served more of a symbolic than a practical function. As Harrison puts it: "[w]e are unfortunately almost wholly in the dark on the duties of a *prostates* beyond that of appearing in court."[8] Nevertheless, metics did receive a certain measure of legal protection. Specifically, the *Archon Polemarchus* was given jurisdiction over cases involving metics. The exact details, however, of a metic's legal capacity are unknown. Unfortunately our sources often fail to distinguish between metics and other non-resident aliens when describing legal status. We do know, however, that, as a general rule, metics could not own real property unless they had received a special exemption called *enktesis*. In addition to the privilege of *enktesis*, it was also possible for a metic to be granted *isoteleia*, an exemption from the obligation of paying the metic's tax. It also seems likely that, on some occasions, a metic could be exempted from the obligation of maintaining a *prostates*. A census taken around 315 B.C. placed the number of metics in Athens at about 10,000.

§ 3.03 Slaves & Freedmen

Most slaves in ancient Athens were considered personal property (chattel slavery). Therefore, they could be bought and sold. But, as Harrison advises, "we should recognize that there was a pervasive ambiguity about the legal status of a slave which made him both a chattel and something more than a mere chattel."[9] Scholars estimate the number of slaves in Classical Athens between 20,000 and 75,000. Athenian slaves were usually foreigners. We may classify slaves in ancient Athens as either public or private. There were only a handful of public slaves. Caretakers of public buildings, the public "coin-tester," and a group of slaves who functioned somewhat like a police force (the Skythian

---

6. TODD, SHAPE 196.

7. The metic's tax was twelve drachmas per-year for a man and six drachmas per-year for a woman. *See also infra* § 9.06.

8. HARRISON, THE LAW OF ATHENS (Vol. I) 193.

9. *Id.* at 163.

archers) were the public slaves. Most private slaves were slaves by virtue of having been captured in war or by having descended from a war captive. Tradition has it that Solon abolished debt slavery in Athens. It is possible that a child's status as a slave depended on the mother. If a child's mother was a slave, the child would be a slave, but not otherwise.

Theoretically speaking, Athenian slaves had no rights. For example, Athenian law did not recognize their family relationships. A slave could not own property in Athens. Slaves could not sue in court and could not enter the *gymnasia* (exercise grounds) or *palaistrai* (wrestling grounds) reserved for citizens. But some slaves routinely worked outside of the owner's home and could earn money. Those slaves working outside of the household were required by law, however, to pay their owners an established payment called *apophora*. Some evidence suggests that it was illegal for owners to kill their slaves; although the law did not prohibit severe corporal punishment. Using a legal theory substantially similar to our modern *respondeat superior* (*i.e.,* vicarious liability), one of Solon's laws made slave owners liable for the offenses committed by their slaves against others. It is also likely that owners were responsible for debts incurred by their slaves as well. Harrison, however, is cautious on this point: "Where an obligation had arisen out of contractual dealings by a slave the rules are far from clear, and they had certainly not been worked out at Athens with anything like the detail and subtlety that obtained in Roman law."[10] Occasionally a slave owner freed a slave in his will. Otherwise, a slave owner could also manumit a slave during his lifetime without going through any formal procedure. According to Harrison, "[i]t was probably fairly common practice for a slave to purchase his freedom out of accumulated earnings."[11] Freedmen were generally permitted to attain only *metic* status, not citizen status. Thus, for example, a freedman could not own land in Attica. Furthermore, a patron had to represent freedmen in judicial proceedings, and the Polemarch had jurisdiction in cases relating to them.

§ 3.04 Chapter Summary

After Pericles in the middle of the 5th century, in order to be considered an Athenian citizen, an individual's mother and father both had to have been Athenian citizens. Kleisthenes reorganized Athenian citizenship so that a per-

---

10. *Id.* at 174. *See also infra* § 12.03.
11. HARRISON, THE LAW OF ATHENS (Vol. I) 182.

son's citizenship depended on local *dēme* membership (which thenceforth became hereditary). Athenian boys, at age 17, gained citizenship status only after a formal review process called *dokimasia*. Among other things, citizenship entitled a person to vote, to hold public office, to conduct business in the Agora, to own property, to participate in the legislative process and court proceedings, and to marry. Citizens were obligated to serve in the military and to pay taxes. Foreigners may have been granted citizenship in limited circumstances, but that was a rare occurrence. Foreigners could acquire "resident alien", or *metic*, status, which provided them with some of the rights (*e.g.*, access to law courts) and obligations (*e.g.*, military service and liturgies) of a citizen. Most slaves in ancient Athens were foreigners and were treated, theoretically speaking, as personal property. But there were aspects of slavery that reflected a limited degree of individual freedom and responsibility. Upon manumission, a former slave was considered the legal equivalent of a metic.

CHAPTER 4

PROPERTY

§ 4.01 Introduction

Harrison relates that "the Athenians of the 4th century were still at a relatively simple stage in their legal thinking about property; so much so that they had no general term which could describe this branch of the law."[1] Real property was especially important in ancient Athens.[2] An owner of real property also *ipso facto* owned any improvements (such as buildings), any crops, and any animals on the land. Aliens were not allowed to own real property in Attica. In addition to real property, Athenian law also authorized ownership of various kinds of tangible personal property (household items, clothing, tools, *etc.*). But Athenian law never refined legal categories of property to a degree even remotely similar to that of Roman law.[3] Still, some ancient writers distinguish between property that was visible *versus* invisible and between property that was ancestral (*patrēia*) *versus* acquired (*epikēta*). There seem to have been some restrictions on the alienability of ancestral property even as late as the 4th century B.C. Since, slaves were considered personal property, it was only logical that slaves themselves could own neither real nor personal property.[4] Slave owners could sue for injuries inflicted on their slaves by others (*e.g., dikē aikeias*). An owner could also sue someone who murdered a slave (*dikē phonou*). Although the Athenians "had no abstract word for ownership,"[5] corporate entities (*e.g., dēmes, phratries*, religious bodies, and the State) were, nevertheless, legally capable of owning any kind of property that an individual could own. According to Aristotle, the benchmark of ownership was the capacity to alienate. Two

---

1. *Id.* at 200.
2. *See* MacDowell, The Law in Classical Athens 133. *Also see* Todd, Shape 236 ("Astonishingly few surviving speeches, however, are concerned generally with property or obligations involving property.").
3. *See infra* § 13.01.
4. *See supra* § 3.03.
5. Harrison, The Law of Athens (Vol. I) 201.

or more people could own property jointly; but in order to sell—or otherwise alienate—property that was jointly owned, all joint owners had to agree. If they were unable to concur on the proposed disposition, a joint owner who wished to alienate his property could bring suit to request that the property be divided for purposes of sale. Athenian property owners could transfer possession—as opposed to outright ownership of property—by a loan or lease.[6] And Harrison asserts that "the Athenians were fully aware of the judicial importance of the distinction" between possession and ownership.[7]

According to Sealey, "[t]he law of property is mainly concerned with ways of acquiring property."[8] In the first instance, we presume (and that is all it is, a presumption) that Athenian law acknowledged original occupation as a source of ownership. Indeed, Aristotle specifically asserts that one could acquire property by fishing, hunting, and seizing in wartime. Otherwise one of Solon's laws allowed that someone who left an object—for example, at a roadside—remained the owner of it so long as he could be identified as the owner. In addition, Athenians could transfer ownership of property by gift, sale, or by operation of inheritance. During the 5th and 4th centuries, a man was not permitted to leave his property in a will to whomever he wished. Instead, the laws of succession established immutable inheritance rights during the Classical period.[9]

In the 6th century B.C., the Greeks first began using coinage as a medium of exchange. The introduction of coinage had a profound effect on the Greek economy and, therefore, on the transfer of property. The availability of metal coins as a medium of exchange greatly facilitated all conveyance of property.

§ 4.02 Real Property

Because agriculture dominated the ancient Athenian economy, many unique laws governed the ownership and use of real property. However, there was neither a collection of public records nor a registration system that evidenced a person's title to his real estate. In 5th century B.C., Athenian citizens could legally sell real property. An alien could only own real estate under exceptional

---

6. *See* Todd, Shape 250. MacDowell, however, notes that there was "no Greek noun for ownership as distinct from possession...." MacDowell, The Law in Classical Athens 133.

7. Harrison, The Law of Athens (Vol. I) 204.

8. Sealey, Justice 60.

9. *See infra* Chapter 6.

circumstances; if he was granted a special privilege called *enktesis*.[10] Generally speaking, an owner of real property was legally permitted to do whatever he wished with his own land. One exception to a land owner's freedom had to do with olive trees. Because olive oil was such an important commodity in the Athenian economy, property owners were limited to cutting no more than two olive trees per year. A violation of this restriction gave rise to a fine of 100 drachmas per tree. In addition, some olive trees (even some on property that was otherwise considered private property) were designated as sacred to the goddess Athena. Even at the beginning of the 4th century B.C., if someone cut down a sacred olive tree, he could face trial before the *Areopagus* and the death penalty. Technically, the olives of the sacred trees belonged to the Athenian State, and the landowners in the late 4th century still paid a royalty of a little less than 3/4 of a pint of olive oil per tree per year.

Property owners also were not permitted to plant trees or excavate ditches so close to their boundary lines that it would hinder their neighbor. Because of the scarcity of fresh water on the Greek mainland, several laws controlled the manner in which land owners could use water on their property. Solon is credited with establishing laws that permitted citizens to obtain water either from public wells or from their neighbors, depending on availability. Thus, under certain circumstances, a citizen was obliged to allow neighbors to enter his property and take specified amounts of water on a daily basis. This type of law is roughly analogous to what modern law might characterize as an easement appurtenant; that is, a right, based on the proximity of two parcels of land, to enter another's land. In order to protect landowners downstream, laws prohibited polluting the rivers upstream. In addition to pollution, Athenian law also imposed penalties (damages of at least 1,000 drachmas) on upstream owners who diverted water in such a way that it harmed the property of a downstream owner.

§ 4.03 Mines

Attica had valuable silver mines. Issues relating to the ownership and use of mines are complex:

> In what sense the State owned minerals under Attic soil and how precisely it exploited this ownership are highly controversial issues. There is a fair amount of evidence in connection with the silver mines at

---

10. *See supra* § 3.02.

Laureion, but it has not yet produced clear and generally accepted conclusions. The main question is whether the Athenians achieved the abstraction of separating out from rights of ownership in the soil the right to exploit the minerals below the surface and vesting this latter right as such in the state.[11]

A great deal of evidence suggests, however, that the State claimed ownership of the subterranean sections of mines. As owner, the Athenian State routinely, through a formal registration process, leased mines to others who then quarried them. The normal lease period for a mine was ten years. When a mine was located underneath the surface of land that was privately owned, some evidence suggests that the State paid a percentage of its lease payment (*i.e.,* the payment from the individual who had registered and was working the mine) to the surface property owner. A special "catch-all" mining law, called *nomos metallikos* forbade anyone from interfering with mining operations.

§ 4.04 Resolving Ownership Disputes Relating to Personal Property

In contemporary American law, when one person claims that a particular property is rightfully his but another person has possession of it, the rightful owner (*i.e.,* the person who does not have possession) can sue for "replevin," thereby asking the court to order the wrongful possessor to return the goods to him (*i.e.,* the rightful owner who for one reason or another has lost possession). When two or more persons disputed a claim to an *inheritance* in classical Athens, one of the disputants could petition the *archon* and the conflict would be resolved in a process called *diadikasia* using a jury trial.[12] Harrison explains *diadikasia*:

> The primary function of the court is to decide which of the two has a better right to own the thing.... This gave to the procedure its characteristic features: there was no plaintiff and no defendant; the two parties stood side by side, trying each to show that his relation to the thing or duty gave him a better right to own the thing or to escape the duty than his opponent.... [13]

---

11. HARRISON, THE LAW OF ATHENS (Vol. I) 234.
12. *See infra* §§ 5.02, 6.01.
13. HARRISON, THE LAW OF ATHENS (Vol. I) 215.

Otherwise, it seems that Athenian law generally permitted A to bring suit against B when A believed that B possessed money or property that A believed was rightfully his. It is likely that such a suit was brought as a *dikē*, and that additional words were used alongside the word "*dikē*" to designate the nature of the property that was in dispute (*e.g., dikē khreēs* (debt), *dikē ousias* (property)). Here, as is the case in a modern action for "replevin," the alleged rightful owner merely was asking that the subject property be returned to him. If the possessor alleged that he had purchased the disputed property from a third party, the defendant/possessor could subpoena the seller to appear at trial. If the court found that the possessor had, in fact, bought the item from a third party, the third party was obligated to repay the possessor/defendant his purchase price, and the possessor had to return the property to the plaintiff who rightfully owned it. Modern American commercial law reaches a different result (allowing the buyer to retain possession but mandating that the seller—presumably the original crook—pay the initial owner compensatory damages) if the possessor legitimately bought the property in good faith.

§ 4.05 Chapter Summary

The ancient Athenians developed advanced property law concepts. For example, they understood various notions regarding real estate, tangible personal property, joint ownership, and possession—as opposed to ownership outright. Aristotle says that the capacity to alienate property is the distinguishing feature of ownership. Athenian law appreciated multiple ways by which one could transfer or acquire property rights, such as fishing and hunting, seizure in war, gift, sale, and inheritance. The advent of the use of coinage in the 6th century B.C. facilitated property conveyance.

Because agriculture dominated the ancient Athenian economy, many unique laws governed the ownership and use of real property. Owners of real property generally had great freedom to do as they wished with their land, but they were forbidden to cut down olive trees. Due to the scarcity of fresh water, special laws regulated the use of wells, rivers, and streams. Although we are unaware of many details regarding the laws relating to mines, evidence suggests that the State claimed ownership of the subterranean portions of all mines. Athenian law also provided formal mechanisms for persons to resolve ownership disputes regarding property (*e.g., diadikasia*—for inheritance, *dikē khreēs*—debt, *dikē ousias*—personal property).

CHAPTER 5

FAMILY LAW

§ 5.01 Introduction: Power & Control

In Classical Athens, the family centered on the *oikos*, the household unit of production and consumption. Adult men were responsible for the protection and well-being of their *oikoi*. Women and children were dependent on their *kyrios*, the adult male who was legally responsible for them. The *kyrios* for a child was typically his/her father, the *kyrios* for an adult woman was usually her husband.[1] Upon marriage, a woman's *kyrios* changed from father to husband. When a woman's husband died, she could decide whether she wished to return to her former *oikos* under the control of her father (or her father's successor as *kyrios*), or she could remain with her married family under the supervision of her husband's heir (typically her own son). This is unusual in Athenian law because, in this special situation, *a woman had an option to make a decision that had legal consequence for herself.* The term *epitropos* is often used for the guardian of boys.

Otherwise, Athenian law typically treated women as children who needed a guardian to administer their property and transact business on their behalf at all times. Women could not make a valid will but apparently could, under certain circumstances, testify on legal matters, although not as a court witness.[2] Women could be tried in court as defendants. Women could own personal property and could buy and sell it if the value of the transaction was

---

1. Speaking in general terms about all ancient Greek women—not just women in classical Athens, Professor Sealey remarks:

> Her *kyrios* might be her father, her brother, her grandfather, or her uncle; in consequence of marriage her *kyrios* would be her husband or eventually her adult son or son-in-law. But in any one city at any one time the degree of authority exercised by the *kyrios*, whoever he might be, was uniform. A Greek woman was subject to *kyrieia* solely because she was a woman.

SEALEY, JUSTICE 82.

2. SEALEY, WOMEN AND LAW 43 (Sealey gives an example of women testifying regarding the authenticity of a document in an arbitration).

below a certain modest amount. And, although much evidence suggests that
a woman was not legally capable of owning real property, Sealey argues that a
woman was capable of "owning" real property such as her dowry and inherited real estate.[3] Her "ownership" was restricted in the sense that it was technically administered by her *kyrios*. Nevertheless, the *kyrios* may have functioned
something like an agent for the woman (*i.e.*, the principal) who legally owned
the property.

§5.02 Marriage & Divorce

Harrison warns that "there is no single Greek word which can be taken to
stand for 'marriage.'"[4] Ancient Athenian law recognized two very different
kinds of marriage: *enguē* and *epidikasia*. Marriage by *enguē*, which required
no formal government sanction, was the more common type. *Enguē* involved
"a transaction between the bride's father and the bridegroom of which the
bride [was] the object."[5] In many respects this type of marriage resembles a
contract between the prospective father-in-law and the groom. *Epidikasia*,
which did require government sanction, was a marriage of a female who had
become an *epiklēros*.[6]

As a rule, the law did not allow a man to marry his mother, grandmother,
daughter, granddaughter, sister, or half-sister (by his mother). He could, however, marry his half-sister (by his father), an adopted sister, niece, cousin, and,
by the mid-5th century B.C., anyone else who was a citizen. Neither *enguē* nor
epidikasia was available when one party was free and the other was a slave. According to Harrison, "[w]here one of the parties was Athenian and the other
a foreigner or metic, the rule differed at different periods."[7] At some point in
antiquity, there seem to have been certain legal drawbacks to being a bachelor
under Athenian law but the evidence is thin and unclear. Girls were usually
about fourteen when they were married and men were much older. A groom
probably had to be at least seventeen in order to take part in a valid contractual arrangement, like *enguē*. And, although we have no direct evidence for a
statute prohibiting polygamy, Athenian law seems not to have permitted it.

---

3. *See Id.* at 43–49.

4. HARRISON, THE LAW OF ATHENS (Vol. I) 1.

5. *Id.* at 2.

6. For a brief discussion of the peculiarities involving an *epiklēros, see infra* this section
and *infra* §6.01.

7. A.R.W. HARRISON, THE LAW OF ATHENS (Vol. II) 24 (1968) (footnote omitted).

In a typical marriage by *enguē*, the man first had to reach a formal agreement called *engyesis* (*i.e.*, an oral contract) with his intended bride's *kyrios*, typically her father. Indeed, it was this formal agreement process between the would-be husband and the girl's father that was called *enguē*. Primarily, the *enguē* consisted simply of the father's formal declaration to the suitor that he (the father) was giving his daughter to the suitor. The girl's wishes were irrelevant to the *enguē*. Later, the actual transfer, *ekdosis*, took place. The *ekdosis* occurred when the woman physically relocated to her husband's *oikos*. It was also possible, though not legally required, for the couple to have a more formal ceremony called *gamos*. And the *ekdosis* and the *gamos* often may have occurred simultaneously.

A bride's father was not legally required to provide a dowry (*proix*) to his son-in-law. Nevertheless, upon divorce, a husband was obligated to return any dowry that had been given. This law, requiring a divorced husband to return any dowry received, had a normative effect. Because the law discouraged divorce when a dowry had been given, it encouraged fathers to give a dowry. In fact we know of no actual instance where there was *engyesis* but no dowry. The dowry served as the functional equivalent of the bride's inheritance. "It was property of any kind, whether money, chattels, land, or claims, made over by a woman's *kyrios* to a man in contemplation of their marriage by *enguē*."[8] Thus, a husband was not completely at liberty to alienate the property that comprised the dowry. If a husband refused to return the dowry upon divorce, his ex-wife's *kyrios* could sue him for its return (*dikē proikos*) and for income or "alimony" reckoned at 18% interest (*dikē sitou*). Otherwise there were few legal impediments to obtaining a divorce if initiated by the husband. Basically, the husband merely had to send his wife away in order to obtain a divorce (*apopempsis*). Divorce was probably more difficult for a wife to secure (*apoleipsis*). She had to leave her husband's house, appear before the Archon with her *kyrios* (*i.e.*, the *kyrios* to whom she returned upon leaving her husband—typically either her father or a brother), and give a written notice. Otherwise, "[v]oluntary dissolution of marriage might arise from agreement to separate between the husband and wife."[9] If a married woman died without surviving children or grandchildren, her husband was required to return the dowry to her *kyrios*. However, if she had any children, the children inherited the dowry.

In addition to the ordinary marriage by *enguē*, an Athenian marriage was also legally valid when accomplished through *epidikasia*. The necessity for this kind of marriage arose in cases where a father died leaving no male heirs—no

---

8. *Id.* at 46.
9. HARRISON, THE LAW OF ATHENS (Vol. I) 39.

sons, no grandsons, and no great-grandsons. If, however, such a man did have a daughter, granddaughter, or even a great-granddaughter, it was theoretically and practically possible for her to give birth to a male child who would thereby become the deceased's grandson, great-grandson, or great, great-grandson. The ancient Athenian legal term for a woman in such a position was *epiklēros*; a term that some legal historians have translated "heiress." In order to facilitate the deceased's inheritance lineage, the closest male relative of the deceased was entitled to marry the *epiklēros*. He (the closest male relative) could, if he wished, decline the opportunity to marry the *epiklēros*. However, at the other extreme, he could also legally force her to divorce her current husband. The orator Isaios claims, indeed, that the nearest male relative commonly invoked this privilege, and required the *epiklēros* to divorce and remarry. The Archon was responsible for ensuring that the *epiklēros* married an appropriate husband. Frequently, more than one relative laid claim to marry the *epiklēros*, and a legal proceeding (*diadikasia*) was necessary to select a husband. Once a male relative had married the *epiklēros*, the court was required to ratify the marriage (*epidikasia*). According to tradition, one of Solon's laws required that an *epiklēros'* husband have intercourse with her a minimum of three times a month for the purpose of producing legitimate heirs. And anyone could prosecute (by *eisangelia*) a person who mistreated an *epiklēros*.

Athenian law regarding fidelity was extremely sexist by today's standards. According to Demosthenes, prostitutes were available for a man's "pleasure" and concubines were necessary for the daily needs of a man's body, but the purpose of wives was to bear legitimate children and to tend the house. During marriage, a man was not required to be faithful to his wife, but a wife was required to be faithful to her husband. Elsewise, as Harrison puts it, "her misconduct might introduce an adulterine bastard into the family."[10] A husband was even allowed to have another woman actually live in his *oikos* and have sexual relations with him. Such a woman was called a *pallakē*. The term *pallakē* was also used for a woman who lived with a man more or less permanently (but in circumstances where there had been no *enguē*). Nevertheless, a woman who was divorced or widowed could legally remarry if she desired.

§ 5.03 Children

As a rule, in order to be considered legitimate, a child had to be born of parents who were married either by *enguē* or *epidikasia*. When one parent was

---

10. *Id.* at 32.

a citizen and the other was not, or if a child was born when the parents had not been married by *engue* or *epidikasia*, such a child was called a *nothos*. Although *nothoi* clearly did not enjoy the rights of full citizens, they had some rights superior to metics and foreigners (*e.g.*, certain rights of inheritance). A citizen boy remained under the control of his *kyrios* (usually his father) until his 18th year. A girl remained under her *kyrios'* control until marriage. "Until a son came of age his father represented him in every kind of legal transaction, whether procedurally before a court or in matters of contract, since a minor was incapacitated from entering into any contract."[11]

Children's rights were few. Parents were legally permitted to practice population control by exposure of an infant. "He [*i.e.*, a father] could ... expose the child, that is, abandon it in some place where there was a chance of its being found and nurtured by another person. There seems no reason to doubt that the father had this absolute discretion and that the right of exposure was more than a purely formal one."[12] Parents could also, before the time of Solon, sell or pledge their children (*e.g.*, for a debt). Solon's laws subjected a son to prosecution for neglecting or mistreating his parents in their old age. The punishment for such neglect or abuse was *atimia*.[13]

When a child's father died, the Archon was responsible for appointing a substitute *kyrios* to serve as guardian. It was common for the Archon to appoint several guardians who shared the responsibilities. A guardian was responsible for the ward's food, clothing, housing, and education. Guardians also had to maintain their ward's property and represent him in matters relating to taxes and law. The guardian-*kyrios* was required to keep careful financial records and accounts of his management of his ward's estate. At the end of the term of guardianship, a ward could bring a private action against his guardian for mismanagement of the estate. Technically speaking, there were several different kinds of legal theories which a ward might advance, and we have evidence for at least three different types of lawsuits—the details of which need not concern us here—(*dike epitropes*, *dike sitou*, and *phasis*). Furthermore, a public cause of action, *eisangelia*, was available against a guardian-*kyrios* (or anyone else for that matter) who mistreated a youth whose father had died.[14] But the details of such a prosecution are uncertain. We do know, however, that a volunteer prosecutor who brought suit in an effort to protect the rights of a child in this manner did not risk the fine that ordinarily accompanied the failure to

---

11. *Id.* at 73.
12. *Id.* at 71.
13. *See supra* § 3.01.
14. *See supra* § 2.02.

garner one-fifth of the jury's votes.[15] This exception to the one-fifth-vote-of-the-jury rule illustrates a paternalistic desire on the part of the State to protect the interests of children whose fathers had died.

§ 5.04 Chapter Summary

The physical center of the Athenian family was the *oikos*. The father was often the principal adult male who served as *kyrios* (legal guardian) for his wife and children. Women had few rights, and could not, as a rule, participate in legal affairs. Women were required to have a guardian who could act on their behalf. They could own personal property, and probably, some types of real estate.

Ordinarily, Athenian law did not recognize marriage between close relatives and had certain minimum age requirements for marriage. *Enguē* was the typical type of marriage in ancient Athens. This marriage occurred simply by virtue of an agreement (*engyesis*) between the bride's father and the groom. Later, the bride physically relocated (*ekdosis*) to the groom's *oikos*. The bride's father usually gave a dowry (*proix*) to his son-in-law. Ordinarily, however, upon divorce, a husband was required to return the dowry. Husbands could divorce their wives by simply sending them away (*apopempsis*) but wives had to use a formal, State-sanctioned procedure (*apoleipsis*) to effectuate a divorce. When a father died leaving a female heir (*epiklēros*) but no male heir, Athenian law provided for a special kind of marriage called *epidikasia*. In this circumstance, a close male relative usually married the *epiklēros* in order to preserve the family and its property. A husband was not legally required to be faithful to his wife but a wife was legally required to be faithful to her husband. Societal custom permitted men to visit prostitutes and even to have a live-in mistress (*pallakē*).

As a rule, in order to be considered legitimate, a child had to be born of parents who were married either by *enguē* or *epidikasia*. Children lived under their father's control and enjoyed little independence. When a child's father died, the Archon was responsible for appointing a substitute *kyrios* to serve as guardian. A guardian had strict legal duties and was held legally accountable for his management of his ward's affairs.

---

15. *See supra* § 2.11.

CHAPTER 6

INHERITANCE AND SUCCESSION

§6.01 Intestate Succession

Although there are many fundamental, theoretical rules of inheritance that we can discern from the speeches of orators, nevertheless, as a practical matter, many inheritance disputes degenerated into unfettered fabrication and self-serving testimony, as relatives and pseudo-relatives presented false testimony, forged wills, and forged adoption documents, while they jockeyed for a piece of a decedent's property. "Athenian inheritance cases should not be treated as the product of a system where clear rigid rules of kinship are authoritatively interpreted and mechanically applied."[1]

When a man died—without a will and without having adopted an heir[2]—and only one legitimate son survived him, that son inherited all of his father's assets and liabilities (public debts in particular). If the deceased had more than one surviving son, the sons inherited equally, without preference for the eldest. Although the inheriting sons could agree to share and keep their inheritance jointly in an undivided whole, brothers under such circumstances usually physically divided and separated their father's goods and property (*i.e.,* the estate, or *klēros*) as equitably as possible. When a son predeceased his father, his sons (*i.e.,* the grandson's) were entitled to inherit their deceased father's share (*i.e.,* his share of their grandfather's estate) on a *pro rata* basis.

One of the more interesting problems of Greek inheritance law occurred in situations involving an *epiklēros.*[3] In the circumstance of an *epiklēros,* marriage by *epidikasia* ensured that the *oikos* of the deceased would continue and that his estate would be secure. When a man died leaving no sons, grandsons, great-grandsons, and no female descendant eligible to be an *epiklēros,* Athenian inheritance law then permitted the man's nearest living relatives, his *anchisteis,*—in a predetermined order of preference—to inherit his property. Brothers (and

---

1. COHEN, LAW, VIOLENCE AND COMMUNITY IN CLASSICAL ATHENS 176.
2. *See infra* §6.02.
3. *See supra* §5.02[B].

his brothers' descendants) were first in line, along with half-brothers by the same father. Sisters (and his sisters' descendants) followed, along with half-sisters by the same father. After brothers and sisters, inheritance law defaulted to the following: 1) All other relatives on the father's side of the family "as far as the children of cousins"[4]; 2) half-brothers (and their descendants) by the same mother; 3) half-sisters (and their descendants) by the same mother; 4) all other relatives on the mother's side of the family "as far as the children of cousins." The real losers in the Athenian inheritance scheme were the widow (she could not become an *epiklēros*), parents, and grandparents, who, because they had no inheritance rights whatsoever, were not even left holding an empty bag, but no bag at all. In 403 B.C., a new law prohibited illegitimate children from inheriting.

Athenian inheritance law did not function with the rule of primogeniture. Thus, sons of the deceased inherited equal shares without regard to birth order. In addition, inheritance was *per stirpes* not *per capita*. For example, suppose the deceased, for purposes of illustration, let us call him Aeschylus, had two sons named Sophocles and Euripides. Now suppose that one of the sons, Sophocles, had predeceased his father, Aeschylus. Suppose also that, prior to his own death, Sophocles had had two sons of his own, Aristophanes and Menander. In this scenario, there would be three individuals, a son, Euripides, and two grandsons, Aristophanes and Menander, who stand to inherit the estate of Aeschylus. The ancient Athenian *per stirpes* system gave Euripides 50% of Aeschylus' estate and gave Aristophanes and Menander 25% each (representing an equal portion of what would have been Sophocles' 50% share had he not died before his father, Aeschylus). A *per capita* system, which the Athenians did *not* use, on the other hand, would have divided Aeschylus' estate equally according to the total number of heirs (three in this hypothetical). Thus, a *per capita* system would have given Euripides, Aristophanes, and Menander each 33 1/3% of Aeschylus' estate.

Sons and grandsons were permitted simply to take possession of any property that was rightfully theirs (by inheritance laws) without having to resort to any formal or legalistic procedure. Anyone else who might claim an inheritance right had to petition the Archon in writing and give notice of his alleged claim through the *Ekklēsia*. This process was called *epidikasia*. If, for some reason, an individual's claim was disputed by another, the

---

4. In ancient Athenian law, the word "cousin" probably means "first cousin." But even ancient cases disputed the actual meaning of this word. *See* MacDowell, The Law in Classical Athens 106–07. *See also* Cohen, Law Violence and Community in Classical Athens 178.

claim was called a *diadikasia*. Of course, it was entirely possible that more than one person could emerge to dispute an inheritance claim. As a consequence, a *diadikasia* might prove to be an exceptionally complicated process. Further confounding this process was the prospect that a man's estate might pass through an *epiklēros*.[5] Several speeches of the orator Isaios, an orator who appears to have specialized in Athenian estates law, reveal just how intricate this field of law was. One well known contested inheritance lawsuit was still raging in the courts more than 50 years after the decedent's demise.

In those instances when inheritance claims were disputed (*diadikasia*), the legal machinery struggled with profound problems of proof. A jury needed sound evidence to serve as a basis for its factual determinations. Because there were neither marriage nor birth certificates, any claimant necessarily experienced difficulty proving genealogy and/or legitimacy. Whenever someone offered into evidence a document purporting to be the deceased's will, there was the distinct possibility that it was a forgery. Credible and persuasive oral testimony from witnesses obviously made or broke many inheritance cases in ancient Athens.

§6.02 Adoption & Wills

Even prior to the laws of Solon (*c.* 594 B.C.), men who had no biological sons had begun the practice of adopting a son during their lifetime. They adopted a son in order to create an heir. According to Harrison,

> Solon seems to have made two closely related rules; he allowed a man who had neither son nor daughter to choose an heir, whom he adopted; and he allowed a man who had only a daughter to choose for her a husband, whom he adopted. There seems now little doubt that this was the essence of what was later regarded as a law conferring complete freedom of testament on a man who had no legitimate issue.[6]

In order to adopt, an adopter had to be a male adult citizen who had no living sons. In Athenian law, adoption was an institution designed primarily to benefit the adopter not necessarily the adoptee. Adoption was a contractual mechanism employed to preserve the adopter's *oikos*. "[T]he normal effect of any adoption was to make the adopted son ... heir to the whole of the estate

---

5. *See supra* §5.02.
6. HARRISON, THE LAW OF ATHENS (Vol. I) 82.

of the adopter."[7] Therefore, most adoptees were adult males, and most adopters were so old or so infirm that they considered themselves incapable of siring a son. Upon adoption, an adoptee legally acquired the same rights as if he had been a natural child of the adopter (except that he, himself, was not permitted to adopt children).

During the 4th and 5th centuries B.C., adoption was the only means by which an Athenian could transfer his estate to a person other than those persons designated in the inheritance laws. An ancient Athenian could not, as we can today, bequeath property to anyone whom he pleased in his will. If he wished to do so, he had to adopt that person as a son. Interestingly, even a man who already had a natural son was permitted to adopt a son in his will. In the event that the natural son predeceased his father (or died simultaneously—in a common accident, for example), the testate adoption became effective. Otherwise, the adoption by will was considered merely contingent, and was thus deemed invalid (*i.e.*, in cases where a natural son outlived his father).

It was not until centuries later that Athenian law permitted testamentary disposition in a manner roughly analogous to modern wills and estates practice. When an Athenian did make a will—for example in order to posthumously adopt an heir—he usually did so in writing. Witnesses were ordinarily present and the testator commonly sealed the document too. Nevertheless, neither a writing, witnesses, nor seals seem to have been required in order to give legal effect to an Athenian will. Instead, those formalities were often used for the purpose of deterring forgeries.

§ 6.03 Chapter Summary

Although the speeches of the orators have preserved a number of legal principles regarding Athenian inheritance, many inheritance disputes degenerated into ugly, mendacious quarrels that were waged by means of perjured testimony and forged documents. As a rule, sons—without regard to their order of birth—inherited their father's estate equally, and they ordinarily divided his estate (*klēros*). In the circumstance of an *epiklēros*, marriage by *epidikasia* ensured that the deceased's *oikos* would continue and that his estate would be secure. When a deceased man had no sons and no *epiklēros*, there was a strict order of inheritance: brothers and half-brothers by the same father; sisters and

---

7. *Id.* at 95–96.

half-sisters by the same father; the father's other relatives; half-brothers by the same mother; half-sisters by the same mother; all other relatives on the mother's side. Athenian inheritance was based on a *per stirpes* system; allowing a deceased's grandchildren to inherit their father's share. The procedure called *epidikasia* permitted persons who had uncontested inheritance claims to petition the Archon. The procedure known as *diadikasia* was used to resolve contested claims. Athenians who had no living sons routinely adopted sons to secure heirs. Ordinarily ancient Athenians used what we might call a "will" only to adopt an heir, but not to bequeath property.

CHAPTER 7

CRIMINAL LAW

§7.01 Introduction

Most scholars who specialize in Athenian law agree that criminal law, in its modern sense, did not exist in Classical Athens.[1] Although there was a group of Skythian archers who performed some of the duties of modern police, and although the "Eleven" "had charge of prisons and executions ... [and] also had the power summarily to arrest offenders...," the State on the whole lacked the basic institutions necessary to operate a criminal justice system.[2] There were no district attorneys, no criminal courts, and no categories of "crimes" *per se*. Nevertheless, there were many laws that were designed not only to remedy a wrong but also to punish offenders, and also laws that required the guilty to pay fines to the State. Indeed, modern criminal law scholars recognize punishment as one of the paradigm purposes of criminal law. Furthermore, the Athenians had numerous laws designed to protect the interests of the community as a whole; a goal also frequently found in modern criminal laws. Therefore, although criminal law may not have existed in ancient Athens in a technical sense, it is useful for modern readers to consider, as a group, those Athenian offenses that are most closely analogous to and that correspond with the objects of our modern criminal laws; such as homicide, theft, sexual offenses, and criminal battery.

---

1. "[I]t is widely agreed among scholars that the concept of crime cannot be properly applied to Athens at all, where prosecutions were almost invariably brought by private individuals acting on their own behalf even for offences committed directly against the state." TODD, SHAPE 263.
   2. *Id.* at 79.

§7.02 Homicide

A. General

Undoubtedly the most famous Athenian law relating to homicide was Draco's (*c.* 621 B.C.). Well into the 4th century B.C., the Athenians still claimed to be applying Draco's homicide law. Athenian homicide law had at least three objectives: 1) deterrence; 2) revenge; and, 3) religious purification. As to the third, the ancient Greeks believed that a killing itself precipitated a "pollution" sent by the gods, *miasma*. MacDowell explains: "[p]ollution was a kind of supernatural infection, which was liable to spread from the killer to others who consorted with him, and to the whole community, unless they took steps to bring him to justice."[3]

B. Categories

Classical Athenian law differentiated between intentional and unintentional homicide. Like contemporary American law, Athenian law recognized that a person who kills another on purpose commits a more culpable act than one who kills accidentally. Consequently, the Athenians punished someone who killed by design more severely than one who killed through some unforeseeable mishap. A slayer's state of mind at the moment of the lethal act, then, determined the manner in which Athenian law treated any given homicide. Modern jurisprudence distinguishes varying degrees of an accused's state of mind. We use terms such as premeditation, intent, recklessness, and negligence to classify diverse kinds of mental states. To better appreciate the Athenian law, it is useful first to summarize how modern criminal law treats the different mental states that a killer may have.

In contemporary homicide law, "premeditation" is ordinarily considered the most blameworthy state of mind; encompassing both the notions of planning and deliberation prior to killing. A person is usually said to kill with "intent" when he either desires to cause death or serious bodily harm, or when he acts while being substantially certain that his act will produce death or serious bodily harm. A person kills "recklessly" when he kills knowing that his conduct will produce an unusually high degree of probability that it will cause death or serious bodily harm. And, a person kills "negligently" when his conduct fails to conform to that of a reasonably prudent person.

---

3. MacDowell, The Law in Classical Athens 110.

The ancient Athenians used at least three terms that may be translated "intentionally": 1) *ek pronoias* ("with forethought," "with design," "purposely"); 2) *hekēn*; and, 3) *hekousios* ("voluntarily"). Scholars disagree about the precise nuances of these terms. Nevertheless, a homicide that was described by any one of these terms was treated differently from a negligent or otherwise accidental homicide. A homicide that could be described as *ek pronoias, hekēn,* or *hekousios* was punishable by death and the confiscation of the murderer's property. Athenian law punished unintentional homicide by exile (permanent, pending pardon). But, in the case of unintentional homicide, the victim's family retained the right to pardon the killer. Punishment for killing a slave was less severe than for killing a citizen.

Athenian law appreciated certain mitigating factors that modern criminal law characterizes as affirmative defenses. The affirmative defenses that are most evident in Athenian homicide law are assumption of risk, self-defense, defense of property, and "heat of passion." For example, when an athlete killed a competitor while wrestling or boxing, such a homicide was excused. Today we would say that the victim had assumed the risk of death or serious bodily harm simply by voluntarily engaging in such a violent and inherently dangerous sport. Curiously, the same rationale apparently applied to doctors and their patients. When a patient died, the doctor was not held responsible. Perhaps, in such a primitive state of medicine, a patient was considered to assume the risk of death when being treated by a physician. Interestingly, this exception stands in stark contrast to several ancient Mesopotamian law collections that severely punished doctors under similar circumstances.[4] In situations where a victim actually was the initial aggressor (*i.e.,* the first to strike a blow) and the killer responded in self-defense, Athenian law permitted the killer a complete defense. If a man killed a thief who was either using force or attempting to rob him at night, he was excused under the theory that a man is entitled to defend his property in such circumstances (*i.e.,* forceful or nocturnal attempts of robbery). A complete defense was available for a man who killed another *in flagrante delicto* with his mother, sister, daughter, or a concubine kept "with a view to free children."[5] One other kind of justifiable homicide was the murder of a person who had been declared a "public enemy."

Abortion was, technically speaking, not treated as a kind of homicide. In many respects the Athenians considered abortion a wrong committed against

---

4. *See* Russ VerSteeg, Early Mesopotamian Law §9.07, 139 (2000).

5. *See* Harrison, The Law of Athens (Vol. I) 13 (Harrison refers to this "concubine" as a *pallakē* "whom a man had taken to himself with the purpose of breeding free children from her.").

the father. Thus, it was possible for a father to bring an action for abortion by *dikē*. But a *graphē* was also possible. Harrison notes, "the fact that a *graphē* was available might suggest that abortion was regarded as a public wrong...."[6]

C. Procedure

There was no district attorney who initiated criminal proceedings against an alleged killer. Rather, a victim's family bore the responsibility of starting the trial process. Generally, a close male relative introduced the legal proceedings against an alleged killer. If the victim was a slave, then it was the owner who brought suit.

The prosecuting relative was first required to make an accusation against the alleged killer in the Agora. As part of that allegation, he demanded that the accused "keep away from things laid down by law." The prosecuting relative next brought his accusation to the Archon Basileus, the official principally responsible for religious matters. The Archon Basileus also proclaimed that the person charged with the homicide must stay away from the things laid down by law. This formulaic prohibition—that the accused had to "keep away from things laid down by law"—required that he must refrain from entering temples, public religious ceremonies, the Agora, all public meetings, and the law courts. If someone charged with homicide violated the terms of this prohibition—for example, if an accused entered the Agora—he was subject to the procedure called *apagogē*. Using *apagogē*, anyone was authorized to make what amounted to a citizen's arrest, and could escort the accused to "the Eleven," the prison wardens, who then incarcerated the accused until he could be tried on the homicide charge. If he did not violate the terms of the prohibition, the accused seems to have been free to go about as he pleased while awaiting trial.

There were primarily two adjudicative bodies that tried homicide cases: the *Areopagus* and the *Ephetai*. The *Areopagus* was the council composed of ex-*archons* (perhaps as many as 200 members at times during the 5th and 4th centuries B.C.) who were given life-tenure. Because of the status of its members, the *Areopagus* maintained an outstanding reputation for sound opinions (although there were some notorious exceptions). It generally heard cases where a defendant was accused of intentional homicide. Interestingly, the *Aereopagus* was known for considering and analyzing the facts of cases more than other ordinary courts. The *Areopagus* held court only on the last three days of every month.

---

6. *Id.* at 72.

The *Ephetai*, a special court of 51 men over the age of 50—perhaps a subgroup of the Areopagus—tried other homicide cases in four distinct courts: 1) the *Delphinion*; 2) the *Palladion*; 3) the *Prytaneion*; and, 4) the *Phreatto*. Homicide cases were tried in the *Delphinion* when the defendant was asserting an affirmative defense (*i.e.*, arguing that the homicide was excused on grounds of assumption of risk, self-defense, defense of property, *etc.*). Cases were heard in the *Palladion* when the homicide was clearly unintentional or when the victim was either a slave or a foreigner. The *Prytaneion* was the site for cases where a death was caused either by an unknown person (*i.e.*, the victim's family had no suspects), an animal, or an inanimate object. There the Archon Basileus conducted a special trial accompanied by the four kings of the tribes.[7] This unique court officially denounced the undetermined killer. In the case of death by animal, the court denounced it and then either killed it or drove it from Attica. Similarly, if the homicide had been caused by a lifeless object, they physically ejected it outside of Attica's borders. Presumably, this process achieved a cleansing and ritualistic function. Lastly, the *Phreatto* was the location where cases were heard when the accused had already been convicted and exiled for a prior homicide. Thus, the defendant had to plead his case from a boat while the judges sat on the beach. The defendant was not permitted on Attic soil lest he pollute it.

As was noted, it was the victim's family that was responsible for instituting legal proceedings against an accused killer. The procedural stages of an Athenian homicide trial, then, were roughly as follows.

1) The victim's relative, in the role of prosecutor, files a charge against the accused with the Archon Basileus, and proclaims that the accused must henceforth keep away from things laid down by law.

2) The Archon Basileus formally and officially proclaims that the accused must keep away from things laid down by law.

3) The Archon Basileus holds three separate pre-trial conferences (*prodikasiai*) in three successive months.

4) In the fourth month immediately following the three *prodikasiai*, the Archon Basileus convenes and presides over the actual trial on the merits.[8]

---

7. *See supra* §2.10.

8. The same individual Archon Basileus was required to preside at all four hearings (*i.e.*, the three pre-trial conferences and the trial itself). Therefore, since archons were only in office for one calendar year at a time, a homicide trial could only be started during the first nine months of the year—not during the last three months. Otherwise, the Archon Basileus would be unable to see the trial through to completion. *See* MacDowell, The Law in Classical Athens 118.

During the trial on the merits, the prosecutor presented his case first. The accused was next allowed to make his speech in reply. After the accused had completed his first speech, he was allowed to go into exile voluntarily rather than proceeding to judgment. Thus, if the accused perceived that the case was going poorly and acquittal seemed unlikely, he could at least save his skin by choosing exile rather than risking death as a result of conviction. If the accused chose not to go into exile, then the prosecutor made his final speech followed again by the defendant's closing argument. Both parties swore oaths attesting to the veracity of their respective statements. And, unlike other trials, women, children, and slaves could testify as witnesses in homicide cases. The jury voted immediately after the defendant's closing, and the Archon Basileius announced the jury's verdict.

§ 7.03 Theft Crimes

Even in modern American law it is difficult to distinguish tort theory from criminal law theory in situations where one individual takes personal property that belongs to another without permission. When one person takes another's property, criminal law regards the former's conduct as "theft" and tort law considers his conduct "conversion." For purposes of this chapter, we shall consider such conduct as criminal.

When a property owner caught a thief red-handed, he could employ the procedure known as *apagoge* to take him before the Eleven for punishment. The cause of action for theft in classical Athens was called *dikē klopēs*. Common street thieves probably were tried before the Eleven using "summary procedures and punishments" rather than having a trial on a grand scale repleat with logographers and extensive procedures.[9] Athenian law required a person found guilty of theft to return the object stolen and to pay the plaintiff twice its value. One speech of Demosthenes suggests that the guilty defendant paid the plaintiff and the State equal amounts. In today's terms, then, we would say that the remedy for theft involved both a civil and a criminal element (compensation and a fine). A jury could also penalize a thief with confinement in the stocks; a form of public humiliation. A more serious degree of theft was *dikē biaiēn* (theft by force). A defendant found guilty of *dikē biaiēn* paid damages to the plaintiff in any amount that the jury deemed appropriate. In addition, the guilty defendant paid the same amount to the State as a fine. Finally,

---

9. *See* COHEN, LAW VIOLENCE AND COMMUNITY IN CLASSICAL ATHENS 139.

the most serious degree of theft was a kind classified by the Athenians as having been committed by the *kakourgoi* ("malefactors"): those thieves who: 1) stole at night; 2) stole from a gymnasium or other location where men disrobed to exercise; 3) stole more than ten drachmas from a harbor; or, 4) stole more than fifty drachmas from anywhere else. Those thieves found guilty as *kakourgoi* received the death penalty.

In addition to these three private causes of action (*dikē*) for theft, Athenian law also permitted a *graphē* to be brought against someone accused of stealing from a sacred treasury (for example by embezzlement). Furthermore, robbing from a temple (*hierosylia*) was punishable by death.

§7.04 Sexual Conduct

If a man forced a woman to have extramarital sexual intercourse against her will, the woman and her *kyrios* could bring a private case against the rapist. A *kyrios* might bring an action before the thesmothetai called *graphē moicheias* or an action before the Forty with the suit known as *dikē biaiēn* (the same type of suit that a person brought if his property had been stolen through violent means). Unfortunately, we are certain of precious few details about the laws dealing with rape in ancient Athens. Solon established the compensation for rape at 100 drachmas. By the 4th century B.C., the penalty for rape had acquired aspects that today we would characterize as both civil and criminal. The jury used its discretion to determine the money damages that a rapist had to pay; but he paid an equal amount to the victim (compensatory damages) and to the State (a fine). Of course, the victim, since she was unwilling, was not criminally liable. [→head of house?]

Evidently a *kyrios* had the right to kill anyone caught in the act of sexually violating a member of his household. Our sources, however, emphasize this remedy against the adulterer, not the rapist. If a man had extramarital sexual intercourse with a woman who was not forced but instead seduced, Athenian law, at least according to Lysias, treated the seducer more harshly than a rapist.[10] The rationale for punishing a seducer more severely than a rapist was that a rapist only abused and injured a female's body but a seducer perverted her mentally. This distinction is roughly analogous to the difference between taking an enemy as a prisoner of war *versus* convincing an enemy to desert and join the other side as a turn-coat. As was noted, if a woman's *kyrios* caught the seducer in

---

10. *See* Lysias 1.32–33. *See also* HARRISON, THE LAW OF ATHENS (Vol. I) 34.

Could nearly do anything to a seducer!

the act, he (the *kyrios*) legally was entitled to kill the seducer on the spot without being subject to penalty for murder. If the *kyrios* so desired, instead of killing the seducer, he could seize him and demand money as compensation. He could even subject him to torture. "[T]he husband could inflict on the adulterer various bodily humiliations, or he could accept compensation from him, holding him a prisoner until he could provide sureties for the payment of the sum agreed."[11] According to Cohen, "we possess no references to actual prosecutions (*graphai*) brought for adultery."[12]

Evidence suggests that Athenian law punished a woman who willingly had extramarital sexual relations. A husband immediately divorced his wife if she was found guilty of adultery, and an Athenian woman found guilty of adultery was automatically denied access to public religious ceremonies. If, after a successful prosecution for adultery, a man still refused to divorce his wife, he suffered *atimia*.[13] In addition, the laws prohibited the adulteress thenceforth from wearing any adornments. Some legal historians have hypothesized that this prohibition was intended to decrease the likelihood that other men would find her attractive. But female prostitution itself was not illegal,[14] and so extramarital intercourse with a prostitute was not considered seduction. Similarly, slave owners could (and frequently did) have sex with their female slaves without violating any laws.

As a final note, it is worthwhile to appreciate that, as Cohen states, "adultery, rape, and seduction all would have fallen within the purview of the law of hubris because they all involve insults to the honor of the family to which the woman belongs."[15]

§ 7.05 Criminal Battery

A kind of battery serious enough to classify under criminal law rather than tort was called *trauma ek pronoias* ("wounding with intent" to kill). In fact,

---

11. Harrison, The Law of Athens (Vol. I) 33.

12. Cohen, Law, Violence and Community in Classical Athens 155.

13. *See supra* § 3.01.

14. Athenian law permitted homosexual activity. Male prostitution was legal for a non-citizen. A male citizen who was a prostitute, however, could be punished by a loss of certain citizenship rights, *atima*. *See* MacDowell, The Law in Classical Athens 125–126; Cohen, Law, Violence and Community in Classical Athens 155; Harrison, The Law of Athens (Vol. I) 37–38.

15. Cohen, Law, Violence and Community in Classical Athens 151. For a brief description of *hubris*, *see infra* § 7.06.

trauma ek pronoias was probably similar to the modern criminal offense of aggravated assault. Speeches of Demosthenes and Lysias suggest that *trauma ek pronoias* was battery with a weapon—not just with fists. Procedurally, a suit for *trauma ek pronoias* was brought by *dikē* before the *Areopagus*, and if found guilty, the defendant was punished with exile and his property was confiscated.

§7.06 *Hubris*

According to Demosthenes, it was technically possible to prosecute someone, by *graphē*, for *hubris*. A legal cause of action for *hubris* could be predicated on behavior that had been directed toward any man, woman, or child (free or slave). As a practical matter, however, very few cases for *hubris* were ever brought to trial. The paucity of cases brought alleging *hubris* was probably due, in part, to the difficulty of defining *hubris*. The Hellenic concept of *hubris* was complex. No single English word functions as an appropriate synonym. *Hubris* combines a number of unsavory characteristics. For purposes of law, the ancient Greeks considered a person's conduct to be hubristic if it was arrogant, self-righteous, irresponsible, indulgent, taunting, and insulting. *Hubris* often also involved a measure of sexual oppression, domination, aggression, and degredation. Cohen characterizes "essentially unproblematic," "standard cases" of *hubris* as "[a]busive and humiliating public assaults and rape (whether heterosexual or homosexual)...."[16] It was easier, nevertheless, in most cases, simply to prove that a defendant had committed battery or slander, and to obtain redress using those simpler legal theories. Otherwise, to prove *hubris* a plaintiff needed to prove that the defendant had displayed an arrogant, self-righteous, irresponsible, *etc.* attitude at the moment that he had injured the plaintiff.

§7.07 Religious Offenses

A. Introduction

In the 4th century B.C., religious officials, called *exegetai* ("expounders"), memorized sacred laws so that they could advise others about them. Unlike today, persons accused of violating religious laws could be prosecuted in the State court system.

---

16. COHEN, LAW, VIOLENCE AND COMMUNITY IN CLASSICAL ATHENS 153.

B. Laws Related to Festivals

When someone violated a rule of conduct regarding religious festivals, anyone else could prosecute the transgressor using the procedure called *probolē*. A person conducting a prosecution for *probolē* brought his case to the *Ekklēsia*, but the *Ekklēsia's* vote was merely a straw vote. After the *Ekklēsia's* vote, a *probolē* prosecutor had to bring the case to another jury in the court of the *nomothetai*. "Any 'wrong action concerning the festival' could be the subject of a *probolē*; this expression was not defined in the law, and it was for the *Ekklēsia* and subsequently the jury to decide whether the defendant's behavior should be so described."[17] It was, for example, illegal to try to collect debts during festivals. In fact this was a particular problem.

C. Impiety

In the 5th and 4th centuries B.C., a prosecutor generally used the *graphē* procedure to prosecute someone for *asebeia* ("impiety"). *Asebeia* included offenses such as the following: 1) the wrong person performing a sacrifice; 2) battery, violence, or other misbehavior in a temple; 3) performing magic; 4) honoring religions other than those traditionally recognized by the State; 5) mutilation of statues of deities; and, 6) parodying secret religious ceremonies (*e.g.*, those of the Eleusinian Mysteries).

For cases that were especially serious, a prosecutor alleging impiety might use *eisangelia* before the *Ekklēsia* and *Boulē* instead of using a *graphē*. *Asebeia* was probably not carefully defined. Thus, juries were left to interpret it on an ad hoc basis; determining whether any given conduct should be construed as impious. The famous trial of the philosopher Socrates in 399 B.C. was a *graphē* for "impiety." The penalty was usually severe; either death or permanent exile coupled with confiscation of property. Apparently, a plaintiff/prosecutor often brought a charge of impiety in an attempt to destroy a political rival.

D. Atheism

Prior to the 430's B.C., it was probably not a punishable offense for a person simply to express that he did not believe in the traditional gods. Then, in the 430's, the Athenians passed the Decree of Diopeithes, a decree which forbade both stating a disbelief in the traditional gods and the teaching of as-

---

17. MacDowell, The Law in Classical Athens 195.

tronomy. The procedure contemplated to enforce these prohibitions was *eisangelia*. At least two well-known ancient philosophers were prosecuted under this law: Anaxagoras and Protagoras. This law is probably best understood as a prohibition of "atheistic speech."[18]

§7.08 Miscellaneous Crimes

A. Arson

To recompense injury by arson, it is likely that an individual whose property had been damaged by fire brought a *graphē* before the *Areopagus*. But perhaps cases only went before the *Areopagus* if the blaze had actually injured a person (in addition to merely property).

B. *Prodosia* (Betrayal)

An Athenian general could be subject to prosecution for *prodosia* for the loss of ships, troops, or territory.

C. Deception of the People

If someone persuaded the *Ekklēsia* to make a particularly bad decision, that person could be prosecuted for deception of the people and receive a death sentence.

D. *Eisangelia*

It is possible that, as early as the 5th century, *eisangelia* was a procedure used for "new wrongs"—things that were arguably wrong, but for which no rule or law yet existed. It was also used for some other offenses, such as treason, that were pretty well defined. In the late 4th century B.C., *eisangelia* was the procedure used to prosecute three distinct types of conduct that were considered injurious to the State: 1) subverting the democracy; 2) betrayal; and, 3) (an orator) misleading the people. This, in many respects, sounds like a basic law against treason. It is probable that during the Reinscription (*c.* 410–403

---

18. *Id.* at 200.

B.C.) the custom of using *eisangelia* for treason was codified. At about this time, *eisangelia* may also have been used *only* for treason and *not* (like before) for any wrongs committed for which there was no adequate cause of action.

§ 7.09 Chapter Summary

The ancient Athenians did not have a body of law that technically was analogous to modern criminal law. Nevertheless, they did have some laws—laws that imposed punishment or fines—relating to homicide, theft, sexual conduct, and the infliction of injury that were similar in many respects to modern criminal law. Draco is famous for establishing the foundational principles of Athenian homicide law. In addition to a desire for revenge and deterrence, the Greeks punished homicide because they believed that homicide caused a pollution (*miasma*) that damaged an entire community. Thus, formal, legal resolution was needed for homicide. Athenian law punished intentional homicide that was characterized as *ek pronoias*, *hekēn*, or *hekousios* (we might say "murder") by death and loss of property, but treated unintentional homicide ("manslaughter") less severely—with exile. They accepted self-defense, defense of property, assumption of risk, and "heat of passion" as justifiable excuses for homicide. Although abortion was, technically speaking, not treated as a kind of homicide, in many respects it was treated as an offense against the father.

Using a specific legal process (including a formal declaration made in the Agora, requiring the accused to "keep away from things laid down by law"), a close relative of the homicide victim ordinarily prosecuted the case. As a rule, the *Areopagus* tried a person accused of intentional homicide and the *Ephetai* heard all other cases of homicide. The *Ephetai* tried cases in four distinct venues: 1) the *Delphinion* (when a defendant asserted an affirmative defense); 2) the *Palladion* (cases involving a homicide that was clearly unintentional, or when the victim was a slave or foreigner); the *Prytaneion* (when the death was caused by an unknown person, an animal, or inanimate object); and, 4) the *Phreatto* (when the defendant had already been convicted or exiled for a prior homicide).

An Athenian homicide trial ordinarily proceeded through four distinct stages: 1) a relative of the victim initiated the complaint with the Archon *Basileus*, proclaiming that the accused must "keep away from things laid down by law"; 2) the Archon *Basileus* made the same formal pronouncement; 3) the Archon *Basileus* held three pre-trial conferences (*prodikasiai*); and, 4) the *Basileus* presided over the trial on the merits. At trial, the prosecution presented its case first, followed by the defense. Prior to final arguments, the accused was given the opportunity to go into exile rather than proceeding to the jury.

The punishment for theft varied, depending upon the amount stolen, the location of the theft, and whether force was involved. For simple theft (*dikē klopēs*) a thief had to return the stolen object and pay the victim twice its value. For theft by force (*dikē biaiēn*) a fine paid to the State was usually imposed as well. The death penalty was given for more serious types of theft (*kakourgoi*) and theft from the treasury or a temple.

Rape was punished by payment of money damages to the victim (100 drachmas under Solon's laws) and also a fine to the State. A *kyrios* might bring an action before the *thesmothetai* (*graphē moicheias*) or an action before the Forty (*dikē biaiēn*). Seduction, because it entailed mental subversion, was considered more heinous than rape. The victim's *kyrios* was permitted to kill or torture a seducer who was caught in the act; or he could seize him and demand a payment of money damages. Adultery committed by a married woman was considered wrongful, but we possess few details regarding it. The husband was required to divorce an adulteress, and she was, thereafter, forbidden to wear jewelry and forbidden attendance at public religious ceremonies. Female prostitution, however, was permissible both legally and socially.

Trauma ek pronoias was a kind of criminal battery involving either unusual force or the use of a weapon with intent to kill. One of the more enigmatic wrongs that may be considered criminal was *hubris*. The Athenians categorized certain types of abusive behavior as *hubris*. *Hubris* has no modern analogue, but it encompassed a broad range of activity that included arrogant, insulting, and sexually aggressive acts. The most obvious kinds of wrongs relating to religion were offenses committed in connection with a religious festival, impiety (*asebeia*), and atheism. For offenses committed in connection with a religious festival (*e.g.*, collecting a debt at a festival), a prosecutor brought his case using the procedure known as *probolē*. A prosecutor could use *graphē* to prosecute someone for impiety (*asebeia*). Since *asebeia* was not well defined, juries had broad latitude to interpret it as they wished on an ad hoc basis. After 430 B.C., a prosecutor could use *eisangelia* to allege atheism.

In addition to these "crimes" clearly there were others recognized in Athenian law, such as arson, betrayal by a general, and "misleading the people." The procedure called *eisangelia* was perhaps once used to prosecute a variety of "new" wrongs, but by the beginning of the 4th century, *eisangelia* was the procedure used in cases alleging treason.

CHAPTER 8

TORTS

§ 8.01 Introduction

Modern American law recognizes tort as a distinct field of substantive law. Although there is no one unifying principle of modern tort law, most lawyers are content to define torts as non-contractual civil wrongs. In contemporary tort doctrine, defendants, generally speaking, become subject to liability when they intentionally cause harm, or when their conduct causes foreseeable harm (negligence), or when their conduct causes harm in such a manner that they will be deemed strictly liable (*i.e.,* usually for reasons of public policy and risk management—without regard to whether the consequences of their conduct were either intentional or reasonably foreseeable). There was no directly analogous group of laws in ancient Athens, yet many *dikai* seem roughly similar to modern tort categories; such as battery, false imprisonment, and defamation. In addition to these, the Athenians of the classical era used a particular cause of action, *dikē blabēs*,[1] as a legal mechanism for redressing several types of conduct that we today would classify as tortious.

§ 8.02 Battery (*Dikē Aikeias*)

Modern tort law clearly distinguishes assault from battery. Battery is the act of intentionally causing harmful or offensive contact with another person. Assault occurs when a person intentionally causes another to apprehend that harmful or offensive contact is imminent. Athenian law in the 5th and 4th centuries B.C. did not really recognize so fine-tuned a distinction. An Athenian committed battery (*dikē aikeias*) when he struck another. If a fight ensued between the two, only the initial aggressor (*i.e.,* the one to strike the first blow) was subject to liability for battery. Generally, intentional personal injury did

---

1. *See infra* § 8.05.

not occur in isolation. Cases such as these were ordinarily the result of an extended feud, or ongoing enmity between the parties. In any event, the jury assessed compensation to the victim with money damages.

§ 8.03 False Imprisonment (*Dikē Heirgmou*)

Although details are few, it appears that Athenian law recognized a wrong akin to the modern tort of false imprisonment. This cause of action was called *dikē heirgmou*,[2] and we can only guess that the jury used its discretion in fixing damages for each such case.

§ 8.04 Defamation (*Dikē Kakegorias*)

Solon's laws prohibited maligning anyone who was deceased. Solon's laws also punished speaking ill of anyone while in a temple, in court at trial, in public offices, or while at festival contests. Damages for these types of slander under Solon had both civil and criminal components: the slanderer had to pay five drachmas; three to the person slandered and two to the State.[3] By the end of the 4th century B.C., the Athenians had modified and updated the law of slander, *dikē kakēgorias*. From the speeches of Lysias and Demosthenes, we know that it was considered slander to allege falsely that someone had beaten or killed his father or mother, and it was also deemed slanderous to allege falsely that someone (presumably while a soldier in battle) had thrown away his shield. Furthermore, it was defamatory to deprecate the work of a citizen in the Agora. Although some recent scholarship has cast doubt on whether truth was a defense as it is in modern doctrine,[4] most legal historians have believed that such statements were regarded defamatory only if they were false.[5] Thus, if an Athenian accused of slander could prove that his assertion was true (for example, if the plaintiff had, in fact, beaten his father as the defendant

---

2. Or it was also called *graphē adikēs heirkhthēnai*. This would be the remedy in cases where a husband has wrongly seized a supposed adulterer.

3. But Professor Sealey doubts whether the payment to the State was really a criminal fine. He suggest instead that it may have been a payment to the State officer as recompense for the plaintiff wrongfully requesting the officer's protection. *See* SEALEY, JUSTICE 127.

4. *See* TODD, SHAPE 260 ("Independent evidence, however, tends to confirm that 'truth' was not admissible as a defence in cases of defamation at Athens.").

5. *See* MACDOWELL, THE LAW IN CLASSICAL ATHENS 128.

had alleged), then he (*i.e.*, the defendant) had a complete and effective defense. At any rate, the plaintiff certainly argued that the assertions were false.

Athenian law in the late 4th century fixed damages for slander at 500 drachmas. But we do not know whether the guilty slanderer paid the entire 500 drachmas to the plaintiff or whether the same 60%–40% ratio established by the laws of Solon still operated (in which case a slanderer would have been required to pay 300 drachmas to the plaintiff and 200 to the State as a fine).

It is likely that the laws regarding slander applied with equal force to false statements that were written (*i.e.*, not only words merely spoken). The Athenians apparently had no *dikē* for libel that was distinct from slander.

Modern American defamation doctrine has had to be sufficiently flexible to accommodate our First Amendment right to free speech. Courts have afforded considerable latitude, for example, to political satire. In a similar manner, Athenian defamation law seems, generally speaking, to have exempted the playwrights of Old Comedy during the 5th century (at least prior to 414 B.C. when, evidently, the scope of this exemption was severely narrowed). Some of Aristophanes' characters, for example, say things about contemporary politicians that clearly would have been slanderous had there been no "comedy exception."

§ 8.05 *Dikē Blabēs*

Dikē blabēs was a cause of action used to redress a wide variety of civil wrongs, many of which involved an allegation by the plaintiff that the defendant's conduct (*i.e.*, either action or failure to act) caused him (plaintiff) some type of harm. The torts that modern American law labels as "trespass to chattel" and "conversion" were, in part, addressed by *dikē blabēs*, because the property owner (*i.e.*, the owner whose property had been damaged) had suffered an economic loss. In these cases, the loss was a reduction in his property's value. *Dikē blabēs* also was the most common cause of action for breach of contract.[6] In addition, it was used in circumstances where modern doctrine would employ nuisance, both intentional and unintentional harm, and even strict liability.

§ 8.06 Chapter Summary

As was the case with criminal law, the Athenians did not distinguish a discrete category of tort law. Many types of *dikē*, however, were analogous to

---

6. *See infra* § 9.04.

"wrongs" that modern law catalogs as torts; and courts typically imposed money damages for these wrongs. *Dikē aikeias* was similar to the modern concept of battery (*i.e.* intentionally striking another), *dikē heirgmou* was similar to what we call false imprisonment, and *dikē kakēgorias* was an action for defamation. The laws regarding defamation were more specific than general. Solon's laws prohibited maligning anyone who was deceased, anyone while in a temple, court, public office, or at a festival. Other laws punished (*i.e.,* by the 4th century B.C., damages were fixed at 500 drachmas) those who falsely alleged that someone had beaten or killed his parents or that he had discarded his shield in battle. The political satire of Attic Comedy seems to have been permitted without recourse to the law of defamation. *Dikē blabēs* was a rather broad cause of action that the Athenians used in circumstances where modern litigants would bring suit for property damage of one sort or another.

CHAPTER 9

TRADE, CONTRACTS,[1] AND COMMERCIAL LAW

§9.01 Introduction

In the *Iliad*, characters use oxen as a medium of exchange. Homer refers to objects as being worth X-number of oxen to describe their value. Once coinage was invented by the Lydians in the 7th century B.C., the Athenians found that the sale of goods was much easier using coined money. Under Athenian law, title passed from seller to buyer at the moment when the buyer physically gave cash to the seller. Many historians have maintained that ancient Athenian law did not sanction sales on credit. However, we know of at least one instance when a seller of slaves loaned the purchase money for the sale to the buyer. Obviously, this arrangement was functionally the same as a sale on credit. Todd explains that "freedom of contract" was a powerful principle in ancient Athens:

> The doctrine of freedom of contract was so strong at Athens that it was possible to contract out of the protection of the law, or to agree that a contract should take precedence over law, or to expect a court of law to uphold a contract which is publicly admitted to have constituted a conspiracy to commit an unlawful act.[2]

In order to make a valid contract, Athenian law required the existence of four elements: 1) the parties had to agree; 2) their agreement had to be voluntarily; 3) their agreement had to be made in the presence of witnesses; and, 4) their agreement had to be just. Quite obviously, the requirement that an agreement be "just" is extremely subjective. Contracts did not have to be in writing. Ev-

---

1. Todd maintains that it is "inappropriate" to refer to "contract" as a category of law in classical Athens. TODD, SHAPE 72, 263–67. With all due respect, as someone who regularly teaches contract law in an American law school, I find his "arguments" (for a lack of contract theory in classical Athens) unpersuasive.

2. TODD, SHAPE 264 (footnote omitted).

idence is strong that Athenian contract law bound buyers and sellers from the moment of their agreement forward. For example, once a buyer had paid a deposit (*arrabon*) to his seller, the seller was legally obligated to hold the property secured by the deposit until the time fixed by their agreement for final payment.

Several laws proscribed misrepresentation in sales transactions. First, sellers in the Agora were not permitted to say things about their goods that were untrue (*i.e.*, false advertising). In a more particularized context, slave sellers were legally obligated to disclose to their buyers any of the slave's bodily faults. A buyer could return for a refund any slave whom he (*i.e.*, the buyer) later discovered had a defect that the seller had failed to disclose at the time of the original sale. Prior to selling real estate, Athenian law required that a prospective seller give 60-days' written notice (to a State official) of his intent to sell. Since there was no land registration procedure in Athens to protect prospective buyers, this requirement of written notice provided the public an opportunity to catch a swindler in advance.

§ 9.02 Lease Contracts

In ancient Athens a landowner could lease his property to another This could be done either orally or in writing. A lease arrangement might include a payment schedule for lease payments and specific provisions detailing a lessee's obligations. Landowners routinely leased agricultural property to be farmed. We have some examples of leases—from public entities to private individuals—that were actually recorded on stone. One such lease required the lessee to whitewash the building's walls, to husband the trees on the leased property, and provided for liquidated damages in the event that the lessee failed to fulfill his obligations under the lease. When a lessee did breach a lease agreement, the lessor could bring suit (*dikē enoikiou* or *dikē karpou*).

§ 9.03 Loans

It was lawful for one Athenian to loan money to another. But of the hundreds of loans that we know about from ancient documents, only about a dozen are loans borrowed from a banker, the rest are from private individuals. Although it was common for creditors to charge interest at a rate of 1% per month, the law dictated neither the amount of interest nor the duration of a loan. And, although Solon abolished debt slavery, a creditor could, nevertheless, confiscate his debtor's property in the event that the debtor failed to pay back his loan.

In order to foster the making of loans, for the benefit of debtors, while at the same time providing protection for the benefit of creditors, debtors soon discovered the utility of giving their creditors collateral (*enekhuron* or *hypothekē*) as security for loans. We know of Athenians using items both of personal property (*e.g.*, a gold cup, a horse, slaves) and real property (*e.g.*, land itself or a house) as collateral for loans. Ship-masters, for example, routinely used their ships and cargo as collateral for loans. Scholars have identified no less than four distinct types of collateral arrangements; each with its own peculiar rules relating to the nature of the collateral and the ownership and possession of it.

It would be an understatement to say that the "law" on this topic is both complex and ambiguous. According to Harrison, however, "sale with right of redemption is, for the classical period, the predominant and typical form of real security."[3] Archaeologists have even unearthed stones (*horoi*) that were placed on land that had been used as collateral for loans. These stones have inscriptions detailing the conditions of the loan agreements. Some texts also show the use of sureties (*enguētai*), people who promised to pay in the event that the debtor defaulted. *Dikē khreēs* was the cause of action for failure to repay a debt. *Dikē parakatathēkēs* was the cause of action for refusal to repay a deposit.

§9.04 Breach of Contract

Dikē blabēs was used as a cause of action to recover, as a general theory, for any kind of economic loss that one might incur.[4] Thus, plaintiffs could and did use *dikē blabēs* as a theory to recover for breach of contract (*e.g.*, failure to repay a loan). If a plaintiff could convince the jury that the defendant had caused the economic loss *intentionally*, the defendant had to pay twice the amount of the loss. Thus, *dikē blabēs* was a popular cause of action with Athenian plaintiffs.

§9.05 Commerce

Most commerce was retail and most took place in the Agora. As a rule (except during part of the 5th century B.C.), an alien could not trade in the Athenian Agora unless he paid a special tax (*xenika*). The "controllers of the market" (*agoranomoi*) served as a specialized court to arbitrate disputes brought in the

---

3. Harrison, The Law of Athens (Vol. I) 271.
4. *See supra* § 8.05.

market. There were five *agoranomoi* in the Agora and five in the Athenian port, the Peiraeus. Some particular laws that the *agoranomoi* applied in their court were laws that: 1) prohibited misrepresentation; 2) prohibited selling adulterated goods; and 3) prohibited fish sellers from sprinkling water on their fish in an effort to fool prospective buyers into thinking that the fish were more fresh than they really were. Some fish prices also seem to have been established by law.

The "guardians of grain" (*sitophylakes*) were a specialized panel, consisting of 5–20 men selected by lot, that enforced laws concerning the sale of grain. Some grain laws dealt with prices and others regulated the quantities of grain that any one seller was allowed to stockpile. Another unique judicial authority was that of the *epimelētai tou emporiou*, a commission that superintended the sale of grain in the wholesale market that was conducted in the Peiraeus at the *Emporion*.[5]

The board called the *metronomoi* (ordinarily five board members in the Agora and five in the Peiraeus) inspected measures and weights. In addition to the *metronomoi*, Classical Athens had a State-owned slave who held the position of "official coin tester." He sat in the Agora and inspected any suspect coins to judge their authenticity. The penalty for making counterfeit coins was death. But clearly death was not the penalty for merely *trying* to use a counterfeit coin. Any person attempting to use an imitation coin could always allege that he had received the fake from some third party.

For some violations of market laws, an offender could be subject to a legal procedure called *phasis*. Details of this process are not complete, but apparently *phasis* was initiated simply by publicly denouncing or exposing contraband or illegal gains. The procedure was then similar in some respects to *graphē*. For example, anyone could bring suit (*i.e.*, not just the individual injured), and a successful prosecutor received a bounty of half of the fine that the offender had to pay.

§ 9.06 Taxes

A. Introduction

The ancient Athenians considered the imposition of direct taxes on citizens the act of a tyrant. Therefore, the only taxes that they levied on citizens were indirect taxes, such as harbor dues, and irregular taxes, such as a tax on the wealthy, only imposed when there was a severe financial shortage. The purchaser of a house had to pay a real estate sales tax of 1% of the purchase price.

---

5. *See supra* § 2.05.

Metics paid a special metic's tax, the *metoikion*. The *metoikion* was a direct and regular tax on metics of one drachma per-month for men and one-half drachma per-month for women.[6] During the 5th and 4th centuries B.C., one drachma, the monthly *metoikion*, equalled, on average, a day's pay or less for a skilled laborer.

As a rule, the State auctioned off tax collection rights annually to the highest bidder. Legally, then, the State assigned its collection rights to the tax collector. Thus, the tax collector owed the State and the taxpayer owed the tax collector. The collector paid the State and kept whatever surplus he could as profit.

B. Liturgies (Compulsory Philanthropy)

Athenian law required the wealthiest citizens to foot the bill for a number of expensive public services. This compulsory philanthropic duty was called a "liturgy." For example, public officials appointed wealthy men, on an annual basis, to: 1) support public religious festivals; 2) maintain an Athenian warship (which included serving as its captain); and, 3) pay taxes for a group of taxpayers (and then the individual who had been appointed had to try to collect taxes from his designated citizens in order to reimburse himself). If an appointee wished to challenge his appointment to a liturgy, he could claim that another man was in a better financial position to take on the task. In so doing, he had to suggest a replacement (*i.e.,* another, more wealthy, Athenian to take his place) and challenge that person whom he had proposed to a procedure called *antidosis*. If the proposed substitute refused to accept the liturgy, the *antidosis* would compel him to exchange all of his property with the original appointee. Demosthenes once was involved in an *antidosis* action, and he decided to accept the liturgy rather than to transfer estates. It is doubtful whether anyone ever swapped property instead of taking on the liturgy.

§9.07 Chapter Summary

The Athenians had tremendous faith in freedom of contract; permitting individuals to fashion many kinds of agreements. Although parties did not have to write down an agreement in order for a contract to be considered valid, they did have to voluntarily agree to a just deal in the presence of witnesses. Specific laws concerning the sale of slaves, sales in the Agora, and sales of real property curbed fraud and various forms of misrepresentation. Other laws governed a lessee's

---

6. *See supra* §3.02.

obligations to his lessor, and we have a number of examples of lease contracts (*e.g.*, for farming agricultural land). Creditors (mostly private individuals) loaned money and charged interest. Although Solon abolished debt slavery, a creditor could, nevertheless, confiscate his debtor's property when the debtor defaulted. Collateral (*enekhuron* or *hypothekē*) was often given as security for loans. Scholars have identified no less than four distinct types of collateral arrangements; each with its own particular rules relating to the nature of the collateral and the ownership and possession of it. *Dikē blabēs* was the cause of action used for most breach of contract cases. For intentional breach, a breaching party had to pay double damages.

The Athenians established unique institutions to handle commercial disputes that occurred in the Agora. The *agoranomoi* ("controllers of the market"), *sitophylakes* ("guardians of grain"), *epimelētai tou emporiou*, and *metronomoi* (inspectors of weights and measures) adjudicated controversies arising from fraud, grain prices, and weights and measures in the marketplace. For some violations of market laws, an offender could be subject to a legal procedure called *phasis* which allowed a successful prosecutor to recover half of the offender's fine as a bounty.

The Athenian government imposed little in the way of direct taxes on its ordinary citizens. The State usually gathered the taxes that were collected by farming them out to independent tax collectors (who kept a portion for themselves as profit). There were some indirect taxes and sales taxes (*e.g.*, on real estate). And metics paid a special tax called the *metoikion*. Otherwise, a great deal of government expense (*e.g.*, funding for public religious festivals and maintenance of warships) was borne by the wealthy by means of liturgies.

Law in Literature:
The *Iliad*, The Trojan War, and Contract Law

Introduction

This examination of Law in Literature considers the myth of the Trojan War from a legal perspective, focusing on reciprocal agreements (contracts). Here we examine several "contracts" and potential contracts (unrealized) between characters in the *Iliad*. These examples include successful contracts between Achilles and Calchas, Hector and Dolon, Hupnos and Hera, and Achilles and Priam; as well as a rejected offer between Agamemnon and Achilles. We then consider the two major contacts that drive the myth, the "Prince's Contract" and the "Paris-Aphrodite Contract." This exploration concludes by reflecting on the role of the gods in contracts and the policies and values promoted by each of the contracts that animate this famous myth.

The extensive scope of Athenian contract jurisprudence suggests that this legal system had been developing over the previous centuries. Thus, many basic principles of Athenian contract law probably find their antecedents in Homer's *Iliad* and the myth of the Trojan War.

I. Contracts in the *Iliad*

From the perspective of modern American contract law, four of the contracts examined below appear to be agreements where both parties intended to benefit from reciprocal promises supported by consideration. The fifth interaction is actually the rejection (by Achilles) of an offer (by Agamemnon). Generally, four of these contracts are intended to advance one side's goals in the war: two seek information; one involves a trade of goods for services; and, one is an exchange of tangible goods.

A. Achilles-Calchas

Achilles and Calchas agree to exchange information for services. Achilles asked Calchas to reveal the cause of Apollo's anger towards the Achaean army. In return for this information, Calchas wanted to insure his own personal safety; once he revealed that Agamemnon was largely to blame for provoking Apollo's wrath. This behavior is similar to witnesses seeking police protection prior to giving information, and has the same effect as a modern whistleblower statutes in the United States, which protect an individual who reveals information for the public good but that is prejudicial to another party and might cause them to retaliate. Although we do not hear from Calchas again, Homer never suggests that he is harmed after revealing this information. This seems to illustrate that in preliterate/protoliterate Greece, a reciprocal agreement involving an exchange of information for services was a completely legitimate contract premise.

B. Hector-Dolon

Hector, the greatest Trojan warrior, and one of his soldiers, Dolon, agree to exchange wealth for services. Hector asks a group of soldiers for a volunteer to go on a dangerous spy mission for him. He offers numerous rewards and goods in return. Dolon volunteered to undertake this task. However, Dolon insisted that Hector take an oath in order to formalize his promise, which was accomplished by Hector holding his sceptre before Dolon and swearing precisely what rewards he would give. It is noteworthy that this is done in front of the assembled soldiers, providing witnesses to the agreement. It is also possible that this act of oath swearing could have constituted a more formal, direct offer to Dolon, as opposed to a general offer to the crowd. From a modern American contract perspective, this would be analogous to the difference between a direct offer between an offeror and an offeree versus and a unilateral contract open to the general public that would be consummated only upon completion of the task. From this perspective, Dolon may have utilized the oath to narrow and formalize the contract to be directed specifically towards him as the only one who could perform and then reap the benefits. In the new bilateral form, Dolon could still only receive the rewards if he performed the contract (*i.e.*, which was to provide Hector with the information that he requested). However, Dolon failed to obtain the information to fulfill his part of the bargain, and thus received nothing.

C. Agamemnon-Achilles: The Rejected Offer

The *Iliad* also contains several examples of rejected contract offers. One example of such a rejection occurs when Chryses attempts to buy back his daughter, Chryseis, who had become Agamemnon's war prize. Unlike most rejected offers in the *Iliad* which never surface again, Agamemnon's offer to Achilles represents something of a unique departure from this norm. Agamemnon offers Achilles great wealth in exchange for his return to battle. However, Achilles refuses Agamemnon outright because of his (Agamemnon's) earlier insult to him.

In modern contract law, such a rejection normally terminates an offeree's power of acceptance, so Achilles could not change his mind later and accept. However, when Achilles does return to battle—for reasons entirely unrelated to Agamemnon's original offer—Agamemnon still bestows everything he had initially promised. Before taking the gifts, Achilles reminds Agamemnon that he has no obligation to provide these riches because he (*i.e.,* Achilles) did not return to the fray on account of the king's offer. Agamemnon, however, feels morally obligated (and perhaps politically motivated) to grant Achilles these gifts anyway. Still, this acknowledgement that rejection makes an offer no longer valid parallels modern American contract law and releases the offeror from further obligations.

D. Hera-Hupnos

A fourth contract worth examining occurs between Hera and Hupnos (the god of sleep). Hera seeks to put Zeus to sleep in an effort to halt his assistance to the Trojans. She asks Hupnos to knock Zeus unconscious, but he is reticent to help her due to a past experience wherein Zeus expressed his profound displeasure at being put to sleep. Hera then offers Pasithea, one of the Graces, to Hupnos in marriage in return for his services, to which Hupnos agrees, contingent on Hera's sworn promise to perform her part of the contract—"Come then! Swear it to me on Styx' ineluctable water." Hera acquiesces to Hupnos' request, and a contract is formed. There is no written agreement here, but a sworn oath with the presence of witnesses (the "undergods" or Titans), which is more formal than a simple oral agreement.

E. Priam-Achilles

King Priam and Achilles agree for the return of Hector's lifeless, abused, and quite dusty body in exchange for goods. It seems inherent in the preliterate/protoliterate rules of war that battle winners are expected to retain possession of the dead and losers are expected to give a ransom for the return of the bodies. At first glance, the interaction between Priam and Achilles fits these unspoken rules perfectly—the Trojan King offers Achilles a generous ransom in exchange for the return of his dead son. Achilles subsequently gives Hector's body back to Priam, an act that clearly would constitute acceptance of a unilateral contract through performance.

However, underneath this seemingly normal war transaction lies a simpler, natural motivation—the desire of a son to abide by his mother's wishes. Zeus, the king of the gods, wants Achilles to return Hector's body. But he does not personally speak with Achilles nor does he send another high-ranking god. Instead, he sends Achilles' mother to persuade the angry warrior to acquiesce to King Priam's supplications. Achilles is an interesting figure because he is a hybrid, a mythical warrior with immortal qualities attempting to live in a mortal world. Part god, he must reconcile the natural tendencies of Zeus, Thetis, and the other gods to not conform to the rules that mortals are bound to follow. Yet he lives in a mortal world governed by the constraints of process and procedure. He is partially divine yet subservient to the wishes of the fully empowered. Motivated not by Priam's ransom, but rather the wishes of his mother, Achilles acquiesces and returns Hector's body saying, "No longer stir me up, old sir. I myself am minded to give Hector back to you." Perhaps even without the promise of riches, Achilles would have done what most sons have been taught to do throughout the course of their lives, mind their mothers.

F. Lessons Learned

After examining these four contracts in the *Iliad*, a further consideration of the transactions between Hera-Hupnos, Hector-Dolon, and Agamemnon-Achilles illustrates the separate legal expectations of gods and mortals. In each agreement, one party offers tangible wealth in return for intangible services; and in all three cases, the intangibles are designed to give a military advantage.

Dolon does not benefit from his arrangement. He was unable to obtain information and failed to return. Moreover, his failure could very well be social commentary, suggesting that this type of contracting behavior did not befit a soldier. The apparent disapproval of Dolon's conduct is somewhat reminiscent of the modern American contract principal of the preexisting duty rule, which would dictate that Dolon, a soldier, should not be paid extra for duties a soldier is already bound to undertake. However, in this case the comparison may not be apt since Hector seeks a volunteer for a particularly dangerous spy mission that may fall outside the normal "duties" expected of a soldier.

Hupnos, on the other hand, accepts Hera's offer, knocks Zeus unconscious, thus temporarily preventing the furtherance of the Trojan's success, and receives his reward. These two cases may present an important dichotomy between a soldier versus a god accepting personal wealth in return for services that advance the war effort. Although it may be unbefitting of a soldier, perhaps there is nothing wrong with a god doing it.

The Achilles-Agamemnon contract, however, creates a separate question: what rules govern demigods? Achilles rejects Agamemnon's offer, yet, upon returning to the fight, Agamemnon pays Achilles the rewards he originally offered. Achilles is a soldier, and, under the precedent set by the Hector-Dolon example, ill-fit to receive personal wealth in exchange for his battlefield accomplishments.

Under American contract principles, it might be tempting to apply the preexisting duty rule to Achilles since he is a more appropriate candidate for application of this rule than Dolon. Achilles refused to take part in any normal soldering activities while sulking. However, it is doubtful that he has the same duties to fight for Agamemnon (as proxy for his brother, Menelaus, Helen's husband) under the Princes' Contract (see below). Achilles was not a party to the original Princes' Contract but joined the fight at Troy willingly upon being presented with the choice of either living a long, happy life or becoming eternally famous but dying young. Thus, it seems he seeks riches of a kind Agamemnon cannot offer. Still, even if Achilles were somehow bound to fight, he might escape any "breach" since he allowed Patroclus and the rest of the Myrmidons, his own soldiers, to participate in battle. In this sense, Achilles fulfills any obligation to participate since he has temporarily sub-contracted out his efforts to recover Helen to his subordinates.

But perhaps Achilles' status as a hybrid—partially mortal and partially divine—leaves him somewhat privy to certain advantages of the gods, such as the ability to ignore normal societal constraints on mortals; perhaps, for example, receiving treasures for actions that are generally expected of an ordinary soldier without repercussions.

Alternatively, another key distinction between the examples of Dolon and Achilles might be the *intent* of these individuals. Dolon, who died on his quest, agreed to perform his mission specifically with the goal of wealth in mind. Conversely, Achilles explicitly rejected the offer to fight in return for riches, and only rejoined the action to avenge his dear friend, Patroclus. Agamemnon subsequently felt honor-bound to reward him, creating the implication that Achilles' actions were estimable. Therefore, while it may have been looked down upon to condition one's performance of soldierly duties on the receipt of rewards, if one performed one's duties admirably and honorably, it was proper and right to be rewarded afterwards for the valor and skill displayed in battle. This explanation seems logical in light of the Homeric warrior's view that honor and prowess in war were principal goals; therefore one could be rewarded, but only after proving worth in the field.

The Hector-Dolon and Hera-Hupnos contracts share similarities. In both cases, the offeree demanded that the offeror reaffirm their promise with a formal oath in front of witnesses, utilizing a symbolic object. Both offerees who demanded the oath were in weaker bargaining positions than the offeror. Since they could not enforce the promise themselves via self-help, the demand for additional formalities might operate as a means to legally bind the other party in a concrete manner. This likely underscores the requirements of oaths and witnesses in Greek contracts as far back as the protoliterate era.

II. Contracts That Shape the Myth as a Whole

In addition to the contract examples in Homer's text itself, two contracts essentially animate the plot of the *Iliad*: the "Princes' Contract" and the "Paris-Aphrodite Contract." Each of these agreements, independently, gave all parties something they desired; however, once these two agreements collided, one of the most storied wars in literature resulted. Ironically, the Princes' Contract was originally a pact intended to deter and prevent violence. Nevertheless, it ultimately became the mechanism that ignited the spark that began the Trojan War.

A. Princes' Contract

This contract originated when as many as 50 Greek Princes were courting Helen. Helen had to choose one suitor, and, being the most beautiful woman in the world, this would obviously displease the rest of the suitors, probably to the extent that one or several of them would then try to seize her by force. All the Greek Princes accepted this basic premise. To escape this conundrum, Odysseus proposed that the princes enter into a compact whereby they all agreed that those who were not picked to be Helen's husband would take up arms against anyone who tried to take Helen away from her chosen suitor. This both created the benefit of added security to the lucky prince selected, as well as a disincentive to any disgruntled, rejected suitor, since 49 princes would now protect Helen instead of just one. This agreement allowed each Prince both to gain security and also to advance his own self interest if he were selected, while also avoiding the potential chaos of war by means of this built-in deterrent. This contract reflects a number of positive values and encouraged a peaceful, pre-designed mechanism to avoid armed conflict. It appeared to be an effective way to prevent war and resolve what seemed to be an intractable dispute.

However, one, perhaps unintended, consequence of this contract was that it did not specify that the princes only aid Helen's husband against other suitors. This meant that if some outsider, a third party threatened or seized Helen, all the princes would be bound to honor their compact and go to the husband's aid in getting her back. While this provided a double security to Helen's husband, it also bound the suitor-princes for the entire foreseeable future should anyone attempt to abscond with Helen. This circumstance also undercuts one of the initial goals of the Princes' Compact: to deter aggression. While this aim was achieved among the Greek princes, a third party interloper thwarted this very goal.

B. Paris-Aphrodite Contract

The basis of the Paris-Aphrodite was the fated wedding between Peleus and Thetis (ironically Achilles' mortal parents), wherein the uninvited and jealous goddess Eris ("Dischord") tossed a golden apple that was inscribed "For the fairest" among Hera, Athena and Aphrodite. The vanity of each goddess led her to desire the apple. Someone was needed to judge and to decide who should get the coveted apple. But Zeus, seeking to avoid any involvement in the dilemma of picking a winner, recommended the Trojan prince, Paris. Each of the three goddesses promptly offered him bribes to declare her the winner: Hera offered power and wealth, Athena offered glory in battle, and Aphrodite offered the most beautiful woman on Earth as a wife. Paris selected Aphrodite, and with her help, traveled to Greece, stole Helen from Sparta, and took her back to Troy.

From a contractual perspective, the Paris-Aphrodite Contract consisted of an offer and an acceptance between two assenting parties. However, unlike the contracts in the *Iliad*'s text wherein the offeree demanded oaths and formalities, Paris required no oath and there were no witnesses to verify or formalize Aphrodite's promise. Given the end result of the contract (*i.e.,* failure, since Paris ultimately loses Helen), Paris may have neglected these steps at his peril. In addition to his failure to observe the proper contractual forms, the Judgment of Paris can also be seen as reprehensible in a manner similar to the Hector-Dolon contract. In the ancient Greek World, judges were acclaimed for judging matters the "straightest." But simply pronouncing the best bribe-giver the winner is probably the antithesis of such a sentiment. From this perspective, perhaps the failure of the Paris-Aphrodite Contract serves a dual purpose. It could be both a normative lesson, illustrating the negative consequences of such 'bad actor' behavior on the part of a judge who is supposed to be neutral and fair, as well as a cautionary warning, illustrating the importance of following the proper contractual forms, especially when dealing with someone more powerful.

C. Conflict of Two Contracts

The Paris-Aphrodite Contract activates the trigger in the Princes' Contract, resulting in the mobilization of the Greek princes (now kings) and the onset of the Trojan War. In modern contract language, Paris seizing Helen was the condition precedent to the princes' obligation. Upon this (unanticipated) triggering of the compact, several princes try to escape their obligation. Odysseus feigns insanity, but is found out; and Achilles is disguised and hidden away in an attempt to avert his involvement. Neither ploy works, but demonstrates that, as is often true today, insanity or lack of capacity may excuse performance of a contract. None of the princes appear to have argued that this situation was fundamentally different from the Princes' Compact as it was initially understood.

Conclusion

Parties used contract law to make various deals—for information, services, goods, and more. Before the preliterate/protoliterate period in Greece, fighting was a common means of dispute resolution. Nevertheless, this examination of Law in Literature illustrates that, although specific contract laws may not have been written, civilized dispute resolution procedures were practice, and contract principles that seem modern in many respects governed contract disputes.

CHAPTER 10

Background and Beginnings of Roman Law

§ 10.01 Introduction

A. Public Law & Private Law

One traditional way of studying Roman law is to divide its contents into public law (*ius publicum*) and private law (*ius privatum*). In Roman law, criminal law and administrative law were categorized as *ius publicum*. The *ius privatum* included rules of property, succession, contracts, and laws relating to the family.[1] According to the Roman jurist Ulpian,[2] the *ius publicum* is that which deals with the interests of the entire community whereas *ius privatum* deals with the interests of separate persons. Indeed, even if a crime victim were to forgive the criminal, we today believe that the interests of the entire community have been infringed by a crime, and thus must be vindicated. On the other hand, it is merely a private matter, for example, when a borrower fails to return money that he owes to his lender.[3]

---

1. It is common for students to study the Roman *ius privatum* rather than the *ius publicum*, because many scholars and legal historians have taken the position that Roman lawyers did not really create anything worth borrowing in the realm of *ius publicum*. *See e.g.*, Hans Julius Wolff, Roman Law: An Historical Introduction 53 (1951) [hereinafter "Wolff, Roman Law"](According to Wolff, Roman private law is the law that has most influenced the Western legal tradition. "Criminal law and procedure were slow in their development and never attained the importance comparable to that of private law and civil procedure.").

2. *See infra* § 10.04[B].

3. This distinction between public and private law exists in most European continental countries (but not in the United Kingdom). The United Kingdom countries reject this distinction because of its peculiar legal history. Specifically, the manner in which appeals were originally heard and appealed to the king affected the United Kingdom's approach; only

One of the greatest gifts that ancient Rome has bequeathed to the world is its private law. Although the Roman Empire eventually collapsed, Roman private law has survived and still permeates many legal systems in the world. In particular, Roman law is the *basis* for all of the laws in Western Europe (including Scotland), except England and Scandinavia. There is even a significant *influence* in English law.

B. Periods of Roman Law: Pre-Classical; Classical; & Post-Classical

Modern scholars traditionally classify Roman legal development into three stages: 1) Pre-Classical; 2) Classical; and, 3) Post-Classical. The Pre-Classical period lasted from the beginning stages to the 1st century B.C. This was a time when the pontiffs (priests) kept law as a secret. The pontiffs hid the law, in part, because it was profitable for them. Later, laws were codified and published, and the priests lost their monopoly. The Classical period of Roman law began in the 1st century B.C. and lasted through the 3rd century A.D. This is probably the most important and interesting period of Roman law. Roman jurists developed legal forms that were abstract and, many have argued, universal (*i.e.*, capable of being applied at any time in any society). The Post-Classical period runs from the beginning of the 4th century A.D. through the 6th century A.D. From the end of the Classical period to Justinian in the 6th century A.D., the law was characterized by bureaucratic administration more than the ingenuity or consideration of jurists. Some have called this the bureaucratic period of Roman law.[4] Few if any significant new legal ideas developed during this period but it is still engaging because this is when the Romans organized, classified, and wrote down a great deal of their law. Thus, students customarily consider the Post-Classical period because of the important codification that occurred during the 6th century A.D.[5] At this juncture it is useful also to mention that Roman history itself is marked by three major periods: 1) Monarchy (753–509 B.C.); 2) Republic (509–27 B.C.); and Empire (27 B.C.–5th century A.D. in the Western Empire and 27 B.C.–1453 A.D. in the Eastern Empire).

---

when the king had an interest in a case was it deemed public. But the Roman law public *versus* private distinction is still important in most western European countries.

4. *See* WOLFF, ROMAN LAW 130 (Citing Schultz).

5. *See infra* § 10.05.

§ 10.02 Early Roman Legal History

A. Laws of the Kings

Prior to any codification, the earliest Romans prospered using custom as the basis for law. According to the ancient Greek authors Plutarch and Diony- sus of Halicarnassus, the seven kings who ruled Rome from 753–509 B.C. (Monarchy) enacted quite a bit of law dealing with family law and sacred law (*i.e.*, relating to religion). Although many scholars doubt the veracity of Plutarch and Dionysus, others take the position that there may be a fair degree of truth to their assertions.[6] Romulus, the first king, required that each plebeian had to select a patrician to serve as his patron. Each patron was responsible for the legal affairs of his plebeian-client (bringing lawsuits and explaining laws). There were other legal rights, duties, and obligations between a patron and his client as well. Romulus prohibited a wife from divorcing her husband. It was also Romulus who formulated the law that decreed that a son was considered to have been freed from his father's paternal power if his father sold him three times. Numa, the second king, decreed that individuals were to mark the boundaries of their property. He also differentiated between murder and manslaughter. Servius Tullius, the sixth king, established that manumitted slaves automatically became Roman citizens. He also set up different trial pro- cedures, depending upon whether they were public or private.

B. The Laws of the Twelve Tables

1. Traditional Background

In the first half of the 5th century B.C., Rome saw the beginnings of what came to be known as the "struggle of the orders": a conflict between the pa- tricians (originally the upper class) and plebeians (originally the lower class). Many plebeians believed that it was unfair for the priests to keep the laws se- cret and for the judges to put themselves above the law. In 462 B.C., a tribune of the Plebs named Gaius Terentilius Harsa proposed that a commission be established to codify laws to bind the consuls. After a period of stalling and inactivity, tradition has it that the Romans then sent a committee to Athens to research Solon's laws (written about 594 B.C.).[7] The second century A.D. ju-

---

6. *See e.g.*, ALAN WATSON, ROMAN LAW & COMPARATIVE LAW 9 (1991) [hereinafter "WAT- SON, ROMAN LAW & COMPARATIVE LAW"].

7. *See supra* § 1.03[C].

rist, Gaius, identifies some laws that he says reflect influence from Solon; but few modern scholars are convinced of such a connection.[8] There is no mention of it in the Greek sources and the Romans had very little contact with the rest of the Mediterranean world at the time.[9] Nevertheless, when the committee returned from Greece, in 451 B.C., ten patricians, the decemvirs, were elected to write new laws for Rome. The decemvirs produced ten tablets of laws written on either bronze or wood. Supposedly, they allowed the populace to comment on their laws and then amended them accordingly. In the next year, another ten decemvirs (including some plebeians) were elected, and they wrote two additional tablets of laws. These decemvirs, however, expressed the desire to remain in power, and after the plebeians seceded in protest, the people ejected the decemvirs. Their work, however, was retained. Many have observed, nevertheless, that the Laws of the Twelve Tables are extremely well written. They are so succinct and clear that the drafters must have had considerable legal expertise.

2. Content of the Laws of the Twelve Tables

The ancient Romans considered the Twelve Tables as the basis for their laws. According to Cicero, schoolboys memorized them. We do not possess the original copies. Tradition has it that the originals burned when the Gauls sacked the city in 390 B.C. Because we no longer have the first bronze (or wooden?) tablets, historians have had to piece the laws together like a jigsaw puzzle from various alternative sources.

The provisions in the Twelve Tables tend to be concerned with unusual circumstances rather than ordinary ones. The beginning parts of the Twelve Tables contain numerous statements about suitable legal procedure. Indeed, procedural laws are prominent. The laws provide that, in cases of conflicts between statutes, the most recently enacted controls. The Twelve Tables establish procedures to substitute for self-help or outright retaliation. In some instances, private vengeance is allowed by retaliation in kind (*lex talionis*), but only in the form of pure retaliation in the event that the wrongdoer and his victim are unable to agree on financial terms. Otherwise, many laws provide for public punishments for a wrongdoer or require that the wrongdoer compensate his victim. It is significant that the laws reflect an appreciation for the subtle distinction between intentional and accidental homicide. The laws establish

---

8. *See* WATSON, ROMAN LAW & COMPARATIVE LAW 13–14. *Cf.* WOLFF, ROMAN LAW 60 ("It is not impossible that the decemvirs consciously took over some Greek ideas.").

9. *See* WATSON, ROMAN LAW & COMPARATIVE LAW 11.

guardians for persons incapable of taking care of themselves and their concerns (such as children, women, "prodigals", and those who are mentally unstable). The Twelve Tables grant a man the right to make a will to control the distribution of his things upon death. There are laws that fix predetermined payments as compensation for personal injuries. The Twelve Tables also give effect to the *stipulatio* form of contract (a face-to-face contract that originally required one party to ask *Spondesne?*—"Do you promise?"—and the other to respond *Spondeo*—"I promise").[10] And, there is a law concerning the settlement of boundary disputes.

§ 10.03 The Role of the Praetor & Aedile in the Development of Roman Law

The Romans established the office of praetor in 367 B.C. Praetors, who were second in magisterial rank and power only to the consuls, were responsible for much of the operation of the judicial system. The aediles were in charge of the streets and marketplace. When these magistrates issued their edicts—usually at the beginning of their terms in office—they ordinarily explained how they intended to carry out the laws, and in so doing, changed the face of Roman law. Roman praetors did more for the development of Roman law than any other Roman officials. Simply stated, they were responsible for matters relating to justice. Praetors were not judges themselves but were officials who administered the legal system and instructed judges concerning how to resolve certain questions of law.

Because the State was interested in dealing with foreigners and in further developing foreign trade, the Romans added a second praetor, called the *praetor peregrinus* in 242 B.C. From that point forward, the *praetor urbanus* (city praetor) took charge of matters concerning Roman citizens and the *praetor peregrinus* (foreign praetor) concerned himself with matters relating to disputes between citizens and foreigners or strictly between foreigners. But in addition to these few facts, we know precious little about the distinctions between the urban praetor and the peregrine praetor. But after 242 B.C., there were two praetors: peregrine and urban.

The praetor urbanus, however, was actually the more important of the two. Each praetor served for only one year. Upon entering office, he promulgated an *edictum* (edict). His edict gave judges general instructions about how to re-

---

10. *See infra* § 18.02.

solve cases. Although each edict of the new praetor urbanus repeated much of what his predecessors had said, he inevitably implemented a little addition, subtraction, and modification. Praetors were not actually empowered to change laws, but because of their office, they could control a great deal of legal *interpretation*. The praetor urbanus, in his discretion, had the authority, therefore, to waive various formalities in the law and to recognize new or variant causes of action, and to disregard others.[11] Legal historians refer to the laws that resulted from the praetors' edicts as the *ius honorarium*. Thus, by adaptations through their edicts, the urban praetors molded Roman law and created the law that has come to be known as the *ius honorarium*. The final century of the Republic (*i.e.*, roughly 140–40 B.C.) was the most active and significant period for the development of the *ius honorarium*.

The *ius gentium* (law of peoples/nations) that the praetor peregrinus administered was not used between different states but only between a Roman citizen (*civis*) and a foreigner (*peregrinus*) or between two foreigners who were involved in a dispute on Roman soil. Thus, in a restricted and limited sense, the *ius gentium* was the Roman predecessor of International Law.

As Rome's influence and territory expanded, the State added more praetors for the provinces (Sulla, Dictator 82–79 B.C., raised the number to eight in 81 B.C.) and six additional praetors in Rome itself to handle the increased caseload.

In the course of their duties, Roman praetors created a number of notable legal institutions. For example, the praetors were responsible for the procedural device called the *exceptio* (exception). The *exceptio* actually operated as a method of protecting rights indirectly as a kind of defense to an action. Indeed, in a contract where a seller sells goods to a buyer for a certain price, if the contract is silent as to when payment is to occur, the law implies that payment will be simultaneous with delivery of the goods. If the seller sues the buyer for payment, the buyer, rather than denying the existence of the contract, might, by *exceptio*, plead that the seller failed to deliver the goods. In essence, it is easier for a buyer to wait for the seller to sue him (and then defend by *exceptio*) than it is for the buyer to sue the seller and plead that the seller failed to perform. Another example of the praetor's innovation is *restitutio* (restitution), by which the law forced a party who had been unjustly enriched to return the unjustly-obtained money. For example, very early in Roman Law, even a contract entered into under duress was considered valid. The Romans said *"Coactus voluit, tamen voluit"* ("Although he was coerced

---

11. *See infra* §11.01 regarding causes of action.

when he assented, nevertheless, he assented"). Eventually, the praetors realized the injustice of this approach to contract interpretation. To mitigate the harshness, then, the praetors determined to acknowledge the existence of the contract, but also decided that it could not be enforced as written, given that the agreement was concluded under duress. Hence, the praetors invented the concept of *restitutio* so that the party who had been coerced could be entitled to restitution. In terms of the big picture, however, the two most significant things that the praetors did to affect the substance of Roman law were: 1) to fashion their edicts (on an annual basis); and, 2) to fashion formulae—as part of what was known as the formulary system of procedure—(on a daily basis).[12]

In addition to the office of praetor, the office of *aedile* was also created in 367 B.C. The four *aediles* kept the State archives, and supervised the streets, aqueducts, buildings, bridges, and the public marketplace. Because of their role in maintaining order in the market, the aediles gradually influenced laws relating to the sale of goods. Like praetors, aediles issued edicts at the outset of their terms. Thus, they too had a certain degree of flexibility to adapt the laws of the marketplace by creative interpretation through the *ius honorarium*.

During the Empire, the praetor's edict brought about very little in the way of significant change. Ultimately, the jurist Julianus, under the Emperor Hadrian (117–138 A.D.), put the praetorian and aedilician edicts into their final, frozen forms. Later the classical Roman jurists referred to Julianus' version of the praetor's edict as the *edictum perpetuum*, and considered it established law.

§ 10.04 Legal Interpretation: Advocates, Jurists, & Emperors

A. Background

Very early in Rome's history, only the pontiffs (*pontifices*) had access to the archives containing the specialized legal forms and phrases that were necessary to conduct a lawsuit. They regulated the specialized rules for initiating and carrying out lawsuits. Only patricians were allowed to serve as pontiffs until the passage of the *lex Ogulnia* in 300 B.C. The first plebeian pontifex maximus was elected in 253 B.C. The pontiffs could interpret laws broadly or narrowly to suit their own purposes. Thus, they had a monopoly on legal advice and law. The pontiffs eventually lost their exclusive grip on legal inter-

---

12. *See infra* § 11.03[B].

pretation. Tradition has it that they lost that grip all at once in 312 B.C. when Gnaeus Flavius, the secretary of Appius Claudius (the famous censor) stole (aided by the collusion of Appius) and published the forms of action.

B. Advocates & Jurists

The wealthiest young Romans generally selected one of three careers: military; politics; or, law. These three professions were closely related. According to Cicero, the jurists of the first century B.C. had three functions: 1) *ad respondendum* (answering legal questions and giving legal advice); 2) *ad agendum* (preparing a case for court); and, 3) *ad cavendum* (drafting documents). The function called *ad respondendum* ("to respond") was the private function of a lawyer—perhaps the ancient jurist's most important task—explaining to a praetor, aedile, judge, or layperson what a particular law meant. Since all legal disputes assumed personal participation by the parties, one needed an attorney for consultion. This was the role known as *ad agendum* (literally "to drive/perform"). *Cavere* actually is Latin for "to warn." Because early Roman procedure was very formal,[13] one needed to use proper legal language in order to create valid documents. *Ad cavendum* was the process of drafting written formulae (either using a standardized form or creating a new one) for lawsuits or business transactions.

Roman *advocates* were those who were more likely to conduct the business of court cases (*ad agendum*) whereas *jurisconsults* (jurists) were more like academics who rendered opinions (*ad respondendum*). Advocates were not allowed to accept payment—at least theoretically—for their services. Jurists did not receive fees for their advice either, but rather performed their services as a contribution to society. The jurists tended to be conservative in their approach. They ordinarily were from families that were of the senatorial class, and thus they were highly respected. Since the *praetors* and *aediles* were politicians who were usually not trained in law, they relied heavily on the *responsa* of jurists. From the time of Hadrian (*c.* 117–138 A.D.) forward, Roman jurists thought of themselves as a special, privileged class who were above the advocates in the courtrooms.

The early Roman jurisconsults (*i.e.,* those in the Pre-Classical period) developed the essential principles of Roman law mostly during the second and first centuries B.C. There were a number of early attempts to impose a semblance of order on Roman law. The *Ius Flavianum* (*c.* 312 B.C.) consisted of a collection

---

13. *See infra* Chapter 11.

of formulae for lawsuits. The *Ius Aelianum*, another collection of formulae, was issued by Sextus Aelius Paetus (consul, 198 B.C.). He also published the first attempt at a systematic treatment of Roman law: a major legal work called the *Tripertitia*. In the *Tripertitia*, Paetus presented first the text of each provision of the Twelve Tables, second, the interpretations by pontiffs and jurisconsults of these provisions, and, third, written formulae appropriate for lawsuits applicable to each provision (*i.e.*, the written words necessary to bring a cause of action under that law). Around 150 B.C., Manius Manilius published forms for sales transactions. The consul Quintus Mucius Scaevola (95 B.C.) is given credit for having divided civil law into *genera* (classes). He wrote an 18-book commentary about the civil law which was the first legal treatise that attempted to impose structure on Roman law. Scaevola organized the text into sections based on related legal principles. His students continued his tradition. The consul Servius Sulpicius Rufus (51 B.C.) wrote the first commentary on the praetorian edict.

The Emperor Augustus (27 B.C.–14 A.D.) granted certain jurists a right called the *ius respondendi* (*ius respondendi ex auctoritate principis*—the right of responding based on the authority of the emperor). Although we do not know precisely what the *ius respondendi* entailed, it apparently entitled the jurist on whom it was bestowed to give his opinion on legal questions. Clearly the opinions of the jurists who possessed *ius respondendi* were given great weight. The opinion did not, in actuality, bind a judge, but as a matter of practice, judges typically adhered to the opinions rendered by jurists with *ius respondendi*.

The jurist Marcus Antistius Labeo (who died about 10 A.D.) is credited with being the first great jurist of the Classical period. He supposedly wrote over 400 works (though very little of his work has survived). Also in the Classical period, Gaius wrote the *Institutes* or *Institutiones* (composed about 161 A.D.). The *Institutes* served as a relatively short and direct introduction to law for students. Indeed, law students in the Empire used the *Institutes* as their principal handbook for learning substantive law. When the Emperor Justinian had his *Institutes* written in the 6th century A.D., the drafters closely followed Gaius' *Institutes*.

Domitius Ulpianus (Ulpian) and Iulius Paulus (Paul) are known for their great legal works on Sabinius and the Edict. Wolff describes their works as follows:

> Ulpianus's and Paulus's commentaries came to be considered as final statements of *ius civile* and *ius honorarium* and thus became the standard works of the post classical period. A very large part of Justinian's Digest consists of fragments taken from these four commentaries. Showing Roman law as it was after two centuries of incessant and in-

tensive development by a group of outstanding jurists, Paulus's and Ulpianus's commentaries are therefore our primary sources for classical law.[14]

Supposedly, the Emperor Hadrian (117–138 A.D.) expanded the *ius respondendi*. Under Hadrian, if the jurists who were questioned agreed—naturally these were jurists with *ius respondendi*—, then their opinions were binding. If they were inconsistent, then the judge was free to adopt whichever jurist's opinion he wished. The last of the great jurists of the Classical period was Aemelius Papinianus (died 212 A.D.).

In 426 A.D. Theodosius II (Eastern Empire) and Valentinian III (Western Empire) enacted the "Law of Citations," which regulated the use of citations in court of the classical jurists and Gaius. Simply stated, this law provided that the writings of Papinianus, Ulpianus, Paulus, Modestinus, and Gaius could be used as precedents. Judges were directed to follow the majority opinion of these writers. If there was a tie among these authors on a point, the position of Papinianus controlled. If Papinianus was silent on the issue, then the judge was to apply his own judgment.

C. The "Schools": Sabinians & Proculians

Two schools of jurists dominated the first 150 years of the Empire: the Sabinians and the Proculians. Labeo[15] is considered the founder of the Proculians and Gaius Ateius Capito is considered the founder of the Sabinians. We know very little about the operation or structure of these schools. It is likely that these "schools" were not schools in the strict sense; that is, they were probably not actual teaching institutions *per se*. Rather, they were probably loose associations of jurists and their pupils. Presumably they met and discussed various topics and questions of law as a means of instruction. Interestingly, although these are the two traditional "schools," and there are isolated instances of differing opinions on specific points of law, scholars have been unable to pin down any general, overarching theoretical disparity between the two. Apparently, shortly after Hadrian, the schools no longer operated, and ultimately no longer influenced Roman jurisprudence.

---

14. WOLFF, ROMAN LAW 122.
15. *See supra* § 10.04[B].

D. The Role of the Emperor

By 150 A.D. it was taken for granted that the emperor was empowered to issue legislation of his own accord. Even before then, emperors affected law in four distinct ways. First, an emperor could issue edicts (*edicta*). Second, an emperor could actually take a case himself—acting as judge and jury. By giving *decreta* (legal decisions rendered by the emperor in any given case that had been brought before him), the emperor's decision (*decretum*) superseded all other decisions, and became precedent. The Emperor Claudius (41–54 A.D.), in particular, enjoyed exercising this power, and did so regularly. Third, emperors influenced law by answering, in writing, legal questions for officials and private citizens. This answer was called a *rescriptum* (rescript) or *epistula* (letter). Lastly, emperors routinely issued *mandata*, the emperor's orders to officials (*e.g.,* provincial governors). In these four ways, the Roman emperors themselves exerted significant influence over the development of law. Eventually, the law developed by the emperors superseded even the *ius honorarium*.

§ 10.05 Justinian & the *Corpus Iuris Civilis*

After one initial false start, a commission appointed by Theodosius II compiled a code of Roman law, the *Codex Theodosianus*, in 438 A.D. Theodosius made the code effective in the Eastern Empire at the beginning of 439 A.D. and soon thereafter Valentinian III adopted it in the Western Empire as well.

In 528 A.D. the Roman emperor, Justinian, created an ad hoc commission to codify all of Roman law. Justinian appointed a lawyer named Tribonianus (Tribonian) to take charge in producing what we know today as the *Corpus Iuris Civilis*. It took Tribonian and his commission seven years (528–534 A.D.). Justinian endeavored to strike a balance between the old, time-honored jurisprudence of the classical jurists and the practical requirements of the sixth century A.D. The *Corpus Iuris Civilis* is divided into four parts. In ascending order of relative importance, they are as follows. 1) *Codex Iustiniani*. First, the least important is the *Codex Iustiniani* (Justinian's Code), promulgated in April of 529 A.D. The *Codex* consists of constitutions of emperors (*i.e.,* bureaucratic legal regulations and various legal acts). 2) *Novellae*. Next are the *Novellae*. Justinian added various amendments, called *novellae* (new laws adopted after the entire *Corpus Iuris* had been written). His successors also issued *novellae* of their own. 3) *Institutiones*. Of penultimate importance were the *Institutiones*, or *Institutes* (535 A.D.). Justinian's *Institutes* were intended as a first-year student textbook but the text was actually enacted into law by imperial statute. Thus, the *Institutes* served both as an official textbook on Roman Law and as a functional code that could be consulted for subsequent decisions (*i.e.*, it had the force of law). 4) *Digest*. Most scholars consider the *Digest* the most important part of the *Corpus Iuris Civilis*. It became effective as law at the end of December, 533 A.D. It consists of approximately two thousand fragments (quotations) of works of 39 different Roman jurists going as far back as the 1st century B.C. Over half of the quotes are from Ulpian and Paul (about 33% are from the former and nearly 20% from the latter). Justinian's codification of Roman law provided a brief but comprehensive summary of Roman law. His synopses served as useful prototypes for later generations to imitate.

§ 10.06 The Reception of Roman Law (*Receptio*)

One of the principal reasons that it is worthwhile for modern students to study Roman Law today is its importance to and incorporation in modern legal systems. Scholars traditionally refer to this incorporation by the countries of the world as the "reception of Roman law."

After the Barbarian invasions at the close of the 5th century A.D., the invaders retained Roman law for their relations with Romans and retained their own *lex Barbarorum* only for relations among themselves. Of course, there was a gradual amalgamation of these, and then, for the next two to three centuries, Roman law began adjusting and taking on new qualities as times changed. Roman law thus evolved into a different form in the 7th, 8th, and 9th centuries A.D. In the 11th century A.D. in Bologna, Italy, two professors (one of whom was especially important—Irnerius 1055–1130 A.D.) found a copy of the Justinian Code obscured underneath another text. They studied and commented upon these laws (explaining and cross-referencing). These comments came to be called *glossa*, and thus the scholars who created these comments were called *glossators* (this was primarily an academic enterprise). The work of the *glossators* continued from the 11th to the 13th centuries A.D. By the 14th century, lawyers had to reinterpret and add further comments in addition to what the *glossators* had done. These scholars were called the *post-glossators* or *commentators*. They further modified Roman law to adapt to new circumstances and an expanding capitalistic system.

Before the French Revolution (1789 A.D.), France did not have its own legal code, even though at the time it was probably the most developed capitalistic society. France was officially divided by north and south. The south was *le pays du droit ecrit* ("the country of the written law") and the north was *le pays des coutumes* ("the country of customs"). When Napoleon ascended, he created an ad hoc commission to draft a civil code. On the commission there were representatives of both north and south. According to tradition, when Napoleon was a young officer just over twenty years of age, he read and virtually memorized the *Corpus Iuris Civilis* (while serving a brief stint in a military stockade). Thus, Napoleon relied on Justinian's laws for his French law. Of course, today the Napoleonic Code has been expanded and modified, and there have been many attempts to do away with it entirely, but the only substantial change has been that dealing with family law. In Belgium and Luxembourg (and for a time in Italy and other countries) the Napoleonic Code has been adopted.

Early Prussian emperors adopted Roman law. Thus, it became the basis for German law. Even when the German civil code was rewritten in 1900 A.D., almost two-thirds of the new code mirrored Roman law. In 1942, Italy borrowed a great deal from that German code for its laws.

The United Kingdom is the most notable exception to the Reception of Roman law. English law was not as greatly affected by Roman law as were Germany and France. The king's judges invented the Common Law beginning in about the 11th century when the judges heard cases for the Crown and resolved disputes according to their understanding of equity. This created the Common Law system and *stare decisis*. The English system was not a system of general abstract rules, but primarily case law. Roman law, on the other hand, is mostly statute law. But in the 10th century A.D., two important books were published in England; one by Bracton and the other by Glanvill. Both were dedicated exclusively to Roman law and described Roman law, in a systematic way. Later, when the kings' judges came across difficult cases, they appealed to Bracton and Glanvill for authority (not Roman sources directly). Thus, Roman law became integrated into the law of the United Kingdom rather indirectly. Therefore, the tradition that English law avoided the influences of Roman law is patently untrue. Roman law has also had a major influence on the laws in Scotland, Quebec, and Louisiana (thanks to its French roots).

It is especially important for lawyers to study Roman law today. It is virtually impossible to survive in isolation, using purely domestic legal thinking. We must understand the legal systems of other nations in order to exist (especially concerning economic and cultural aspects of other nations). Foreign law affects the world. As has been seen, the general principles of Roman law permeate many of the laws of the world.

§ 10.07 Justice & Jurisprudence: the Role of Law

Watson takes the position that custom was relatively unimportant "as a source of new law" during both the Republic and Empire.[16] Most legal historians agree, nevertheless, that laws ordinarily are rooted in custom.[17] The Romans did segregate secular law from law relating to religion. Thus, there was not necessarily a strong correlation between law, religion, and morality. And, although the Roman jurists had studied philosophy and rhetoric, their principal interest in law was practical not theoretical.

Still, many of the classical jurists were strongly influenced by the philosophy of Stoicism. Zeno (350–260 B.C.), the founder of the Stoics, made nature the key to his philosophy. For Zeno and the Stoics, a pervasive reason dominated and controlled the universe. Equality was an integral precept in the Stoic concept of natural law. In his *Institutes*, Gaius states that natural reason establishes laws that men follow. These laws, brought about by natural reason, constitute the *ius gentium* (law of nations) whereas the laws created by state legislation are *ius civile* (civil law).

Cicero (106–43 B.C.) held fast to the Stoic ideal of a natural and universal law. In his *De republica*, he described true law as right reason that works in concert with nature. It exists among humans and is constant. True law's principles encourage citizens to perform their duties while discouraging illegal acts. According to Cicero, law is the same everywhere and it governs all people. It is everlasting and immutable. In *De Legibus*, he says that law is the highest reason. It emanates from nature and dictates what men should do and prohibits those things that they should not. Natural law depends on intelligence and human reason. It is a higher law that began before governments and the written law of mortals. As Wolff states, Cicero believed that there were certain "legal institutions and conceptions inherent in human nature and therefore reasonable and shared by all mankind."[18] In sum, for Cicero, justice is a single nature-based unity that governs all people. It is right reason applied to command and prohibition.

---

16. WATSON, ROMAN LAW & COMPARATIVE LAW 15.

17. *Id.* ("Of course, if one goes back to the beginning, one will find that most fundamental rules derive from custom.").

18. WOLFF, ROMAN LAW 83. For more on Cicero's views on the nature of law, *see infra* p. 113–18.

§ 10.08 Chapter Summary

The Romans categorized criminal and administrative laws as public law (*ius publicum*) and laws relating to individuals—such as property, contracts, and family laws—as private law (*ius privatum*). The private law of the ancient Romans has significantly influenced a great deal of modern law. We traditionally categorize Roman legal development in three major periods: 1) Pre-Classical (up to the 1st century B.C.); 2) Classical (1st century B.C. through the 3rd century A.D.); and, 3) Post-Classical (4th century A.D. to the 6th century A.D.). During the Monarchy (753–509 B.C.), the seven kings of Rome established laws relating to matters such as legal procedure, religion, the patron-client system, property, family law, and citizenship. According to tradition, in 451/450 B.C., the Romans sent a delegation to Athens to study Solon's laws. As a result of that research, two groups of decemvirs produced the Laws of the Twelve Tables. In addition to many procedural rules, the Laws of the Twelve Tables also address issues such as punishments, compensation for personal injury, homicide, guardianship, wills, and contracts.

Praetors were the officials in charge of the judiciary—the legal system as a whole. By the middle of the 3rd century B.C., the Romans had established two praetors: 1) the *praetor peregrinus*, who administered disputes that involved foreigners; and, 2) the *praetor urbanus*, who was responsible for law relating to Roman citizens. Through their annual edicts, the praetors played a significant role in the development of both Roman law, the *ius honorarium*, and also the antecedent of international law, the *ius gentium*. By the 1st century B.C., there were more than a dozen praetors in Rome and the provinces. The praetors were responsible for numerous legal innovations that allowed procedure and business to operate more smoothly. In addition to the praetors, the aediles—who were in charge of the marketplace—directly affected laws relating to the sale of goods. Under the Emperor Hadrian, the jurist, Julianus, polished the praetorian and aedilician edicts into their final forms.

Although the patrician pontiffs originally controlled legal procedure through secrecy, at the close of the 4th century B.C., plebeians became eligible to serve as pontiffs and, thus, henceforth had access to the rules governing lawsuits. Eventually, Roman jurists developed distinct roles: 1) *ad respondendum* (answering legal questions and giving legal advice); 2) *ad agendum* (preparing a case for court); and, 3) *ad cavendum* (drafting documents). As a rule, the advocates (who were not permitted to accept fees) litigated cases in court and the jurisconsults (who, likewise, received no fees) gave legal advice to praetors, aediles, and judges. During the 2nd and 1st centuries B.C., a number of jurists (such as Paetus, Manilius, Scaevola, and Servius Sulpicius Rufus) began organizing and summarizing the fundamental principles and rules that were developing in Roman law. Augustus granted the *ius respondendi* to certain jurists—giving them the authority to render non-binding, but highly influential opinions to judges. Later the Emperor Hadrian made such opinions binding. In the Classical Period, Gaius composed his *Institutes*, which were later used by law students and subsequent scholars as a basis for study and as authoritative statements of the law. Soon thereafter, Ulpian and Paul wrote important commentaries that later were used extensively in the preparation of Justinian's *Digest*. Early in the 5th century A.D., the Emperors Theodosius II and Valentinian III formally elevated the writings of the jurists Papinian, Ulpian, Paul, and Modestinus to that of binding authorities.

Labeo, whom many consider the first great jurist of the Classical Period, is thought to have been the founder of the Proculians; while Gaius Ateius Capito is regarded as the founder of the Sabinians. These—the Proculians and Sabinians—were the two most prominent "schools" of Roman jurisprudence. The emperors themselves influenced the direction of law by issuing edicts (*edicta*), by writing opinions in cases brought before them when acting as judges (*decreta*), by giving formal written opinions on legal questions (*rescripta/epistula*), and also by issuing orders to administrative officials (*mandata*). The Emperor Theodosius II appointed a commission that compiled a law code (*Codex Theodosianus*) which became the rule of law in 439 A.D. Nearly a hundred years later, the Emperor Justinian enlisted the aid of several jurists (most notably Tribonian) who produced the *Corpus Iuris Civilis*; comprised of four important works which constituted the most comprehensive codification of Roman law: 1) *Codex Iustiniani* (529 A.D.); 2) *Novellae*; 3) *Institutes* (535 A.D.); and, 4) *Digest* (533 A.D.).

From the 5th to the 13th centuries A.D. various European nations adapted and used Roman law. The glossators (11th–13th centuries) and post-glossators/commentators (14th century) renewed interest in Roman law by trying to explain it and trying to put it to use in the context of a changed Europe. In France, Napoleon used Justinian's laws as the basis for his Code, which, in turn, profoundly influenced the later development of law in Italy, Belgium, and Luxembourg. German law also employed Roman law as its foundation. Even the United Kingdom—with its reliance on Common Law—indirectly borrowed from and absorbed a great deal of Roman law through its reliance on authorities such as Bracton and Glanvill. Thus, even today Roman law and legal thinking permeate much of the law in the Western World.

Roman law was dependent, to a degree, on both custom and practicality. Nevertheless, Greek philosophy, such as Zeno's Stoicism, influenced Roman jurisprudence and its reliance on the concept of natural law. Cicero, for example, shows in his writing an adherence to immutable, universal natural laws shared by all humans.

Law in Literature:
Discovering More About Legal Philosophy
Cicero's *De Legibus* and Natural Law

There are few classical authors who have influenced modern concepts of justice and natural law as much as Cicero. Marcus Tullius Cicero was a prominent orator, lawyer, and writer. Born in 106 B.C., he was assassinated in 43 B.C. He was active in Roman government and served as both a consul and proconsul. Legal historians often fail to recognize the impact that Roman law has had on the English, and in turn, the American common law systems. Yet, especially with the growing sense of legal consciousness, Ciceronian concepts of natural law and innate justice have become turning points in major American cases.

In Cicero's major work that explains his viewpoints on law and legal philosophy, *De Legibus,* he notes at the outset that people who study law without an understanding of natural concepts of right and wrong are merely learning the skills necessary to construct arguments and to speak in court, but they are not learning the basic concepts that underlie the construction of legal arguments. "Those who teach the civil law in any other way [other than through an understanding of natural justice] are teaching not so much the path of justice as of litigation." Cicero compares and contrasts "lowly" practitioners who merely know the law as far as it can be useful to clients to legal philosophers who concern themselves with deeper conversations, such as where law comes from and the ultimate meaning of what is "right" and "wrong." Cicero classifies a practitioner of law as someone who is only concerned with ultimate answers. He suggests, however, that the law should be regarded as a more overarching, binding principle.

Cicero believes that it is important to understand the law not merely to practice the law. He expresses concerned that lawyers "carr[y] their studies of this civil law, as it is called, only far enough to accomplish their purpose of being useful to the people." Cicero worries that practitioners separate the utility of the law from the big picture, diminishing their overall understanding of the law. He then seeks to expand the ideas of man's purpose and nature's gifts to mankind, not to "learn how to protect ourselves legally, or how to answer clients' questions," but to better understand the reasons for law and justice in itself.

Cicero contends that the goal of law is to "promote the firm foundation of States, the strengthening of cities, and the curing of the ills of people." For this reason he pays special attention to his thoughts, to be sure that he will not "lay down first principles that have not been wisely considered and thoroughly investigated." Cicero then seeks through introspection to understand the basis of law and natural justice and their relationship to written law.

De Legibus addresses not what we commonly think of as "civil law" or even the written conclusions known to society as "law," but rather it examines that which is innately human law, "justice." Humans, according to Cicero, inherently have both a need for and an understanding of law. His views encapsulate the commonly accepted Stoic views of Roman Society. Cicero's Stoic views represent what a majority of Romans at the time believed. Stoicism gives credence to a natural order and teaches that there is a purpose for all things. Stoic philosophy easily coordinates with many traditional religious concepts, especially the idea of gods or higher powers. Cicero incorporates the ideas of law and justice into the higher power by concluding that man has a "divine element within him," and that man "will think of his own inner nature as a kind of consecrated image of god." So all men will, therefore, act in a way which is intended to please the gods. Introspection, therefore reveals truth, justice, law, and "the right way." On the other hand, Cicero worries that the Epicurean lifestyle is "the counterfeit of good, which is ... the mother of all evils—pleasure." The Epicureans did not believe in the idea of gods, but believed in living for pleasure's sake, for the joy of living.

As most debates regarding control and structure go, Cicero discusses the concept of right and wrong, and how, as human beings, we inherently know what is right, good, and proper. Cicero states that if law is derived from nature, "then the origin of Justice is to be found in Law, for Law is a natural force." Because law comes from nature, Cicero contends that law itself is inherent in the nature of human beings. "And so they believe that Law is intelligence, whose natural function it is to command right conduct and forbid wrongdoing." When considering this stance on the origins of how we define what law is and where it originates, nature makes sense as its source. In this way, all decisions can be linked to our common source, which is nature. And as Cicero points out, nature is, in essence, the gods.

If human beings are naturally programmed to promote "right" conduct and punish "wrongdoing," then how is it possible that human beings exist who do wrong? Cicero addressed these concerns stating, "The similarity of the human race is clearly marked in its evil tendencies as well as in its goodness." He admits that people do commit wrongs, perhaps due to their desire to seek pleasure (a jab at Epicureans), or because they do not feel fulfillment in other areas of their lives. Whatever the problems individuals may face that lead them to wrongdoing, even when people do something wrong or act inappropriately, it is likely that what they are doing "has some likeness to what is naturally good."

Cicero states that all human beings inevitably want to be happy, and that in order to be happy, they must do good. "But what nation does not love courtesy, kindliness, gratitude, and remembrance of favors bestowed? What people do not hate and despise the haughty, the wicked, the cruel, and the ungrateful." Cicero claims that this is our common nature as humans to love what is good and hate what is bad. He believes that all human beings are not only aware of what is good, but that they want to be good as well. For Cicero, there is no room for opinion about what is good or bad, evil or just. There is only that which is naturally just and naturally good. This point of view reflects the Stoic ideal of a natural plan and reason for everything. Good things, including a sense of justice, are naturally bestowed upon all men if we look hard enough. Therefore, written law is a culmination of and interpretation of natural law. This struggle and desire to be good is controlled by nature, and the gods, and is set out in our laws. Therefore, law controls people by punishing them for bad behavior, thus helping them stay on track and become good, as they want to. In this way law promotes natural justice and therefore human nature.

Because Cicero believes that god created humans to have what he calls "right reason," he also believes that humans analyze problems rationally and arrive at the same conclusions regarding right and wrong. Cicero holds that because all human beings have right reason, all therefore, have the same notions as to what is acceptable and unacceptable behavior. He articulates the general principle that a common human nature enables us both to distinguish between good and bad and also to desire what is right: "Inasmuch as these considerations prove to us that the whole human race is bound together in unity, it follows, finally, that knowledge of the principles of right living is what makes men better."

We have laws which stem from our own nature as humans and which, in a sense, keep human beings on track in their pursuit of goodness. We have laws not only to distinguish what is good from bad but also to remind people of it and to punish them if they veer off course. Law is not, however, intended to scare people into following it. Rather, law announces to the community the inherent concepts of justice for the community's benefit. People follow law because of a desire to be just, not because following the law would benefit them in some way or provide them pleasure. Because laws are inherent in our nature as humans and arise from nature itself, which in turn stems from the gods, laws essentially create rules to remind everyone of the way they should act, although they already know this inherently. Although laws promote doing what is right and punishing what is wrong, they also serve as a reminder and a reflection of inborn natural human understanding.

Cicero claims that "Justice springs from Nature." *De Legibus* reflects a Roman belief that law is a natural force. "Law is the highest reason, implanted in Nature, which commands what ought to be done and forbids the opposite." Cicero explains that justice "is implanted in us by Nature." It is from Nature that man has received the "gift of reason." Cicero regards reason as divine and the highest good. He defines Law as "right reason applied to command and prohibition." Nature gives reason, right reason is Law, and Law, in turn, Justice. It is through this connection that he finds Justice inherent in Nature.

In further examining the nature of Justice, Cicero clarifies that written law does not always produce Justice. "Right is based, not upon men's opinions, but upon Nature." He explains that the laws of Nature cannot be changed by votes. "If a law can make Justice out of Injustice, can it not also make good out of bad?" It is our "natural inclination to love our fellow-men" that is the foundation of Justice. Law is based in part upon societal norms and community expectations. Through societal norms and an understanding of natural justice, the community forms bodies of written law. Moreover, "all good men love fairness in itself and Justice in itself, and it is unnatural for a good man to make such a mistake as to love what does not deserve love for itself alone." Right laws already exist and it is our duty to find them. It is in this way that we work justice; not by creating it but by finding and adopting the laws that already exist naturally, as a community.

Nature teaches humans right from wrong. "Whatever good thing is praiseworthy must have within itself something which deserves praise, for goodness itself is good by reason not of opinion but of nature." Cicero believes that people are born good and that it is unnatural for us to turn against our inclination towards Justice. He explains, "we look upon pain as one of the greatest of evils, not only because of its cruelty, but also because it seems to lead to the destruction of nature." When men act wrongly, it is solely because they are detached from the natural concepts of justice within them. Cicero asks, "who, therefore, would judge a man of prudence and, if I may say so, hard common sense, not by his own character but by some external circumstance?" Humans have the natural capacity to be good. Dishonor and vice occur only when man disconnects from himself. Even today, character is an important way of judging the value and rightness of others. The law seeks to treat men as individuals within their given circumstances. Bad people are aware that they are bad. Goodness reflects a connection with nature but evil reflects a lack of connection with nature. Observing nature will reveal what is right and wrong.

Cicero's concept of virtue embraces the belief that goodness is good naturally because it is meant to be good, not because someone thinks it is good; neither men's thoughts nor opinions dictate what is good. Virtue exists only in men and in god as the common bond between the two. Virtue is a gift that makes man higher than any other creature. Virtue is "nothing else than Nature perfected and developed to its highest point." Both introspection and observation of the natural order of things lead to Virtue and Justice.

Nature provides those things necessary for human survival: grain, fruit, animals for meat, and animals to assist in work. Not only does Nature provide for our existence, but Nature provides it all "conveniently." "[F]or it is by skillful imitation of [Nature] that reason has acquired the necessities of life." Man has also been equipped with "nimbleness of mind ... [and Nature] has also given him the senses to be ... attendants and messengers." Nature has given man "a great many things to serve as the foundations of knowledge." All this has been given to us in a "bodily form which is convenient and well suited to the human mind." Either Nature or the gods has given humans the gifts and the tools not only to survive, as animals, but also to step closer to the gods. We may accomplish this through introspection and observation, by learning about the divine order, and by using the divine order in our everyday existence.

Like Virtue, man possesses other tools necessary to develop and understand Law and to incorporate Justice into positive law. "[T]hat animal which we call man [is] endowed with foresight and quick intelligence, complex, keen, possessing memory, full of reason and prudence." Today these are still the principal tools for lawyers. Foresight, the ability to think on one's feet, and a sound memory, are qualities that all lawyers need. And as Cicero suggests, although these skills can be developed to a certain extent, they are more like gifts from nature. Once man begins to utilize these gifts of nature, "reason, when it is full grown and perfected, is rightly called wisdom."

One may ask whether law comes "directly from the Gods" or whether it is derived from the community. According to Cicero, "Justice does not exist at all, if it does not exist in Nature." The notion that nature teaches right and wrong was a concept familiar to the ancient Romans. Cicero's audience was educated. Many of them were, no doubt, Stoics who believed that the gods endowed humanity with an innate sense of "right reason." They believed they were blood relations with the gods; "it is clear that man recognizes God because, in a way, he remembers and recognizes the source from which he sprang." All of nature obeys "this celestial system, the divine mind, and the God of transcendent power." Hence, both gods and men are central figures within the universe. They follow a path already decided for them and are connected to one another by concepts of natural justice, law, and "right reason."

But there are also hints of legal relativism in Cicero's text. Legal relativism is the theory that written laws are an expression of community standards of Justice. Legal relativism suggests that private and public law are derived from the practices and customs of the Roman people, not the gods. This concept suggests that Justice is not necessarily derived from the gods, because it casts the *people* as judges of right, not an innate sense of reason. But some passages imply that these two apparently contradictory ideas may be reconciled. Cicero believes that the gods give everyone an innate sense of "right reason." Therefore, people use this god-given sense, as a *community* to formulate customs and laws, which are the basis for positive law. Each member of the community has reason and they use it collectively to formulate the laws. "For since an intelligence common to us all makes things known to us and formulates them in our minds, honorable actions are ascribed by us to virtue, and dishonorable actions to vice; and only a madman would conclude that these judgments are matters for opinion and not fixed by nature."

The Romans believed in their gods. And although the Roman concept of religion did not survive and later monotheistic faiths dominated world religions, the "natural rights" principles articulated by Cicero survived and still inform contemporary legal theory. For example, the United States Constitution contains "fundamental rights." In addition, nineteenth century and early twentieth century judges believed that there was an unwritten body of "natural rights" that were so basic that they did not need to be written down. Indeed, given the views of several contemporary United States Supreme Court Justices who have endorsed Natural Law, it appears that Ciceronian legal thinking remains an important factor in the American legal community, even though it is not often overtly recognized. The concept of Natural Law is still an active element of American jurisprudence. Many Supreme Court justices discuss law as an overarching principle that was not derived from man, but from nature and ultimately, God. For this reason, it is important for the members of society who create and enforce laws to understand Natural Law. Although Cicero did not believe in one central god in the same sense that many modern religions espouse, the controlling precept that all human beings have a common understanding of what is considered to be "right" and "wrong" is a basic theme that today still persists in all major religions and cultures.

CHAPTER 11

LEGAL PROCEDURE, INSTITUTIONS, AND ORGANIZATION

§ 11.01 Introduction

In American law, the possession of a right is a prerequisite to beginning a legal dispute. In ancient Rome, the opposite was true. The procedure was the cause of the right. In some respects, this is similar to the old English writ system. Prior to William the Conqueror, all legal disputes in England were resolved by local custom. Before the King became involved in a dispute, he had to have some sort of interest in it (*i.e.*, an interest for the Crown). Then and only then, did the King become involved by using a proper document, the "writ." The commonplace was "where there is no writ, there is no right." Therefore, the King's judges heard a case only if the plaintiff had a writ (*i.e.*, the writ gave the party the right to sue). The same was true under Roman law. Suits in Roman law were called *actiones* (*actio* in the singular). A person's rights came from the *actiones*. One might have said in ancient Rome, "where there is no *actio*, there is no right."

For civil cases between citizens, litigants took their cases to the court of the Urban Praetor. Civil cases involving foreigners were heard by the Peregrine Praetor. Criminal cases in the Republic were heard by various *quaestiones perpetuae* that were established by specific legislation to address particular kinds of criminal conduct. As an antecedent, however, to understanding the nuts and bolts of legal procedure, it is helpful to appreciate something about the nature of the legislative bodies that created laws. Thus, this chapter begins with an overview of the Roman constitution and important early laws that established the basis for much of later Roman law. As regards procedure itself, in early Roman law, it was important that a litigant use the proper form of action. Without a pre-set form of action, a litigant would have no remedy. Therefore, the second section of this chapter examines the three traditional chronological phases of Roman legal procedure: 1) Pre-Classical (*Legis Actiones*); 2) Formulary (*Per Formulam*); and 3) Extraordinary (*Cognitio*). Lastly, we survey the specialized field of criminal procedure and briefly consider the Roman law of evidence.

§ 11.02 The Roman Constitution & Significant Republican Legislation

A. Introduction

When historians speak of the "Roman Constitution," they do not mean a document *per se* like the American Constitution, but rather they mean the totality of customs, principles, and separate legislation that in sum delineated the powers and functions of the Roman government. Scholars have speculated that the Romans borrowed some concepts in their constitution from the Etruscans. Scholars have also speculated—with very little corroborating evidence—that they also borrowed Etruscan concepts as part of their private law. For the purposes of the present study, it is necessary to consider the Roman Constitution in order to understand the nature of the officials and legislative bodies responsible for the development of Roman law.

Roman law originally was a monopoly of the priests, the *pontiffs*. During the Monarchy (*c.* 753–509 B.C.), the early Roman kings created laws that dealt with family law and sacred law. In the 5th century B.C., the Laws of the Twelve Tables constituted the first codification of Roman laws (*c.* 451/450 B.C.). Apparently, the Twelve Tables presented the only expression in writing of old Roman customs that heretofore had been kept secret by the priests.

In addition, two other legal sources supplemented the Twelve Tables in earliest Rome: *leges* and *senatus consulta*. *Leges* were statutes adopted by the *populus Romanus*. A statute generally was binding because it resulted from a positive vote of an assembly of the people. Some ancient Roman *leges* survive in original texts (such as inscriptions on stone) while others have come down to us as quotations by ancient authors. Over 800 are extant. Given that these laws span many centuries, this is actually a rather small number. In many respects the Roman *leges* were designed to honor the *mos maiorum*, the customs of their ancestors. *Senatus Consulta* were not really laws but "advice" from the senate. The Twelve Tables, *leges*, and *senatus consulta*, technically speaking, applied only to Roman citizens.

We often find Roman statutes that have at least two parts: 1) *praescriptio* (a general comment concerning the wrong); and, 2) *sanctio* (the negative consequences which resulted from a person's violation of the *praescriptio*). Thus, theoretically speaking, there can be four basic types of laws based on the relationship between the *praescriptio* and the *sanctio*: 1) *lex imperfecta* (a law which provides a rule without a sanction)(*e.g.*, "A master may not free a slave without first giving the appropriate magistrate 5 day's notice."); 2) *lex perfecta* (here the *sanctio* merely invalidates the act which has been performed but prohibited by the *praescriptio*, *i.e.*, the *praescriptio* is "protected" by the *sanctio*)(*e.g.*, If a master frees a slave without first giving the appropriate magistrate 5 day's notice, the slave is not free but rather remains a slave; the manumission is void and invalid."); 3) *lex plus quam perfecta* (here the *sanctio* both invalidates the act that has been performed and prohibited by the *praescriptio* and it also exacts other negative consequences (*e.g.*, fines))(*e.g.*, If a master frees a slave without first giving the appropriate magistrate 5 day's notice, the slave is not free but rather remains a slave; the manumission is void and invalid, and the master must pay a fine of 10 sesterces."); and, 4) *lex minus quam perfecta* (here the *sanctio* does not invalidate the act prohibited by the *praescriptio*, but instead imposes negative consequences)(*e.g.*, If a master frees a slave without first giving the appropriate magistrate 5 day's notice, the master must pay a fine of 10 sesterces.").

B. Legislative Bodies

The entire Roman citizenry gathered, as an assembly for political purposes, in several different groups. Each such assembly was called a *comitia*. It was the citizenry gathered as a *comitia* that initially enacted statutes. There were three such assemblies worthy of note: 1) *comitia centuriata;* 2) *comitia tributa*; and, 3) *comitia curiata*. The *comitia centuriata* was the assembly comprising all Roman citizens organized into "centuries," or one-hundreds. It was arranged by a wealth-classification. Because of the order of voting in the *comitia centuriata*, the wealthiest citizens could always out-vote the poor. The *comitia tributa* was established on an old tribal/territorial basis. During the Monarchy, Rome was divided into four districts called *tribus* (tribes). Gradually, more tribes were added in the surrounding countryside until there were thirty-one rural and four urban tribes as of 241 B.C. All Roman citizens were considered members of one of these tribes for voting purposes. Eventually, they abolished the geographic distinctions, and instead made membership in the tribes hereditary. We have very little precise knowledge about the *comitia tributa* and its operation. The *comitia curiata* operated in some fashion during the Monarchy but the details are far from clear. By the Republic it served mostly to witness (and perhaps to authorize) wills and adoptions.

The *concilium plebis* was originally an assembly of all plebeians. The *lex Hortensia* of 287 B.C. decreed that the enactments of the *concilium plebis*, called *plebiscita*, had the force of law over all Roman citizens. Prior to 287 B.C., *plebiscita* had legally bound only plebeians. The tribunes of the plebs were the officials who presided over the *concilium plebis*.

In order for the *comitia centuriata*, the *comitia tributa*, or the *concilium plebis* to convene legally, a magistrate had to call the assembly. A consul could call a meeting of the *comitia centuriata*, only a "patrician" magistrate could call a meeting of the *comitia tributa*, and a tribune of the plebs could convene the *concilium plebis*. After the end of the 1st century A.D., neither the *comitia centuriata* nor the *comitia tributa* enacted legislation.

Two *censors* were elected every five years for the purpose of conducting the census. By virtue of their position, they were able to determine the political and social status of all Roman citizens. In addition, they acquired the role of evaluating both public and private moral behavior. Technically speaking, the *censors* selected senators. As a rule, the censors only picked former magistrates to serve as senators. Senators served for life. During most of the Republic, there were 300 senators. In 81 B.C., Sulla increased the number to 600. Usually the senate (which, during the Republic, technically had no power to pass laws itself) debated a bill first. Then, after the bill had been worked out in the senate, a magistrate presented it to an assembly. The assembly only had the power either to accept or reject the bill as presented by the magistrate. As a practical matter, however, the assemblies respected the wisdom and *auctoritas* of the advice given by the senate. The legislative power of the senate waxed during the Empire—a time when decrees of the senate, *senatus consulta*, acquired the force of law. Initially a clause in the praetor's edict was required to elevate *senatus consulta* to the level of statute, but in time—certainly by the time of Hadrian (117–138 A.D.) (*senatus consultum Tertullianum*)—this was no longer necessary. By the 2nd century A.D., the emperor routinely sent bills to the senate for its approval or rejection.

C. Legislation

"[M]ost legislation was political and ... there are in fact few statutes concerned with private law."[1] But there are a few statutes from the Republic that

---

1. WATSON, ROMAN LAW & COMPARATIVE LAW 18. *See also* WOLFF, ROMAN LAW 67 ("Roman legislation served the purpose of adapting the structure of state and law to changed conditions, but never that of radically altering it.").

influenced Roman law to such an extent that they should, at least, be mentioned. The *lex Canuleia*, passed in 445 B.C., gave plebeians the right of intermarriage with the patricians. In 367 B.C., the Licinian-Sextian law provided that one of the two consuls elected every year had to be a plebeian. A very important piece of legislation during the Republic was the *lex Aquilia*, passed by the *concilium plebis* in 287 B.C. The *lex Aquilia* governed most of the law related to damage to property. It established the rights of a master against someone who injured his slaves or animals. Also in 287 B.C., the *lex Hortensia* provided that measures passed by the plebeian assembly (*plebis scita*—plebiscites) were binding on all Romans, and thus, had the force of law. Although we do not know the specifics of the *lex Aebutia* (passed in the latter part of the 2nd century B.C.), we do know that it brought about changes to Roman legal procedure.

§ 11.03 The Three Chronological Phases of Roman Procedure

A. *Legis Actiones*

In the early stages of Roman procedural development, lawsuits were conducted by means of the *legis actiones* ("suits of law"). These were unalterable and only existed in a few forms. The praetor and the judge (*iudex*) were the two most important officials involved in the development of the *legis actiones* system. The praetor was the person to whom a plaintiff first appeared for the initial stage of procedure. This initial stage was called *in iure* ("in accordance with law"). The praetor did not really affect the substance of the case but instead characterized the dispute. In particular, it was he who determined whether a particular type of action addressed the particular dispute in question. He rejected the case if there was no applicable cause of action. If the praetor decided that there was a cause of action, logically, that meant that the praetor had decided that there was, in fact, a protected right which existed. The praetor then spoke directly with the plaintiff and defendant. If the praetor determined that there was a valid cause of action (*i.e.*, he determined that the *in iure* stage had been successful for the plaintiff), the matter then proceeded *apud iudicem* (*i.e.*, the time at which the case would be heard by the judge (*iudex*) on the merits). The opinion of the *iudex* was called a *sententia*. The *legis actiones* system, therefore, involved a relatively passive role by the praetor. He merely decided whether the case could be heard by a judge. Thus, the praetor actually had little impact on the substantive law itself.

B. Formulary Procedure (*Per Formulam*)

The formulary system, a more flexible system of procedure, eventually—perhaps as early as the beginning of the 2nd century B.C.—replaced the *legis actiones*. The *formulae* were less formal and less rigid. This newer legal process permitted expansion of fresh legal concepts and innovative ideas. In the formulary system, the praetors began taking an active role in shaping substantive law.

We are not sure of the precise date of the *lex Aebutia* that legitimated the procedure *per formulam*, but it was probably passed between 150 and 125 B.C. Much later, the *lex Iulia* (17 B.C.) of Augustus established the formulary procedure as the mandatory procedure for virtually all kinds of lawsuits under Roman law. The distinction between *in iure* and *apud iudicem* still existed. In fact, there was no significant change in the *apud iudicem* phase. There were, on the other hand, major changes in the *in iure* step. In essence, the formulary system did away with the rigid *in iure* stage and, instead, substituted the use of a *formula* (written instruction) that delineated the facts and law for the judge. Praetors still determined whether the dispute was sufficiently significant to warrant being heard by a judge. The parties appeared before the praetor to initiate a suit. This appearance was the *litis contestatio*. It was here that the praetor, if he decided that there was a cause of action, wrote the formula that then went to the judge. The praetor's formula summarized the claims and defenses of the parties. The judge was required to make his decision based on the praetor's written formula. It was the formula that, in effect, created the legal rule which the judge was to apply in any given case. Because the formula was not bound by the strictures of the *leges actiones* and the *in iure*, the praetor had a new-found flexibility when considering the claims and defenses of the parties.

A typical formula consisted of three different parts: 1) *iudicis nominatio* (nomination of a judge); 2) *intentio* (the statement of the plaintiff's claim—the most important section of every formula); and, 3) *condemnatio* (the instruction to judge to either find the defendant liable or not, based upon an application of the formula to his findings of fact). The *intentio* made clear exactly what the action was. It could claim either a specific claim (*certum*) or an unspecific one (*incertum*). In terms of later jurisprudence, it was aspects of the formulary procedure which survived (specifically, the distinction between determinations of law and fact as in the distinction between *in iure* and *apud iudicem*).

Almost any adult male could serve as a judge (often called an arbiter). Eminent jurists frequently served as judges. Surveyors often judged cases involving land division and boundaries. The parties could also appoint their own arbiter, extra-judicially, to decide their case. Praetors could appoint a small jury of *recuperatores* (recoverers), usually three to five judges instead of a single *iudex*. We also know of large juries especially for disputes involving inheritance of large estates of nobles or the rich. These were called *centumviri* (100 men). The author Pliny describes a case where there were actually 180 jurors not just 100.

If a defendant, who was found liable, failed to comply within 30 days, the plaintiff could bring an "action on the judgment." The plaintiff then could seize the defendant, personally imprison him, and seize his property and sell it to satisfy the judgment. Otherwise, especially during the Republic (509–27 B.C.), there really was no appeal. The best that a defendant could do was to argue that the judge had not issued an opinion, that the judge had been coerced or was fraudulent, or the defendant could sue the judge for "corruption."

C. Extraordinary Procedure (*Cognitio*)

The final chapter of Roman procedure was the stage called *cognitio*, or as Justinian referred to it, "extraordinary" (*extraordinaria*) procedure. This was the procedure used in the Post-Classical period (certainly the principal process used by the mid-2nd century A.D.). In many respects, it was a regression, falling well below the achievements of the Classical period. Because the Roman Empire had expanded to such an extent, administration was complex. In simple terms, an emperor was incapable of handling everything. The emperor's bureaucrats managed litigation on the emperor's behalf. As was noted, under the formulary system the *in iure* phase was distinct from the *apud iudicem* phase. The *in iure* consisted of the praetor deciding what legal rules would apply to a case. The *apud iudicem* involved the judge who dealt with the facts in order to assess the proofs gathered by the parties, and thus to resolve the problem. Of course the hearing itself was subordinated by specific rules of presenting evidence and the other party's explanation of any potentially damaging evidence. In the end, the judge had to give an opinion along with his conclusions and explanations to articulate his reasoning and support his conclusions. By contrast, in the extraordinary procedure, there was no distinction between the *in iure* and *apud iudicem*. The two were combined. The same official decided both the legal prerequisites and the facts as well. *Cognitio* was a "trial before an official (such as the Urban Prefect or a provincial governor) sitting alone as a judge...."[2] The implementation of a lawsuit was in writing, expounding both the plaintiff's demands and also the testimony of witnesses.

---

2. O.F. Robinson, The Criminal Law of Ancient Rome 7 (1995) [hereinafter "Robinson, Criminal Law"].

§ 11.04 Criminal Procedure

A. Introduction

1. The Early Criminal Courts — Quaestiones Perpetuae

We know very little about the earliest Roman criminal law and procedure. It is not until the time of Plautus and Terence (*i.e.,* during the 2nd century B.C.) that we begin to get a reasonably clear picture. Roman law ordinarily dealt with many types of conduct that modern legal systems treat as criminal (such as theft, battery, and injury to property) instead as torts.[3] Criminal courts were established during the Republic. In 149 B.C. the *lex Calpurnia* instituted a permanent criminal court comprised of senators as jurors. This court decided cases concerning extortion by officials in the provinces. In the period following the *lex Calpurnia,* the Romans began establishing new permanent jury courts known as *quaestiones perpetuae* to handle criminal matters.

The Dictator Sulla set up a system of *quaestiones perpetuae* in 82/81 B.C. As a rule, any given permanent criminal court was established by the vote (a *lex*) of one of the citizen assemblies. We know of at least one pre-Sullan *quaestio perpetua* that was formed as a result of the *lex repetundarum* (law concerning extortion) of the *tabula Bembina* (formerly referred to as the *lex Acilia*—perhaps from about 120 B.C.). The courts that Sulla established tried cases dealing with a variety of topics such as homicide, forgery, counterfeiting, assault, treason, extortion, and embezzlement. Other permanent criminal courts followed during the next thirty years.[4] Augustus created the last of the permanent criminal courts. Augustus' *quaestiones perpetuae* dealt with matters such as election practices, adultery, violence (*vis*), and treason. Sulla saw to it that, in addition to the Urban Praetor and Praetor Peregrinus, other, additional praetors managed the business of the various *quaestiones perpetuae.* Occasionally a former aedile served as a *iudex quaestionis* in the absence of a praetor.

2. Evolution of the Courts and Criminal Jurisdiction

Although a number of *quaestiones perpetuae* continued to operate until the mid-2nd century A.D., they ceased to have their former, Republican significance. In their place, courts convened by the Urban Prefect took precedence. The *quaestiones perpetuae* did not perish wholesale. Indeed, many functioned, and

---

3. *See infra* Chapters 16 and 17.
4. *See* Robinson, Criminal Law 3.

in fact, thrived for at least the first hundred years of the Empire. The Urban Prefect had broad-sweeping jurisdiction in criminal cases. The emperor and the senate also exercised a degree of criminal jurisdiction.

In the 1st century A.D., the senate itself acted as a court for public crimes of the sort that the *quaestiones perpetuae* had heard during the Republic. By and large, the senate only heard cases involving non-political charges when the cases themselves involved either a senator or a senator's family. In the early Empire, the senate took over the legislative functions that had previously belonged to the citizen assemblies. The emperors also wielded a fair degree of personal power in criminal matters. At some point, it appears that the emperor had to approve all death sentences. And, until Hadrian put a stop to it, emperors had the power to put an end to trials and to reverse the senate's verdict. The emperor even conducted some trials on his own. But it is nearly certain that jurists who acted as his advisers actually wrote the emperor's *decreta* (judicial decisions) and rescripts (written responses to legal questions).

The Urban Prefect initially controlled criminal jurisdiction within the city of Rome proper. By 200 A.D., his jurisdiction extended outward from Rome to a radius of 100 miles. Other prefects also acquired criminal jurisdiction during the Empire. The Prefect of the Night Watch, the Prefect of the Grain Supply, and the Praetorian Prefects all supervised criminal cases that pertained to their respective subject matter. Although we are not completely certain, it seems likely that the *tresviri capitales* of the Republic and the Urban Prefect or Prefect of the Night Watch during the Empire would have been in charge of criminal law as it related to foreigners in Rome. In the late Empire (*i.e.,* the Dominate—the Empire after 284 A.D.), the senate ceased to function as a standard court. Instead the Urban Prefect presided over a court of five senators (*iudicium quinquevirale*) to hear capital cases in which a senator had been charged. There was no general right of appeal from a decision of the Praetorian Prefect. In addition, other bureaucratic imperial officials were given jurisdiction over criminal courts at various levels in Rome and the provinces.

B. Juries & Jurors

The earliest jurors in the permanent criminal courts were senators. For a time, after changes wrought by Gaius Gracchus (122 B.C.), equestrians took the place of the senators. Sulla gave the juries back to the senators. The *lex Aurelia* (70 B.C.) established the system that, with minor adjustments, prevailed for the balance of time during which the *quaestiones perpetuae* operated. The scheme of the *lex Aurelia* took prospective jurors from three groups: 1) senators; 2) equestrians; and, 3) *tribuni aerarii* (*i.e.,* probably the citizens whose census wealth was just below that of the equestrians). In order to be eligible, a prospective juror had to reside either in the vicinity of Rome or in Rome itself. In addition, jurors had to be between the ages of 30 and 60. Originally, each law that established a court also established the size of its jury. We know of at least one jury that had 32 jurors in a criminal trial in 74 B.C. After the *lex Aurelia*, most criminal juries appear to have been comprised of 75 jurors— 25 senators, 25 Equestrians, and 25 *tribuni aerarii*.

C. Criminal Procedure & Affirmative Defenses

Ordinarily, any male citizen could initiate proceedings upon application to the president of the court. The prosecutor swore an oath that his prosecution was in good faith. Roman law considered it a criminal offense for an accuser to bring false charges (*calumnia*), to hide legitimate charges (*praevaricatio*), or to abandon charges once formally begun (*tergiversatio*). The legal institution of the prosecution began with the *nominis delatio* (*i.e.*, a kind of initial hearing, or arraignment). The person who was being accused was required to attend the *nominis delatio*. The court president then wrote down an *inscriptio* for the prosecutor to sign. After signing the *inscriptio*, the prosecutor could not turn back without facing severe penalties himself. Thereafter, the prosecutor had a reasonable period of time (a minimum of 10 days) within which to ready his case for trial.

At trial, the prosecutor made a lengthy introductory statement in which he explained the charges against the defendant (or in some cases several speakers were involved). Next, the defendant—or usually an advocate (or advocates) speaking on his behalf—responded to the charges. Thereafter, each side, beginning with the prosecution, presented its evidence. Evidence could be in the form of oral or prepared written testimony by witnesses or documents.[5] Jurors in Republican courts considered the oral testimony of witnesses as the most reliable evidence. In particular *laudatores*, character witnesses, were often pivotal. In addition to giving direct testimony, witnesses were also cross-examined by the opposing side.

Jurors voted by secret ballot using wax-covered tablets. Each juror had a two-sided wax tablet. One side of the tablet was inscribed with the letter "A" for *absolvo* (*i.e.*, acquittal) and the other was inscribed with the letter "C" for *condemno* (*i.e.*, conviction). In order to convict, a prosecutor needed a simple majority of the jury's votes. But even a 50–50 deadlock yielded an acquittal

---

5. *See infra* § 11.05.

for the defendant. If convicted, a defendant was sentenced either automatically by the terms of the relevant statute itself or by the jury in cases where the statute did not provide a compulsory penalty. The most common penalties were fines, banishment (*interdictio aquae et ignis*—denial of water and fire), death, infamy, and forced labor.

Before Augustus, there were, apparently, no statutes of limitations for crimes. As part of his legislation on *quaestiones perpetuae*, Augustus did introduce a statute of limitations of five years for adultery and *peculatus* (embezzlement).[6] About 300 A.D., a twenty-year statute of limitations was imposed for the crime of *falsum* (forgery).[7] Otherwise, there appear to have been few, if any, statutes of limitations for other crimes.

Roman law recognized a number of viable affirmative defenses. For example, self defense could justify homicide. Similarly, a man who killed someone engaged in sexually assaulting a family member had a complete defense. In the appropriate circumstances, duress could also furnish an affirmative defense to conduct that otherwise would have been criminal. The "heat of passion" could function as a defense for a man who killed his wife when she was caught in *flagrante delicto* in adultery. However, Roman law treated "heat of passion" in these circumstances not as an affirmative defense *per se* but rather as a mitigating factor that could reduce his punishment.

§ 11.05 Evidence

"To the Roman lawyer evidence, as a separate division of the law, was unknown.... [T]he Roman law of evidence is scattered throughout Code, Digest, and Novellae."[8] Roman law did not have rules regarding admissibility of evidence. Advocates could introduce nearly any kind of evidence, including what modern law characterizes as hearsay. Quintilian recognized a distinction between oral *versus* documentary evidence. Public documents, for example, were afforded great evidentiary weight. Private documents (*e.g.*, letters) were considered equal in evidentiary value to oral testimony. There was a preference for original documents, as the "best evidence".

Quintilian noted a difference between what he called "artificial" and "inartificial" evidence. This latter distinction is roughly analogous to what modern

---

6. For more on adultery, *see infra* § 16.05[A], on *peculatus, see infra* § 16.07[C].

7. *See infra* § 16.07[E].

8. Carr Ferguson, *A Day in Court in Justinian's Rome: Some Problems of Evidence, Proof, and Justice in Roman Law*, 46 Iowa L. Rev. 732, 740 (1961).

law identifies as the difference between circumstantial evidence (*e.g.*, the discovery of footprints in the snow) and direct evidence (*e.g.*, the direct testimony of an eyewitness who testifies that he saw an individual walking in the snow). In certain circumstances, Roman law gave evidentiary weight to various oaths taken by parties. Statements that a party made that contradicted his own interests and outright admissions by a party were given added evidentiary weight.

Originally the direct testimony of witnesses provided the most important evidence in Roman law courts. It was not until late in the Empire (*i.e.*, perhaps late in the 4th century A.D.) that documentary evidence came to be regarded as more reliable than a witness's testimony. Justinian's corpus reveals a clear distrust towards witnesses and a marked preference for evidence established by documents. As a rule, a lone witness's testimony was insufficient to prove a fact. Some form of corroboration was needed to supplement a single individual's statements. The number of witnesses, also, could be crucial. For example, in order to validate a gift, a contract of *depositum* (gratuitous loan for safekeeping) or *mutuum* (loan of fungibles),[9] prove adultery, or legitimize a child, it was necessary to have three witnesses. One needed five witnesses to validate the contract of *mancipatio* (transfer of *res mancipi*—*e.g.*, Italic land, slaves, cattle, horses, mules, donkeys, and the four praedial servitudes),[10] an amendment to a will, or the manumission of a slave. Both a divorce and a will needed seven.

Certain persons were not permitted to serve as a trial witness. For example, a party, himself, could not testify. For obvious reasons of conflict of interest, husbands and wives, parents and children, and patrons and freedmen could not testify in matters concerning one another. In order to testify in a civil trial, a witness had to have reached puberty, for a criminal trial, he had to be at least twenty years old. Slaves could only testify under torture. Occasionally, Roman courts relied on expert witnesses. For example, handwriting experts could detect forgeries, surveyors could assist in boundary disputes, and doctors could offer testimony relating to illnesses or death. It is a matter of some interest that Roman jurists frequently remarked that men of higher wealth and rank were to be regarded as more trustworthy witnesses than the poor and those of lesser rank. Roman law provided a certain measure of flexibility for the sake of convenience: it permitted a witness who lived a distance from the situs of a civil trial to give his testimony in writing (*i.e.*, such as by an affidavit or deposition). Thus, he was not forced to travel a great distance to testify. For a crim-

---

9. *See infra* § 18.04.
10. *See infra* § 13.04 [A].

inal case, however, he had to appear personally. Perjury was a serious offense. Depending on the circumstances, a witness who lied in court could be put to death, or receive a number of lesser punishments.

§ 11.06 Chapter Summary

In the beginning stages of formal law in Rome, a litigant had to have and use a pre-established form of action in order to obtain legal redress. In addition to the Twelve Tables, the advice of the senate (*senatus consulta*) and laws passed by the people (*leges*) comprised the backbone of early legislation. A number of statutes have a *praescriptio* (a general comment concerning the wrong) and a *sanctio* (the negative consequences that resulted from a person's violation of the *praescriptio*). Originally, the citizens gathered into an assembly (*comitia*) to enact legislation. The *comitia centuriata*, *comitia tributa*, and *comitia curiata* were the three principal assemblies responsible for legislation in the very early Republic. After the *lex Hortensia* (287 B.C.), the *concilium plebis* (under the direction of the tribunes of the plebs) was legally empowered to pass binding laws. The censors selected senators (who served for life). During the Republic (509–27 B.C.), the senate first debated legislation and then presented it to one of the assemblies where it could be enacted into law. During the Empire (27 B.C.–mid-5th century A.D.), the senate itself made law, primarily by means of *senatus consulta*. Among the most significant Republican laws passed were the following: 1) *lex Canuleia* (445 B.C.—plebeian right of intermarriage); 2) the Licinian-Sextian law (367 B.C.—one consul must be plebeian); 3) *Lex Aquilia* (287 B.C.—rules regarding property damage); 4) *lex Hortensia* (287 B.C.—made plebiscites binding); and, 5) *lex Aebutia* (2nd century B.C.—laws governing procedure).

The traditional chronological phases of Roman legal procedure are: 1) Pre-Classical (*Legis Actiones*); 2) Formulary (*Per Formulam*); and, 3) Extraordinary (*Cognitio*). In the Pre-Classical period, the praetor, during a procedure called *in iure*, assessed the dispute brought before him and initially determined whether the plaintiff's suit had any merit. If he decided that it did, he then sent the matter forward to a judge for a decision (*apud iudicem*). In the Formulary system, the praetor took on a more significant role. He evaluated the parties' claims and defenses, and then wrote a formula—a summary of the facts and a statement of the applicable laws—which the judge had to follow when deciding the case. Ordinarily, a praetor's formula consisted of three parts: 1) *iudicis nominatio* (naming of a judge); 2) *intentio* (a statement of the plaintiff's claim); and, 3) *condemnatio* (an explanation of how the judge was to apply the facts to the law). In the Extraordinary Procedure of the Empire, an imperial bureaucrat alone performed the roles that had hitherto been executed separately by the praetor and the judge. In essence, the bureaucrat conducted both the *in iure* and *apud iudicem* functions in the same procedure (presumably in an effort to achieve greater efficiency of process).

The first criminal courts—such as those designed to address extortion by provincial officials—were established in the middle of the 2nd century B.C. Sulla devised a system of permanent criminal courts (*quaestiones perpetuae*) to adjudicate cases involving various matters, and Augustus also was responsible for creating additional permanent criminal tribunals. During the Empire, the courts administered by the Urban Prefect gradually replaced the *quaestiones perpetuae*. The senate and the emperor, probably relying on the advice of jurists, decided a number of criminal cases. The role of the Urban Prefect and other prefects evolved during the Empire. Eventually, the various prefects oversaw the lion's share of all Imperial criminal cases. Although originally only senators were eligible to serve on criminal juries, after the *lex Aurelia* (70 B.C.) criminal juries usually had seventy-five jurors (each between the ages of thirty and sixty): twenty-five senators; twenty-five equestrians; and, twenty-five persons from the class just below the equestrians.

Any male citizen could initiate a criminal prosecution; beginning the process with an arraignment (*nominis delatio*) before the president of the court. After opening arguments first by the prosecutor and next by an advocate on behalf of the accused, each side presented evidence. Jurors in criminal trials voted secretly, using wax tablets. A simple majority was all that was necessary to convict. Even though Augustus implemented some statutes of limitations, as a rule there were few. Self defense, defense of a third party, duress, and, to a lesser extent, "heat of passion" operated as valid defenses for certain crimes (especially homicide).

Roman courts produced few rulings regarding the law of evidence. Although Quintilian did note both the distinction between oral *versus* documentary evidence as well as the difference between circumstantial and direct evidence, advocates generally introduced nearly anything that they wished (including hearsay) in attempting to sway a jury. As the law matured, judges gradually placed greater trust in documents than in the testimony of witnesses. In time, certain types of proof required a specific number of witnesses in order to be considered competent. Due to a presumption of bias, parties themselves, their relatives, and patrons and freedmen were not allowed to testify. Ordinarily witnesses had to be of a certain minimum age, and expert witnesses occasionally gave their professional opinions at trial.

Law in Literature:
Quintilian's *Institutio Oratoria* Book XII

Introduction

Marcus Fabius Quintilianus was born in Spain about 40 A.D. As a young man he studied in Rome under the grammarian Palaemon but returned to Spain thereafter. In 68 A.D. the emperor Galba brought Quintilian back to Rome. There he excelled both in the practice of public speaking as well as teaching. He taught, for example, Pliny the Younger. After 20 years in practice and teaching, he retired from public employment and devoted his time to writing his *Institutio Oratoria*. The treatise did not simply offer a dry list of rules. Instead, he illustrated the text with examples from writers and included observations that readers from all walks of life could understand. His exact date of death is uncertain he may have still been alive in 118 A.D. which would have made him around 78 years old. Book XII contains a great deal of advice that is even applicable to modern legal education.

I. *Quintilian,* Institutio Oratoria, *Book XII, §III*

Quintilian begins part three of Book XII by articulating the types of learning an orator must acquire to achieve eloquence. The orator must possess knowledge of civil law, customary law, and the religion of the State. In order to understand the State, he must understand the essential elements that make up the statehood. He continues by arguing that one should not be a mere transmitter of knowledge. If an orator does not first acquire the necessary knowledge, he cannot cope with unexpected problems that are commonplace in the field of pleading. Quintilian states, "he will be little better than if he were a reciter of the poets." During debate, because argument is not linear in nature, an advocate must have the necessary tools (*i.e.,* information and skills) at his disposal rather than having to ask other counsel for help. Quintilian recommends that an orator should be involved with every stage of the preparation. Who is better than the pleader himself to prepare the points which he will be pleading?

He presents his argument with a military analogy, specifically noting the skill set of a general. A general must have the basic traits of courage and leadership but he must possess other skills as well. He must know the supplies gathered and the supplies needed. He must know what weapons the soldiers have and what weapons they will need. Most importantly, he must at all times be prepared for any situation so that he can properly protect his troops. Quintilian states "preparation for war is an essential preliminary for its successful conduct." As a general must thoroughly know his enemy as well as his own soldiers, an orator must thoroughly know his opponent and his own case, inside and out. Written or customary laws are not difficult to comprehend or to argue since they do not call on the imagination. However, ambiguous laws rest on the principles of equity. In order to deal with situations where established laws or customs are not clear, an orator must be thoroughly prepared.

Quintilian examines the qualities an orator must possess. An orator is a man of virtue and good sense who must anticipate and address counter-arguments of opponents. Because an accomplished orator understands the demands of equity, he will have an advantage in an argument. Quintilian cites Marcus Cato and Cicero as examples of great lawyers and great orators. Through disciplined study, they had acquired the knowledge they needed both to plead and also to teach.

Section III of Book XII concludes with a preemptive argument. Quintilian anticipates the arguments of adversaries who, noting that many in the field of oratory already use the profession as a refuge for sloth, may argue that his advice is not practical. However, he affirms that "philosophy may be counterfeited, but eloquence never." Quintilian maintains that the lazy will not be able to blend in with those who follow his guidance. He also warns against those who might be tempted to use his advice for the wrong reasons. Those who use shortcuts will never become great orators. They are simply too indolent to rise to the proper level of eloquence

II. Quintilian, Institutio Oratoria, *Book XII, §§ IV–VI*

In Book XII of the *Institutio Oratoria*, Quintilian commits himself to a subject which Cicero treated about a century earlier in his essay *De Oratore* ("On the Orator"). Quintilian directs the attention of his target audience (*i.e.,* future orators) to the knowledge and substance they must acquire if they hope to succeed in practicing their craft and perfecting an art.

In Section VI, Quintilian insists that the regimen of a legal advocate must balance formal training and practical experience. He believes that both knowledge of legal theory and an understanding of the law's practical implications are crucial ingredients for developing as an effective legal advocate. Thus he states, "It is only when theory and practice are brought into perfect harmony that the orator reaps the reward of all his study." He does not maintain that there is a certain age at which an orator must begin to practice the law. Rather he suggests that an orator should develop his craft with an eye toward achieving a balance between theory and practice. Quintilian offers Cicero as an example of an advocate who charted the proper course. When early experience at trial taught him that the law required extensive study, Cicero withdrew from practice in order to study further, thereby learning the theory and techniques he would later need to hold sway in the courts.

In Section V, Quintilian articulates specific skills that an orator must obtain. He notes that, although an orator may acquire some, others must be cultivated within oneself. A legal advocate must especially cultivate a certain "loftiness of soul," derived from recognizing the great importance of his task. Quintilian suggests that when a legal advocate maintains such a purposeful view of his role, its attendant "constancy, confidence and courage" assist the legal advocate in overcoming natural inhibitions that might dilute his effectiveness.

He also emphasizes, however, that an excess of either confidence or modesty would undermine a legal advocate's effectiveness. Just as a combination of theory and practice is necessary, a healthy balance between modesty and confidence is essential for success. An excessive regard for one's own "nobility" as a legal advocate may degenerate into "the vices which are its opposites, such as arrogance, temerity, impudence and presumption." On the other hand, he asserts that an excess of modesty masking "a form of fear deterring the soul from doing what is its duty to do," also may obstruct an orator's potential genius. Therefore, Quintilian comments, "the best remedy for such excess of modesty is confidence," as the one moderates the other, and the orator "find[s] strength and support in the consciousness of the nobility of [his] task," without more.

While an abundance of any one ingredient may overpower the rest and spoil the recipe, Quintilian emphasizes that an effective legal advocate also must add ample doses of sugar and spice to "be secure of a kindly disposition in the audience." Such are among the arrows an outstanding orator would fix in his quiver: "a ready store of words and figures, power of imagination, skill in arrangement, retentiveness of memory and grace of delivery," in order to connect with and relate to an audience. Indeed, earlier in Section IV, he had recommended "a rich store of examples both old and new" as an indispensable tool that enriches the prowess of a legal advocate to persuade the audience, by lending authority to his arguments. Section V concludes by identifying the natural instruments, "such as voice, lungs, and grace of carriage and movement," that punctuate an orator's reputation as an effective legal advocate.

III. *Quintilian,* Institutio Oratoria, *Book XII, § VII*

In Section VII, Quintilian turns his discussion from qualities and skills to more practical and ethical considerations of lawyering. According to Quintilian, the "good man" will prefer defense over prosecution. This point of view is interesting given the popular view of lawyers today, where defense attorneys are often portrayed as shady or crooked and prosecutors are commonly depicted as enforcers of the law. Although Quintilian does not explain why defense is a more attractive option to the "good man," he paints a negative picture of the role of accuser. He goes so far as to say that devoting one's life to prosecution with the hope of bringing the guilty to trial is little better than making one's living "by highway robbery."

But Quintilian does defend the task of prosecution as a necessary duty. Indeed, he says "the laws themselves would be powerless without the assistance of advocates equal to the task of supporting them." He equates the failure to prosecute wrongdoing with sanctioning the crime. Therefore the role of accuser is necessary. That task, however, must be undertaken for the right reason: the "desire to correct vice and reform morals," not merely the desire to punish transgressors. When the role of accuser is undertaken as a fulfillment of the orator's duty, prosecution is considered "conduct worthy of comparison with that of heroes, who champion their country's cause in the field of battle." Here again, Quintilian analogizes lawyers with soldiers, a theme common in Book XII.

Whether in defense or prosecution, it is important for an orator to select carefully the cases he chooses. Although the character of both the prospective client himself and the character of those who recommend him may influence an orator, the facts and nature of the specific case are most important. There are two major concerns regarding client selection: soliciting powerful clients against the weaker; and, supporting the weak against the powerful. Both are problematic, Quintilian notes, because the social class of the litigant does not determine whether the case is just. Further, an orator has a duty to his client to give honest advice regarding whether the cause is just or unjust. Thus, if an orator finds that the cause is unjust, he may not defend the client. However, if an orator mistakenly believes his case to be just, then he has still performed honorably.

In addition, Quintilian discusses whether an orator should accept fees for his services. He argues that the most honorable and ideal course would be to perform legal services for the good of society and not to debase the nobility of the orator's duty by selling such services. One who collects fees for his services when he already has enough to satisfy his needs has lessened the value of the orator's services. However, if an orator requires additional income to meet the demands of his duties, then it is permissible for him to accept payment for legal services. In fact, Quintilian says that there is not a more honest way to earn payment.

Nevertheless, the amount of the fee should not depend on the seriousness of the client's situation. Lastly, Quintilian suggests that an orator ought not seek more than is sufficient for his needs. Payment received should be an expression of gratitude rather than a fee. Clearly, such "noble" sentiments have been long replaced in modern society, as today the legal profession is viewed as a business.

IV. Quintilian, Institutio Oratoria, Book XII, § VIII

In Section VIII, Quintilian switches his focus from an orator's ideal characteristics to the need thoroughly to dissect a case. He first warns that, although a case with willing characters and a cooperative client may enhance the strength of a weak orator, it may also trick him into falling into the opposing side's arguments. An orator first must familiarize himself with the facts. He criticizes orators who rarely make adequate time to prepare a case before trial. They often scramble to learn the case either during the trial itself or at best in haste the day before.

He must select his witnesses wisely. For many witnesses only look to add thunder to a story and relish the attention of captivating a crowd. An unfit witness's points will sneak into and weaken the case for an orator who has not taken the time to research. Quintilian notes the importance of preparing witnesses and clients for a rigorous round of cross-examination. Failure to do so can be ruinous.

He warns:

> For a large number of clients lie, and hold forth, not as if they were instructing their advocate in the facts of the case, but as if they were pleading with a judge. Consequently, we must never be too ready to believe them, but must test them in every way, try to confuse them and draw them out. For just as doctors have to do more than treat the ailments which lie hid, since their patients often conceal the truth, so the advocate must look out for more points than his client discloses to him. (Book XII. § VIII. 8–12).

An orator must coach and prepare his client. An effective orator must become a trainer of sorts. As a trainer, an orator subjects his client to hostile interrogation. Since every individual is capable of exaggeration and lying, truth must be extracted from a conflated mixture of statements in a client's version of the facts. An orator's success thus becomes dependant on his time spent preparing his client.

A well-prepared orator will not fall prey to trick questions during cross-examination nor to a hidden document that may take him by surprise. Quintilian notes the importance of discovering concealed facts in advance. Despite the honesty and sincerity of a client, an orator cannot trust his client until he has prodded, poked, and probed every nuance of his client's story and facts. Clients tend to disregard important facts that a knowledgeable orator may elicit.

Once the orator has studied the case, his client, and tested his case and his client's statements regarding the case, the final step is for the orator to project himself into the role of the judge. Thus, in the eyes of Quintilian, the process of successfully handling a case is similar to completing a puzzle; one cannot attain perfection without the patience and knowledge of strategically placing together the pieces.

Conclusion

Even if an orator follows each of the steps and advice Quintilian offers, an orator may still be taken in by the tendency of the human ego to relish in the attention of others. Book XII warns against the devilish tendency of selfishness that may lie dormant in the human ego. It can sneak up upon an orator's flawless performance. He admonishes: "above all it is important that he should never, like so many, be led by a desire to win applause to neglect the interest of the actual case."

Quintilian's warnings and observations address more than merely the potential orator. He is cautioning the entire legal system regarding the evils that lurk in the performance of an orator and the deceptiveness in a client. He speaks directly to the legal system's corrupt tendencies to obsess about performance rather than substance and to those, specifically the jury, who carry other's fates in their hands. Quintilian looks to do far more than inform the orator. He looks to unmask the obstacles that lurk in every legal framework.

CHAPTER 12

PERSONAL STATUS

§ 12.01 Introduction

In ancient Rome, only persons who had "legal capacity" could be rights-holders and obligors (*i.e.*, those capable of having legal rights and duties). The notion of "legal capacity" was known as *caput* (literally "head"). According to the Roman jurist Paul, there were three kinds of status which determined legal capacity: 1) *civitas* (citizenship); 2) *libertas* (freedom); and, 3) *familia* (family).[1] At its most elementary level, the scope of rights and duties of any individual depended on whether he was a citizen or a foreigner, free or slave, and the head of his family or a subordinate.

§ 12.02 Citizenship

A. General

In many respects, citizenship (*status civitatis*) was the most empowered legal capacity. Those who were born as Roman citizens had three very important legal rights: 1) *ius honorum* (the right to hold governmental office); 2) *ius connubium* (the right to marry another citizen); and, 3) *ius commercium* (the right to engage in commercial and property transactions). In early law, these three rights were strictly observed as the province of Roman citizens only. Foreigners (*peregrini*) were required to secure a citizen, as patron, in order to transact business. Eventually the law evolved, primarily for two reasons. First, economic relationships with foreigners rose to such a level that legal capacity for foreigners to contract was needed for foreign trade. Thus, in the Classical period of Roman law, foreigners received *ius commercium* with certain restrictions. But foreigners received neither *ius connubium* nor *ius honorum*. Sec-

---

1. Chapter 12 discusses *civitas* and *libertas*. The discussion of *familia* appears *infra* in Chapter 14.

ond, because the Roman Empire expanded to such a broad geographic extent, in order to function effectively as a state, Rome needed to have more citizens than non-citizens. In the early Republic, the Latins and Junian Latins received varying degrees of citizenship. During the first two centuries of the Empire, army veterans often received Roman citizenship. This altered the nature of Roman citizenship. Then in 212 A.D., the Emperor Caracalla granted Roman citizenship to nearly all of the free persons in the vast Roman Empire. Eventually all adult male inhabitants of the Empire were declared citizens. Hence, the adult men within the boundaries of the Empire received all three rights of citizens.

There is yet another interesting aspect of the Roman law of legal capacity that should be noted. One way that jurisprudence classifies legal capacity is dualistic, as two distinct types: 1) "legal capacity"; and, 2) "dispositive capacity." "Legal capacity" is the capacity which arises at birth. It is, in essence, a passive capacity that entitles a person to have certain rights and duties. On the other hand, "dispositive capacity" is the capacity which allows an individual independently to acquire and exercise rights and duties (*i.e.*, not merely arising at birth, but rather as an active pursuit). Law ordinarily requires that a person attain a certain age (*e.g.*, eighteen) and be of sound mind in order to acquire dispositive capacity. Although Roman law did not employ the terminology of "legal" and "dispositive" capacity *per se*, the Roman concept of *caput* actually included both types. Consider legal regulations concerning children. There is a clear distinction between adults and minors. Roman adults could exercise all rights and perform all duties but minors could not. For example, under Roman law, children under the age of seven could exercise no commercial rights and had no commercial duties; all of their transactions were invalid. Parents or guardians executed all contracts for children under the age of seven. When a child was between seven and fourteen (for boys) or seven and twelve (for girls), s/he could enter into transactions and contracts. But these could only be transactions or contracts that were favorable to the child (*e.g.*, a child of this age could receive gifts). At age fourteen (for boys) and twelve (for girls) Romans were no longer considered children but adults, and thus could fully execute all commercial transactions and contracts.[2] Thus, by birth a Roman child may have received the legal capacity of a citizen but he could not exercise many of his citizenship rights (or perform many of his citizenship duties—such as military service) until he had acquired dispositive legal capacity through the process of aging and attaining or retaining a sound mind. In

---

2. There were certain exceptions. For example, ordinarily, a person had to be at least twenty-five years old to sell or buy a slave. Or an adult under twenty-five could do so with the consent of his curator (*i.e.*, a person who acted as a guardian for an adult—*see infra* § 14.05).

Roman law, the insane had no dispositive capacity. Insane persons always had a guardian of some sort, and only their guardians could execute contracts for them. Roman Law did, however, permit a person who was *lucidiae intervalis* (*i.e.*, someone who had periods of mental clarity) to have dispositive capacity during his periods of lucidity.

B. *Capitis Deminutio*

The legal capacity (*caput*) of Roman citizens could, however, be restricted for a number of reasons. If events warranted it, Roman Law could reduce (or diminish) a person's legal capacity. This reduction in status was called *capitis deminutio*. It could occur on three levels: 1) *maxima*; 2) *media*; and 3) *minima*. *Maxima capitis deminutio* resulted from loss of freedom (becoming a slave). This entailed losing one's freedom and all other status. Fundamentally, one could receive *maxima capitis deminutio* in three ways. First, an individual might become a captive of a foreign war. Second, some criminal punishments resulted in *maxima capitis deminutio*. For example, some punishments for crimes required that a person go into exile "across the Tiber River" (*trans Tiberim*) and others dictated that a convicted criminal be sold as a slave to a foreigner. Lastly, a free woman who had sex with a slave could also receive *maxima capitis deminutio* by being sold as a slave *trans Tiberim*. A Roman citizen who suffered *media capitis deminutio* lost only some of his rights as a citizen. Ordinarily, such a person lost his *ius honorum* (the right to hold political office) and *ius connubium* (the right of marriage) but retained his *ius commercium* (the right to enter into business transactions). Thus, a person who suffered *media capitis deminutio* acquired essentially the legal status of a foreigner. Generally, *media capitis deminutio* resulted from criminal punishment where the individual was exiled but not sold into slavery (for example he might be forced to move to a colony). The term *minima capitis deminutio* refers to a reduction in status with respect to family. Specifically, the expression is only used when a person who had previously been a *persona sui iuris* (person of his own right) became a *persona alieni iuris* (person of another's right).[3] For example, a man could experience *minima capitis deminutio* as a result of adoption. A woman could experience it by marriage *cum manu*.[4] To explain further, suppose that a husband and wife were married and had no sons. If the husband then died, the widow would have become a woman *sui iuris*. Then upon remarriage *cum manu*, she would un-

---

3. *See infra* § 14.01.
4. *See infra* § 14.02[B].

dergo *minima capitis deminutio*. This reduction in legal capacity entailed important legal consequences. For example, all personal property immediately became the property of the new *paterfamilias*, and indeed, all other legal consequences of being a *persona alieni iuris* arose.[5] Nevertheless even a person who had endured *minima capitis diminutio* still retained his *libertas, civitas, ius honorum, ius connubium*, and *ius commercium*—all, of course, within the limits of subordination to his *paterfamilias*.

§ 12.03 Slaves & Freedmen

The most important distinction in terms of legal capacity was that between freedom and slavery. In essence, the Roman jurists said *"servi res sunt"* ("slaves are things"). Slaves were considered means of production, not persons themselves. Legally speaking, however, slaves had attributes of both property as well as attributes of human beings. When a slave made something, it belonged to his master. Slaves were, in essence, *res mancipi*.[6] Slaves did not have legal standing either to sue or be sued. In the Republic (509–27 B.C.), masters had free reign to treat their slaves however they wished. In the Empire (27 B.C.–mid-5th century A.D.), certain laws restrained a master's unmitigated command. In particular, the Emperor Hadrian (117–138 A.D.) prohibited a slave owner from killing a slave unless a magistrate first approved the execution.[7] By the time of Constantine (272–337 A.D.), the State could prosecute a master for murder if his inhumane discipline caused his slave's death. By the time of the Emperor Justinian (527–565 A.D.), a Roman master was only permitted to exact punishment on his slaves that was regarded as "reasonable."

There were three principal ways that someone could become a slave. One could become a slave as a result of: 1) being a prisoner of war; 2) birth;[8] or, 3) debt. In addition, there were certain crimes that could be punished by enslavement. The Twelve Tables declared that a thief who was caught red-handed could be punished by enslavement. Moreover, if a person tried to dodge the census (*i.e.,* trying to escape military duty), he too could be punished with enslavement. Furthermore, the *senatus consultum Claudianum* (52 A.D.) pro-

---

5. *See infra* § 14.01.

6. *See infra* §§ 13.01, 13.04[A].

7. *See* WATSON, ROMAN LAW & COMPARATIVE LAW 40.

8. *See Id.* at 39 (1991) (Watson explains that a child born to a slave woman could legally be considered free (*i.e.,* not slave) if the mother had been free at any point between the child's conception and his birth.).

vided that a freewoman who lived with another's male slave (without the slave owner's permission) automatically became a slave to that owner. Any children born of that union also became his slaves. If an individual was a slave because of any of these reasons, his *caput* was non-free. Interestingly, if a Roman citizen became a prisoner of war in a foreign country, but subsequently was freed, the praetors developed an institution—known as *postliminium* (literally "beyond the threshold")—whereby that Roman was deemed to be free, not a slave. In fact, Roman law considered that such a man had *never* been a slave.

Originally, Roman law treated all offspring of a female slave as slaves themselves, even if their father had been a free man. This was true if the mother had been a slave even temporarily while she was pregnant. Eventually the rule was turned on its head. If the mother had been free even temporarily, the child was considered free. By an interesting twist of legal logic, the children of slaves were not technically considered "fruits" of the slave. This did not mean that a slave's child was not a slave—she certainly was. It simply meant that when a third party had the use of a slave and the slave's fruits (for example by contract), if the slave gave birth during that time, the child became the property of the owner of the slave-mother, not the usufructuary.[9]

Because many slaves served in responsible positions (such as herding sheep or captaining a ship), there had to be some legal means for such slaves to execute valid contracts. To a limited extent, a slave could act on behalf of his master as an agent would. But the analogy to principal and agent is imperfect in many respects. Thus, a distinction was drawn between a "legal obligation" and a "natural obligation." An *obligatio naturalis* created a relationship similar to the type of obligation in modern American law where an adult contracts with a minor. An adult cannot enforce a contract against a minor but a minor can enforce it against an adult if he so desires. Similarly, after the statute of limitations has run on a cause of action, there may still exist an *obligatio naturalis*, even though there is no legal obligation due to the statute of limitations. For example, American law recognizes a natural obligation in the case of a debtor who pays his creditor after the statute of limitations has run: the law will not force the creditor to return the payment to the debtor. Roman law used this same concept of natural obligation to permit slaves to enter into binding contracts. This gave slaves a semblance of quasi-legal capacity (not an *obligatio stricti iuris* but an *obligatio naturalis*).

Another legal problem relating to slaves was their relationship to torts (*i.e.,* injuries to persons or property).[10] For example, when a slave caused damage,

---

9. *See infra* § 13.05 regarding the concepts *usus* and *usus fructus*.
10. For more about the Roman law of torts, *see infra* Chapter 17.

who was responsible? Technically, a slave could not be responsible for damage that he caused because he had no legal capacity (*caput*). Thus, as a rule, a slave's owner was responsible for (*i.e.*, vicariously liable for) damage caused by his slave. But this liability was only limited liability up to the value of the slave. Once the amount of liability rose to or above the value of the slave, himself, the master could choose simply to give the slave as compensation instead of paying money. The basic rule is that of *respondeat superior*. The Romans also used the term *culpa in custodiendo* (guilty in supervising). A master could escape liability in such situations only if he could prove that he had done virtually everything in his power to prevent his slave's damage.

Another institution peculiar to the Roman law relating to slaves—and, in fact, pertinent to their tort liability—is the *peculium*. The *peculium* was a stipend of money or property that a master customarily gave to his slave for the slave's use. It legally belonged to the owner. As a rule, however, a slave owner— and everyone else—dealt with the *peculium* as if it belonged to the slave. Technically speaking, a slave was only allowed to use the *peculium* in accordance with the wishes of his owner. The legal significance of the notion of *peculium* is actually rather subtle. When a master transferred property to his slave as *peculium*, the master was only liable for the slave's actions (*i.e.*, actions relating to the *peculium*) to the extent of the *peculium*. The same general concept operates today in the notion of limited liability in modern corporations law. When an individual buys stock in a company, if the company causes damage or goes bankrupt, the stockholder can only be liable up to the amount of his investment.

Another group with special legal rules was the *libertini*, freedmen (*i.e.*, slaves who had been manumitted or freed in an appropriate manner). During the Republic, there were three legally recognized methods of freeing a slave: 1) manumission by will (very common in the late Republic); 2) *manumissio censu* (a master allowed his slave to enroll in the census); and, 3) *manumissio vindicata* (This was accomplished by collusion whereby a third party—ordinarily a friend of the master—brought a legal action against the master and falsely alleged that the slave was, in fact, free. The owner, playing his part in the collusion, simply failed to contest the suit and the slave became free thereby.). Using an interesting bit of legal fiction (since technically slaves could not enter into binding agreements) a master could agree to free his slave in exchange for the slave's promise to work a specified number of days every year (*operae*) for the master. The only limitation on this type of agreement was that the amount of days could not be unreasonable.

In addition to manumission by will, *manumissio censu*, and *manumissio vindicata*, in time, other less formal methods of manumission came to be accepted as a matter of custom. For example, a master could free a slave by means of a letter or by a declaration in the presence of friends (as witnesses). These methods of manumission, although not technically considered legal, were recognized by praetors as a practical matter. Augustus enacted legislation—the *lex Fufia Caninia* (2 B.C.)—to limit the number of slaves that any one owner was permitted to manumit. The *lex Aelia Sentia* (4 A.D.) invalidated manumission in circumstances where the slave owner was under the age of twenty. This same law provided that if the manumitted slave was not yet thirty, he was not considered a Roman citizen. In addition, the law invalidated a slave's manumission if it had been done in an attempt to defraud the master's creditors.

Manumitted slaves acquired both freedom and partial Roman citizenship. They became clients of their former masters and the former masters became their patrons. A freedman (*libertinus*) could never truly be equal to a person who was free by birth in the eyes of Roman law. Once freed, the freedman and the patron each owed the other certain duties. As former slaves, freedmen—at least up to the time of Justinian—were expected to do some work *gratis* for their former owners. A freedman could obtain neither *ius honorum* nor *ius connubium*. However, he did obtain *ius commercium* as a result of gaining his freedom. Still, this was a somewhat restricted *ius commercium*, since he was unable to make a valid will. In some respects, then, the *libertini* lived as free people but died as slaves (*vivunt liberi moriuntur servi*). At death, a freedman's property went to his former owner. Finally, in the 6th century A.D., Justinian gave freedmen full Roman citizenship upon manumission.

§ 12.04 Chapter Summary

There were three types of status that affected an individual's legal capacity (*caput*) most significantly: 1) citizenship (*civitas*); 2) freedom (*libertas*); and, 3) family (*familia*). Roman citizens—a group which by 212 A.D. included all adult males living in the Empire—enjoyed three important rights: 1) the right to governmental office (*ius honorum*); 2) the right to marry another citizen (*ius connubium*); and, 3) the right to participate in commercial and property transactions (*ius commercium*). The Roman notion of *caput* (legal capacity) encompassed what scholars today characterize as both "legal capacity" (*i.e.*, the legal capacity that one possesses merely by birth) and also "dispositive capacity" (*i.e.*, the capacity that one acquires). It was possible (for example, as a result of criminal punishment or marriage) for a Roman citizen to suffer a reduction in his/her personal status (*capitis deminutio*). In extreme cases, a citizen might lose all citizenship rights, while in others, he might be only partially disenfranchised (*i.e.,* losing only certain rights).

Roman law considered slaves as property. It was not until the Empire that laws restrained a master's freedom to punish or even to kill a slave at will. As a rule, an individual became a slave as a result of being a prisoner of war, as a result of birth, as a result of debt, or as a result of criminal punishment. Generally speaking, the child of a slave was also considered a slave. But, eventually, the law allowed that, if the mother had been free at any time during her pregnancy, then her child was considered free, not slave. Because many slaves served in responsible positions, Roman law permitted them to enter into valid contracts, on the presumption (basically a legal fiction) that their conduct created a "natural obligation" (*obligatio naturalis*). Ordinarily, a master was legally responsible for damage caused by his slaves. But a slave who served in a position of responsibility was not kept on a short leash; rather he was usually given a stipend of money by his owner (*peculium*) that he used virtually as his own.

Manumitted slaves (*libertini*) acquired both freedom and a limited form of Roman citizenship. A master could manumit a slave either legally by formal means (*e.g.,* by will, *manumissio censu, manumissio vindicata*) or extra-legally by informal means (*e.g.,* by letter or declaration in the presence of witnesses). Although freedmen had some citizenship rights (*e.g.,* a limited *ius commercium*), they could neither marry a Roman citizen nor hold public office until the time of Justinian in the 6th century A.D.

CHAPTER 13

PROPERTY

§ 13.01 Introduction: The Most Significant Categories

One of the most striking things that one notices when first studying the Roman law of property (*i.e., res*, "things") is the incredible degree of classification. Roman jurists categorized property *ad nauseam*. We will examine the most significant categories of property first. Gaius divided property into two parts: 1) *res divini iuris* (things under divine law); and, 2) *res humani iuris* (things under human law). Roman law further subdivided things under divine law (which, incidentally, were incapable of human ownership) into *res sacrae* and *res religiosae*. The former were things such as temples that the Roman people had consecrated for the celestial gods. The latter were things such as graves that were dedicated to the gods of the netherworld. There was also a third branch of *res divini iuris* known as *res sanctae*, such as a city's walls and gates.

Roman jurists subdivided things under human law into two categories: 1) *res publicae* (public things); and, 2) *res privatae* (private things). *Res publicae* could not be owned by any one individual. Examples are roads, harbors, and rivers—all of which, of necessity, had to be accessible for all to use. A similar category was *res communes*. These were also things that could not really be owned, such as the air, the seas, and flowing water.

Gaius also classified property as either corporeal (*res corporalis*) or incorporeal (*res incorporalis*) (*i.e.,* tangible and intangible). Most civil law countries did not keep this ancient distinction, but the Common Law countries (*e.g.,* England) did borrow it from Roman Law. The principal import of this differentiation was that only tangible property could be—legally speaking—transferred by the method known as *traditio* (the most common method of property transfer).[1] This was because *traditio* required a physical conveyance in order

---

1. *See infra* § 13.04[B].

to be valid. With intangible property (*res incorporalis*), a different mode of legal transfer had to be used (usually *in iure cessio*).[2]

In addition, Gaius classified property as *res mancipi* and *res nec mancipi*. Property which was classified as *res mancipi* could only be sold by the method called *mancipatio*.[3] *Mancipatio* involved a very specific, formal, and formulaic method of transfer. It is often said that the things that were *res mancipi* were things that were essential for a rustic agricultural subsistence. Examples commonly given of *res mancipi* are slaves, oxen, horses, donkeys, real property, and the four praedial servitudes (*iter, actus, via,* and *aquaeductus*).[4] For example, to sell a slave by *mancipatio* the following had to be present: five witnesses; a person to hold a scale (*libripens*); the owner of the slave; the buyer; and, the slave. The purchaser placed precious metal—often copper—(later a coin) on the scale and one hand on the slave's shoulder, and said "I declare that this is my slave." Simply stated, in order to validly transfer ownership of things that were *res mancipi,* one had to use the formulaic method of transfer known as *mancipatio*.[5] One could transfer things that were *res nec mancipi* using less formal methods such as *traditio*[6] and *in iure cessio*.[7]

Eventually, as Roman society increased in complexity and size, *mancipatio* fell into disuse. In the late Empire the differentiation between those things that were *res mancipi* and those that were not vanished. Justinian officially eradicated the distinction. Nevertheless, some of the formulaic vocabulary of *mancipatio* continued to be used although the procedure itself was not. According to Justinian, however, mere delivery was not sufficient to legally transfer ownership of a *res* unless the buyer first either paid the price or gave security for it.

§ 13.02 Additional Categories

Roman jurists separated property into many, many other classifications. Some additional categories of Roman property (all of which are still used in some fashion in modern legal systems) are the following.

---

2. For more about *in iure cessio, see infra* § 13.04[C].
3. *See infra* § 13.04[A].
4. *See infra* § 13.05.
5. For more on *mancipatio, see infra* § 13.04[A].
6. *See infra* § 13.04[B].
7. *See infra* § 13.04[C].

1) *Res in commercio* as opposed to *res extra commercio*. *Res in commercio* were those things in economic circulation. Anyone was able to buy and sell these types of things. *Res extra commercio*, on the other hand, were things excluded from economic circulation. The majority of things were *in commercio*. Of the very few things that were considered *extra commercio*, the most common was probably the *ager publicus*, the land owned by the Roman State which could not be bought or sold.[8]

2) *Res mobiles* as opposed to *res immobiles*. *Res mobiles* were all things in Rome except land. All else, at least theoretically, could be moved. Thus only land, the most valuable type of property in ancient Rome, was considered a *res immobilis*. In nearly every country where plots of land can be sold today, the legal system classifies land as *immobilis*, and thus, as such, the sale and purchase of land must follow a specific form (*e.g.*, the transaction must be registered and/or recorded with the local government). As a general rule, only a registered landowner can be considered the rightful owner of such real property. A party who buys from a registered owner is considered a bona fide purchaser, and thus gains title to the land. These registration systems for land and the related rules about the sale of land which have evolved from this Roman distinction (*res mobiles/res immobiles*) constitute the principal significance of this distinction in the modern world.

3) *Species* as opposed to *genera*. *Species* were specific things with certain unique peculiarities that made it possible to distinguish them from other things (*i.e.*, things which could be identified by sight or appearance). Legally, *species* could not, for example in a contract, be replaced by another similar thing. If a *species* was destroyed, the contract to sell it immediately became unenforceable due to impossibility. *Genera*, on the contrary, were fungible items which did not have peculiarities that distinguished them from other like or similar items. Therefore, *genera* were considered replaceable. Hence, even if the object of a sales contract were destroyed, the contract was still enforceable if the object of the contract was an item classified as *genera*. The applicable Latin maxim was *genera perire non consentur* (*genera* are not considered to perish). The distinction between *species* and *genera* is roughly the same distinction that exists between non-fungible (*i.e.*, unique) and fungible goods in many modern legal systems today.

4) *Res quae usu consumatum* (things which are consumed by use) as opposed to *res quae usu non consumatum* (things which are not consumed by

---

8. This is not too dissimilar to the public squares, parks, or commons in many modern cities today (*e.g.*, the Boston Common).

use). *Res quae usu consumatum* are those things which, in the process of their use, are consumed (even if the consumption is little by little). Food, for example is a *res quae usu consumatum*. *Res quae usu non consumatum*, however, are those things which are not consumed by use, but instead remain intact (*e.g.,* an ox). They retain their uniformity. One may well wonder why this distinction is significant. In Roman law, it was considered impossible to lease or rent consumables (*i.e., res quae usu consumatum*). This is so, because, by definition, a lessee is required to return the property that he leases. Thus, leases can only occur with *res quae usu non consumatum*.

5) *Divisible things* as opposed to *non-divisible things*. This distinction was a purely legal distinction, not a physical one.[9] For example, grain is divisible because it retains its peculiar identity even if individual granules are physically separated from one another. On the other hand, a chair is non-divisible because, if it is physically split into parts, it loses its identity as a chair. In other words, a thing was deemed non-divisible if, when broken, it was no longer what it started out as. Clearly, that type of thing—in order to retain its integrity—should never have been divided in the first place.

§ 13.03 Legal Titles Connected with Things

A person is legally entitled to keep property because of some type of legal "title" to that thing. Different titles entail different legal consequences. The three most important types of legal title defined by Roman jurists are: 1) *dominium*; 2) *possessio*; and, 3) *detentio*.[10]

Dominium was basically what we today call "ownership." This type of title differs distinctly from all others. The Romans described it as yielding *plena in re potestas* (complete power with respect to the thing). One who had *dominium* of an object (its "owner") had unlimited power over the thing within the bounds of the law.

Possessio (possession) was a very complicated concept. When an ancient Roman had *possessio*, he kept a thing at his disposal; though not necessarily "physically." In order to have *possessio* of a thing, a person had to have it available for his control. There were two principal features of *possessio*: 1) a person kept a thing; though not necessarily physically; and, 2) not only did the per-

---

9. Unlike the case of *res mobiles* and *res immobiles* where the distinction is physical.

10. Of course these three did not exhaust all possible titles (*e.g.,* abstract title—which may be broad enough to include nearly all others).

son keep the thing, but he kept it *as his own thing*. Possession could be accomplished personally or through an agent. Interestingly, a tenant in a Roman lease was not considered to possess the property. Instead, the landlord was deemed to have *possessio* through the tenant.

At this point, it may be helpful to consider the legal difference between *dominium* and *possessio*. Of course it was very often the case that someone had both *dominium* and *possessio* of property. For example, a farmer could have both *dominium* and *possessio* of his ox. But circumstances could also arise where someone had *possessio* but not *dominium*. In basic terms, when a person who has *dominium* keeps a thing, he keeps it because he *really* owns it (with complete, unfettered power over it). However, when a person keeps something *merely thinking* that he owns it—but in reality he does not—he may have mere *possessio*, but not *dominium*. When a person has *possessio*, he is entitled to the legal presumption that he, the possessor, is the owner unless proven otherwise. Thus, a possessor is considered the owner of a thing, unless someone else succeeds in proving that he is not.[11] The same presumption exists in most legal systems today. This presumption is important for people who are the genuine owners of things, because it puts the burden of proof on a non-possessing claimant. Of course, in some cases a true owner will use self-help to "steal" back an item which another person has somehow obtained (as a possessor). Thus the unjust possessor, in order to get the item back (short of stealing it back yet again) would have the burden of proving his ownership in court. This would, no doubt, be a difficult task if the true owner can produce— which he probably could—witnesses who could testify as to his rightful ownership (*dominium*) of the item in question.

Detentio (detention), on the other hand, is a type of title that occurs when a person keeps a thing; but he is not the owner and, in fact, he does not think or even contend that he is the owner. Instead, an individual with *detentio* simply maintains that he has a legal right (of some sort) to possess the thing. Our modern concept of bailment is quite the same as *detentio*. A person keeps another's property but does not claim or imagine ownership. Unlike *possessio*, *detentio* can never ripen into ownership through adverse possession. As far as Roman law is concerned, all property disputes required an analysis of the type of title involved: whether the claimants had *dominium*, *possessio*, or *detentio*.

---

11. This distinction between *proprietas dominium* and *possessio* is significant also for the concept of *usucapio* (adverse possession or "usucaption"). Third parties must be capable of dealing with an adverse possessor just as if he were the true owner. *See infra* § 13.04[G].

§ 13.04 Methods of Acquisition of Property

A. *Mancipatio*

In Roman law, a person could acquire the right of ownership (*dominium*) in a number of ways. For example, a purchase and an inheritance are two rather obvious means of gaining ownership of things. But many ways existed, and some of them still exist in modern legal systems. As has been mentioned above, the earliest and most formal method of acquiring ownership through transfer of a thing was *mancipatio*.[12]

In early Roman law, *mancipatio* was the only valid means of transfer for *res mancipi*[13] (*e.g.*, Italic land, slaves, cattle, horses, mules, donkeys, and the four praedial servitudes; namely, *iter, actus, via,* and *aquaeductus*). There were a number of formalities that were required. There had to be five witnesses present (all Roman citizens who had reached puberty) and a sixth was needed to hold the scale. The transferee held the *res,* struck the scale with a bronze or copper ingot, and proclaimed the object to be his. Presumably the bronze was symbolic of an earlier incarnation of this ritual when that would have been the actual "money" exchanged for the *res.* The transferee probably also stated aloud the purchase price. The transferor, for his part, remained silent as a way of demonstrating that he did not contest the transferee's ownership.

Mancipatio automatically entailed an unwaivable warranty of title. If the true owner successfully sued a good faith purchaser, then the purchaser's damages against the fraudulent seller were twice the price that had been stated during the *mancipatio.* Buyers and sellers soon found a way around this rule by stating a ridiculously low (fictitious) price in the *mancipatio.* In addition to the verbal statements made during the *mancipatio,* it was common for a written record to be made that stated both the genuine value of the *res* as well as the price that had been recited in the *mancipatio.*

B. *Traditio*

Traditio was the most common method of transferring tangible personal property, and it was available for both Romans and foreigners. Apparently *traditio* was recognized as early as the Twelve Tables. It was perhaps the most commonly recognized mode of transfer for *res nec mancipi.* And later, in Clas-

---

12. *See supra* § 13.01.
13. *Id.*

sical Roman Law, it was accepted as a valid means of transferring even *res mancipi*. *Traditio* was a much more simple (and thus more practical) method of ownership transfer than *mancipatio*. Three elements were necessary to effectuate a transfer by *traditio*: 1) the actual, *physical transfer* of the thing; 2) the *intent by the transferor* to bestow all of his rights in the thing to the transferee; and, 3) the *intent by the transferee* to accept both the thing and all of the transferor's rights. These elements (*i.e.*, physical delivery, intent of the transferor to transfer, and intent of the transferee to accept) operated to transfer *dominium*. By the end of the Republic (*c.* 27 B.C.), *traditio* was even accepted by law at the moment that a buyer simply affixed his seal to the goods.

In addition to "ordinary" *traditio*, Roman law also recognized three legitimate variations ("soft" versions) of it: 1) *traditio longa manu* (*traditio* by the long hand); 2) *traditio brevi manu* (*traditio* by the short hand); and, 3) *constitutum possessorium*. If the nature of the goods to be sold made physical transfer impractical (*e.g.*, tons of cut stone stored in a warehouse), Roman law legally admitted *traditio longa manu* (long-handed *traditio*) when the seller, in view of the warehouse, gave the buyer a key to that warehouse. Thus, a person transferred *dominium* by *traditio longa manu* when he (the transferor) pointed out to the transferee the object to be "transferred" under conditions that could enable him (*i.e.*, the transferee) to take it at once. For example, *traditio longa manu* would take place if, while they were standing next to the granary, a seller of corn (*i.e.*, corn that was in the granary) were to give the granary keys to the transferee. A person transferred *dominium* by *traditio brevi manu* when he (the transferor) merely authorized the transferee to keep an object (*i.e.*, an object owned by the transferor) that the transferee already had under his control (*i.e.*, by *detentio*).[14] Thus, in circumstances where a buyer already had possession of the *res*, the law recognized *traditio brevi manu*. For example, *traditio brevi manu* would take place if a lender of a tool were to tell the borrower that he (*i.e.*, the borrower) may keep it for himself. Gaius referred to this type of *traditio* as transfer by *nuda voluntas* (bare desire). *Constitutum possessorium* was, essentially, the opposite of *traditio brevi manu*. A person transferred *dominium* by *constitutum possessorium* if he (the transferor) physically kept the object but *his* power over that object transformed from *dominium* to *detentio*. In other words, the transferor retained physical control of the thing but, without actual movement, his control turned into a mere holding (*i.e.*, *detentio*) for the transferee's benefit. For instance, a seller could sell an ox to a buyer with the understanding that the buyer would actually pick up the animal at an agreed upon future

---

14. For an explanation of *detentio, see supra* § 13.03.

date. In the interim, the seller could retain physical control of the beast by *detentio* but the buyer obtained *dominium* by means of *constitutum possessorium*.

C. *In Iure Cessio*

Another method of transfer of ownership (a method that could be used to transfer both *res mancipi* and *res nec mancipi*) was *in iure cessio*. In some respects, *in iure cessio* was similar to a modern quiet title action. The transferor and transferee would arrange to meet before a magistrate. The transferee then declared that the *res* to be conveyed belonged to him. Playing his part, the owner/transferor simply remained silent. Thus, the magistrate ruled that the thing did, indeed, belong to the transferee. This was an unwieldy way to transfer goods. Consequently, the Romans tended not to use it if other means were readily available. It was, however, practically the only way to transfer certain incorporeal property, such as personal servitudes.[15]

D. *Occupatio*

1. *General*

Occupatio was the acquisition of *dominium* of a thing merely by seizing physical control of it. *Occupatio* was possible in the case of *res nullius* (things that no Roman had previously owned) or *res derelictae* (things abandoned by their owners). For example, objects that one found on an ocean beach (*e.g.*, pearls and shells) were *res nullius*. Wild animals (*ferae naturae*) are the paradigmatic example of *res nullius*; capable of ownership by *occupatio*. In Roman law, the first person to take physical control of a *res nullius* with intent to keep it as his own (*i.e.*, the first occupier) was considered the owner (*res nullius primo occupanti*). As regards *res derelictae*, the Sabinians advocated that, once abandoned, things immediately were considered *res nullius*, and, thus, capable of ownership by someone else through *occupatio*. But the Proculians argued that the former owner did not cease to own an abandoned object until a finder actually seized it. In any case, to become an object of *occupatio*, the original owner must have sincerely forsaken it. If a person merely lost an item, he did not lose his ownership unless and until he gave up trying to find it. This is why cargo that a ship captain jettisoned in the midst of a storm was not capable of new ownership by *occu-*

---

15. *See infra* § 13.05.

patio. Presumably, he tossed his freight wanting to save his ship and those on board, not wanting, necessarily, to abandon it.

2. Thesauri Inventio

Roman law took special interest in what was known as *thesauri inventio* (found treasure). Apparently, the underlying legal justification for acquisition of *thesauri inventio* was *occupatio*, and hence, that is why we consider it here. The jurist Paul defined it as a deposit of money the remembrance of which has been lost, so that it now has no owner. Although Paul only refers to money, it apparently also encompassed many other types of valuables such as jewels and precious metals. The laws regarding *thesauri inventio* evolved over the centuries. As of the 2nd century B.C., the jurists had decided that treasure belonged to the landowner on whose property it was discovered. In the early Empire it was deemed to be property of the Imperial Treasury. The precepts relating to the ownership of treasure that Justinian ultimately embraced were embodied first in laws passed under the emperor Hadrian. Under Justinian, the rules of ownership of treasure were as follows. 1) A person was permitted to keep treasure that he discovered on his own property. 2) A person was permitted to keep half of the treasure that he inadvertently discovered on another's property (the landowner kept the other half).[16] 3) If a person was either willfully searching for treasure on another's property or employing magic to find it, he was not permitted to keep any of the treasure that he found (the landowner kept it all).[17]

E. *Specificatio*

A person secured ownership (*dominium*) of a thing by *specificatio* when he created something completely new (*nova species*) from materials that someone else initially owned. Suppose, for example, that A owns a stone and that B makes it into a sculpture. The simple question in such a circumstance is whether A or B should be considered the owner of the sculpture?

Roman jurists observed that the sculpture in this case was actually a *nova species*, a new kind of thing. The two prominent juristic schools, the Sabinians and the Proculians,[18] initially adopted different points of view on ownership in these situations. The Sabinians gave ownership to A, the owner of the

---

16. If the land was public land, half of the treasure went to the Imperial Treasury.

17. If the land was public land, all of the treasure went to the Imperial Treasury.

18. *See supra* § 10.04[C].

materials. The Proculians gave ownership to B, the person who made the sculpture, the *nova species*. Under Justinian, if the creator had owned part of the materials used to create the new thing, then he was the owner of it. A third approach (*media sententia*) was approved in Justinian's *Corpus Iuris Civilis*. Under the theory of the *media sententia*, if it was practical to return the *nova species* to its original condition, then the owner of the component element(s) was deemed the owner of the new thing. If, on the other hand, the *nova species* could not be reduced to its former state, then the creator became the owner, but he was required to compensate the person who had originally owned the materials for their value. Thus, in our example, since it would be impractical to piece the stone back together, B, the creator, would be deemed the owner of the sculpture. Presumably, the opposite result would be reached if A had owned a bronze ingot, and B had melted and molded that into a sculpture. In that case, it would be practical to melt the sculpture back into an ingot.

In modern law, the relative values of the materials and the *nova species* often determine who will be deemed the owner. In a number of jurisdictions (*e.g.*, France and Germany) whichever (*i.e.*, the raw materials or the new thing) is the more valuable—monetarily speaking—controls. So, if the raw materials are more valuable than the new thing, then the original owner of the materials is considered the owner of the new thing, but, if the value of the new thing is greater than that of the raw materials, then the creator is considered the owner of the new thing.[19]

F. *Accessio*

In rudimentary terms, if B joins a minor object to A's major object (such as painting on a wooden board), the law of *accessio* determines the ownership of the entirety. One of the more interesting debates in Roman law centered around acquisition of property by *accessio*. The Roman juristic controversy took the following form. Imagine that A owns a parchment and that B, in good faith (*e.g.*, without knowing that A owns it), writes a poem on it. Or, suppose that A owns a canvas and that B, in good faith (*i.e.*, not knowing that the canvas belongs to A), paints a picture on it. The simple question is whether A or B is considered the owner of the poem on the parchment and the painting on the canvas? Roman jurists gave answers that appear somewhat inconsistent if not illogical.

---

19. Still the maker/owner in such a scenario must compensate the owner of the raw materials for their value.

It is difficult to justify the inconsistent approaches that Roman jurists took in these situations. The first inconsistency can be seen in the different treatment afforded to writing *versus* visual art. In the case where a writer writes on another's parchment, the general Roman law rule was that the owner of the parchment became the owner of the entirety. On the other hand, in the case where a painter paints on another's canvas, the general rule was the opposite: the painter became the owner of the whole.

In sum, then, a person could obtain ownership of one item of property by *accessio* when it (*i.e.,* that item of property) became incorporated into another item of property that that person already owned. In order for a valid *accessio* to occur, however, two essential elements had to exist: 1) the thing acquired had to have been assimilated with the object already owned in such a way that it was no longer recognizable as what it had been; and, 2) the thing acquired had to be inseparably incorporated.[20] Thus, the newly acquired article ceased to exist in its previous form, due to its merger into the other, already owned, thing. Therefore, for example, since a new leather strap attached to a horse's bridle could be separated without much difficulty, the strap in such a situation would not be acquired by *accessio*. The general rule of *accessio* is clear, the owner of the principal thing gained ownership of the incorporated thing.[21] Hence, the fate of the principal thing determined the fate of the adjoining thing. But as the examples of the writing on parchment and painting on canvass illustrate, it is not always simple to determine which thing should be considered the principal and which the accessory.

G. *Usucapio*

Usucapio was a method of acquiring ownership of property that was similar to the modern concept of adverse possession. In its simplest terms, *usucapio* entitled a person to acquire ownership of property by using that property when its original owner had apparently abandoned it. In terms of public policy, the principle encourages persons to make productive use of property and discourages "sleeping on one's rights" while allowing otherwise productive property to go to waste.[22] In order for a person to acquire ownership of a *res* by *usucapio*, several criteria had to be fulfilled. First, the thing had to be the

---

20. This is also the general the rule that applies in most legal systems today.

21. The applicable Latin maxim was *accessoria cedit principalis* (an accessory yields to a principal thing).

22. *See generally* Roger Cunningham, William Stoebuck, & Dale Whitman, The Law of Property, §11.7, at 814 (1993).

kind of property capable of human ownership. Second, because, by definition, *possessio* ordinarily required good faith on the part of the possessor,[23] stolen items could not be acquired by *usucapio*. Third, the person claiming ownership by *usucapio* had to have started his possession in good faith (*i.e.,* thinking that he was entitled to possession).

A person acquired ownership of a thing by *usucapio* by virtue of uninterrupted *possessio* for a designated amount of time. In Roman law, the time period necessary for *usucapio* to mature into *dominium* was relatively short (especially when compared to modern adverse possession which often takes 15–20 years of possession): two years for land and one year for other property.

§ 13.05 *Iura in re Aliena* (Rights in the Thing of Another)

Roman law recognized certain rights with respect to the things that belonged to others. In particular, Roman law admitted servitudes both that were connected to land (similar to what modern American law calls easements appurtenant) and servitudes that were personal (similar to the American law easements *in gross*).

As early as the Twelve Tables (451/450 B.C.), there were four servitudes that "ran with the land." In order for these to be applicable, the two parcels of land at issue had to be adjacent to one another. These four *praedial* servitudes were: 1) *via* (the general right of passage through a neighbor's property); 2) *iter* (the right to walk through a neighbor's property); 3) *actus* (the right to drive animals through a neighbor's property); and, 4) *aquaeductus* (the right to conduct water from one's own property across a neighbor's property). These servitudes were basically intangible rights that were dependent upon an association with land.[24] They could be established either by *mancipatio* or *in iure cessio*—but not by *traditio*.[25] Because the praedial servitudes ran with the land, they were not tied to individuals. Accordingly, if the parties who created a right of *iter*, *actus*, *via*, or *aquaeductus* were to die, the servitude itself endured; the demise of the mortals who established it being irrelevant.

---

23. *See supra* § 13.03. There were, however, a few exceptions to the requirement of good faith in *usucapio*.

24. In this regard they were similar to our easements appurtenant—such as the right to light and the right to the support of a common wall or roof.

25. *See supra* §§ 13.04 [A]–[C].

Eventually, in addition to these servitudes related to land, Roman law also recognized personal servitudes (somewhat similar to modern easements *in gross*) that were not tied to real property. The Roman personal servitudes, then, were associated only with specific persons for limited periods of time. There could be any number of such personal servitudes (*e.g.,* a life estate, fishing privileges, fruits of an orchard, living in a house). In particular, Roman jurists categorized the following: 1) *usus fructus* (the right to use another's property and its fruits); 2) *usus* (the right to use another's property, but not its fruits); 3) *habitatio* (the right—for life—to live in another's house); and, 4) *opera servorum vel animalium* (the right to have slaves or animals perform work).

Probably the most significant personal servitude in Roman law was *usus fructus*. *Usus fructus* allowed a person both to use a *res* and to reap the benefits of the "fruits" of that thing (*i.e.,* the products of that thing). For example someone who had *usus fructus* of an olive orchard would have both the use of the property itself and would also be entitled to reap the benefits of the olives produced by the trees in the orchard. Roman law forbade a person with the right of *usus fructus* to destroy or significantly alter the property. It was common for a man—in his will—to leave his real property to his children but to leave the right of *usus fructus* to his wife for her life.[26] The other two most important personal servitudes were *usus* and *habitatio*. When a person had *usus*, he had the right to use a property but did not have the right to appropriate its fruits. A person who had *habitatio* had the prerogative to live in a specific residence, usually for life.

§ 13.06 Chapter Summary

Roman jurists classified property by creating numerous dualistic categories. Gaius said that all property was either under divine law or human law. These categories were further subdivided as well. Gaius also classified property as tangible and intangible—a classification which dictated the means by which any given property legally could be transferred from one person to another. It was also Gaius who classified property as either *res mancipi* or *res nec mancipi*. This classification also dictated the potential legal means of transfer (*i.e.,* the formalistic *mancipatio* was the only valid method for transferring *res mancipi*, such as slaves, oxen, horses, real property, and the praedial servitudes). By the

---

26. For more on Roman wills, *see infra* § 15.03.

time of Justinian, however, this distinction was no longer meaningful. Other property dualisms recognized by Roman jurists include: 1) things in economic circulation *vs.* those not in economic circulation (*res in commercio/res extra commercio*); 2) movables *vs.* immovables (*res mobiles/res immobiles*); 3) unique things *vs.* fungibles (*species/genera*); 4) things consumed by use *vs.* things not consumed by use (*res quae usu consumatum/res quae usu non consumatum*); 5) things that could be divided and maintain their basic character *vs.* those that could not.

Roman law distinguished several kinds of legal title. The three most important are: 1) *dominium* (basically equivalent to what we today call ownership); 2) *possessio* (control of a thing—though not necessarily *physical* control—coupled with a belief that one owns the property in question); 3) *detentio* (control of a thing not believing that one owns it).

Certain types of property could only be transferred, legally at least, in certain ways. For example, *res mancipi* (*e.g.,* Italic land, slaves, cattle, horses, mules, donkeys, and the four praedial servitudes; namely, *iter, actus, via,* and, *aquaeductus*) could only be transferred by *mancipatio*—a method of transfer that required specific formalities, including five witnesses, a scale, and certain formulaic statements made by the transferee. Property transferred by *mancipatio* came with an automatic warranty of title. For *res nec mancipi, traditio*—a means of transfer requiring physical delivery of the object, the intent of the transferor to transfer, and the intent of the transferee to accept—was the most widespread and practical method of property transfer. As the law evolved, the Romans validated three "soft" versions of *traditio* which, for a number of practical reasons, relaxed the requirement of actual, physical delivery: 1) *traditio longa manu* ("delivery" by providing access); 2) *traditio brevi manu* ("delivery" which has already occurred); and, 3) *constitutum possessorium* ("delivery" to occur in the future). *In iure cessio*—a form of conveyance somewhat similar to a prearranged quiet title action before a magistrate—was used both for *res mancipi* and *res nec mancipi* (especially for intangibles). Romans could acquire ownership (*dominium*) of an object either that had never been owned by another (*res nullius*) or that had been abandoned (*res derelictae*) simply by taking physical control of it (*occupatio*). Similarly, landowners and discoverers could acquire rights in treasure that had been found (*thesauri inventio*). *Specificatio* was a unique means of gaining ownership that arose when someone created an object that was completely new (*nova species*) from materials that someone else initially owned (*e.g.,* a sculpture created by an artist made from a stone owned by another). Under Justinian, the creator of the new thing—not the owner of the original thing—was considered the owner of the new object only if it was impractical or impossible to return it to its original state (in which case the creator had to compensate the original owner for the value of the raw material). Roman law granted ownership, by *accessio*, to the owner of a principal object when another accessory object was incorporated into the principal thing in such a way that the two became inseparably merged (*e.g.,* writing on a parchment). But it was not always easy to determine which thing should be considered the principal and which the accessory. *Usucapio* was the Roman method of acquiring property roughly analogous to modern law's adverse possession. To obtain ownership by *usucapio*, a person had to maintain *possessio* (*i.e.,* good faith possessory control) of land for two years or of other types of property for only one year.

As early as the Twelve Tables, Roman law recognized certain servitudes that were, in a number of respects, analogous to what modern law calls easements appurtenant (*i.e.,* easements dependent on a relationship to land itself). The four oldest servitudes were the so-called praedial servitudes: 1) *via* (the general right of passage through a neighbor's property); 2) *iter* (the right to walk through a neighbor's property); 3) *actus* (the right to drive animals through a neighbor's property); and, 4) *aquaeductus* (the right to conduct water from one's own property across a neighbor's property). Eventually, Roman jurists also acknowledged personal servitudes (similar to modern easements *in gross*), such as *usus fructus* (the right to use another's property and its fruits), *usus* (the right to use another's property but not its fruits); and *habitatio* (the right—for life—to live in another's house).

CHAPTER 14

FAMILY LAW

§ 14.01 Power & Control: *Paterfamilias*

Probably the most significant feature of the family in Roman law was the institution of the *paterfamilias*. The Roman *paterfamilias* was ordinarily the father and husband who held the right of life and death over his entire family. Legally speaking, a wife was considered "in place of the daughter." In essence, all family members were either: 1) a *paterfamilias* (an independent person of his own right—*persona sui iuris*—who could resolve all issues of a legal nature with his own discretion and without restriction); or, 2) members of the family (persons who were considered *personae alieni iuris*—persons of another's right [*i.e.*, dependent upon the *paterfamilias*]). Family members could not participate in any legal relationships without the permission of their *paterfamilias*. The *paterfamilias* owned all of the family's property. As Roman law and society developed, the institution of the *peculium* came to be used by family members.[1] Family members did have *ius honorum*[2] which was considered a *quasi-peculium* that the State, not the *paterfamilias* granted.

Patria potestas was the power that a Roman father held over his subordinates (*e.g.*, wife, children—both biological and adopted—, grandchildren). A Roman male, if his own father, grandfather, *etc.* were dead, acquired *patria potestas* when he entered into a valid marriage. As long as the father was living, he retained his *patria potestas*. Technically, by virtue of *patria potestas*, a Roman father had complete power over his children. He had the power of life and death. He decided whether to expose an infant at birth. He could, before the Empire, sell them into slavery. His consent was needed to marry and, generally speaking, he could force them to marry and also forbid them to marry. Before Antoninus Pius (138–161 A.D.) changed the law, a father's *patria potestas* even permitted him to dissolve a son's marriage—even a happy one—with-

---

1. A family member's *peculium* was similar in many respects to the *peculium* of a slave. *See supra* § 12.03.

2. *See supra* § 12.02[A].

out his son's consent. A Roman *paterfamilias* owned his children's possessions; although children might have a *peculium* (a fund nominally owned by them).

The Emperor Augustus (27 B.C.–14 A.D.) created an exception for sons who were in the army but technically still under their father's (or grandfather's) *patria potestas*. Augustus granted a son in the army the power to make a will, and to distribute—in any manner that he wished—any money or property that he had obtained as a soldier. This money and/or property was called his *peculium castrense*. The Emperor Hadrian (117–138 A.D.) amended Augustus' law by simply granting complete ownership, outright, of the *peculium castrense* to the soldier-son.

§ 14.02 Marriage & Divorce

A. General Considerations

The earliest marriage contracts were in the form of a *sponsio* (*i.e.,* an early form of formulaic oral contract),[3] and were supposedly actionable. By the 2nd century B.C., Roman marriage contracts were no longer actionable. Generally speaking, an agreement of the *paterfamilias* of both the bride and groom was needed to make a marriage valid. Before the Empire (*c.* 27 B.C.), what the girl wanted made little difference. A prospective husband or his father made the marriage contract. The *paterfamilias* of the prospective wife always conducted the contract negotiations for her—unless she was no longer under the control of her *paterfamilias*—in which case one of her relatives took the place of her *paterfamilias*. Once a marriage contract was concluded, sex with another man was deemed adultery.[4]

Marriage was defined simply as the joining of a man and woman; the incidence of all life (*matrimonium est coniunctio maris et feminae consortum omnis vitae*). A bride's family contributed a dowry (*dos*) for the marriage. The groom's family also contributed marriage gifts, usually equivalent to the *dos*. The intent of the man and woman to create a marriage was essential. Often a dowry served as evidence of such intent, making clear that the couple did not intend merely concubinage. There were certain formal methods of creating a dowry. There were also certain procedures that had to be followed in the event that later the wife's father or the wife, herself, wished to sue for the return of the dowry (*actio rei uxoriae*). One of the principal results of a valid Roman marriage was

---

3. *See infra* § 18.02.
4. *See infra* § 16.05.

that the couple's children were considered legitimate and they were under the *patria potestas* of their *paterfamilias* (*i.e.,* typically, the father, grandfather, or great-grandfather).

Roman law only recognized marriage as valid when it was between Roman citizens or a union between a Roman citizen and a citizen of a state having a right of intermarriage with Rome. Slave marriages were not regarded as legal. Plebeians were not permitted to marry Patricians until the passage of the *lex Canuleia* in 445 B.C. The Emperor Augustus (27 B.C.–14 A.D.) forbade senators—and their descendants—from marriage with freedmen (and freedwomen) and actresses.

Certain blood relatives were legally prohibited from intermarriage. The proximity of relationship that was impermissible vacillated as the societal mores and expectations of the Roman people changed over the years. In early law, second cousins were prohibited from intermarriage. But by the late Republic (*i.e.,* 150–27 B.C.), even first cousins were allowed to marry one another. During most periods, uncles and nieces could not marry nor could great-uncles marry their great-nieces. Still, the Emperor Claudius (41–54 A.D.) had the law changed so that he could marry his niece, Agrippina. Thus, for a brief period afterwards, such a union was considered legal. A Roman girl had to be at least twelve years old to marry. It appears that many girls had not yet reached puberty when they were married, and in fact, whether they had reached puberty seems to have been irrelevant. For boys, the Proculians held the view that eventually was adopted in law; namely, a boy simply had to be at least fourteen in order to marry. The Sabinian view—a view that faded—was that a boy had to have reached puberty as a precondition of marriage. The Sabinians even required that a boy undergo a physical examination as proof that he had reached puberty.

B. Types of Marriage

Fundamentally, there were two recognized, legal types of Roman marriage: 1) *matrimonium cum manu* (marriage with power); and, *matrimonium sine manu* (marriage without power). Marriage *cum manu* was the older of the two. In such a marriage, the wife was considered to be living under her husband's power. A wife was subordinated to her husband. In the event that her husband, himself, still was under the power of his *paterfamilias*, then the bride also was regarded as being under the power of that superior *paterfamilias* (*i.e.,* her father-in-law). In either case, the bride's status was, legally speaking, roughly equivalent to that of being her husband's daughter. He automatically took legal ownership of any property that had previously belonged to her. People still commonly married *cum manu* in the early 1st century B.C. but the practice became the exception by mid-century. Roman law also permitted unmarried persons to live together in concubinage. We know, for example, that the emperors Vespasian and Marcus Aurelius did so.

By the time of the Twelve Tables (451/450 B.C.), the three ways in which marriage *cum manu* could be formed were already in existence: 1) *confarreatio*; 2) *coemptio*; and, 3) *usus*. *Confarreatio* was a religious ceremony that involved two priests and a ceremony with a cake of spelt—the *far* in *confarreatio*. The *confarreatio* was, as a practical matter, exclusively an aristocratic institution. *Coemptio* was marriage using an early ritualistic form of sale (*mancipatio*).[5] It was a mock sale of the bride by the *paterfamilias* to the groom. *Usus* was marriage created when a husband and wife lived together for a complete year, so long as the wife did not stay away from her husband for three consecutive nights during that year. In some respects, this type of marriage is similar to the acquisition of property by adverse possession or usucaption (*usucapio*).[6] Eventually, the law of the three nights fell into disuse by custom. Instead, a woman only came under her husband's power through the consent of her guardian. *Usus* was abolished entirely by legislation during the early Empire. Soon the other types of marriage *cum manu* had all but disappeared.

In marriage *sine manu*, the wife did not fall under the power of her husband (or his *paterfamilias*). Thus, it was a union in which the wife was not subordinated to her husband as *paterfamilias*. Instead, she remained under the power of her own *paterfamilias*, ordinarily her father or grandfather. In the event that she had been independent at the time of marriage *sine manu*, she retained her independent status even upon marriage. Interestingly, if a wife had no *paterfamilias* and the couple wished to avoid marriage *cum manu*, they could invoke the doctrine of *trinoctii absentia* (absence for three nights). In order to accomplish this, the wife moved back and lived with her previous family for three consecutive nights every year. By doing so, she avoided living with her husband continuously for an entire year, which would have resulted in marriage *cum manu*. Marriage *sine manu* was the most common type of civil marriage. By the early 2nd century B.C., marriage *sine manu* was routine.

C. Divorce

During the earliest period of Roman law (*i.e.*, the Monarchy—753–509 B.C.), a husband was allowed, with impunity, to divorce his wife for three rea-

---

5. For more on *mancipatio, see supra* §§ 13.01 and 13.04[A].
6. *See supra* § 13.04[G].

sons: 1) if she committed adultery; 2) if she "tampered with the keys" (*i.e.*, the presumption operating was that she had altered the household keys as a means by which a lover could enter); and, 3) if she poisoned a child. Under these three circumstances, neither she nor her father was entitled to have any of her dowry returned. If a husband divorced his wife for any other reason, the wife was entitled to one-half of her husband's property.

If the marriage had been performed with the *confarreatio*,[7] it only could be dissolved by means of a revocation ceremony, called *diffarreatio*. Otherwise, Roman marriages could be terminated without any special procedure. The most common form of divorce was done by *repudium*, which did not even require mutual consent. *Repudium* was considered a simple withdrawal of the *affectio maritalis* by the couple together (or merely one of them). Augustan legislation required seven witnesses.

In early Roman law there were stiff financial penalties for being found the guilty party in a divorce proceeding. Similarly, there were penalties if a husband or wife divorced without cause. By the late Republic, these penalties were no longer enforced. As a general rule, upon divorce, a husband was required to return most of the dowry to either the ex-wife or to her father. He was entitled to retain specified portions of it unless he was at fault in the divorce, in which case, he had to return the entire dowry. As divorce law evolved during the Republic, a husband was allowed to divorce his wife for no particular reason at all. A wife was able to divorce her husband so long as she was not under his power. The Emperor Constantine (306–337 A.D.) took a dim view of divorce. He imposed severe penalties on spouses who divorced, except for those who divorced for what he deemed legitimate reasons. Under Justinian (6th century A.D.), there were certain legitimate reasons for which a wife could divorce her husband. If she divorced him for another reason, she surrendered all her property and was sent to a nunnery permanently. On the other hand, if a husband divorced his wife for a reason not recognized as legitimate by law, he suffered only fines.

§ 14.03 Adoption

There were two principal forms of adoption discussed in Justinian's *Digest*: 1) *adoptio* and 2) *adrogatio*. It was also possible to adopt by means of a will. Julius Caesar, for example, adopted Augustus in his will. *Adoptio* was the form

---

7. *See supra* § 14.02[B].

used when the adoptee was still under *patria potestas*. The father (or grandfather) went through the formality of "selling" his son (or grandson)(*i.e.,* the adoptee) three times. That act technically freed the boy. Once freed by the triple sale, the adoptive father could secure his own *patria potestas* over the adoptee by a decree of the praetor. *Adrogatio* was the form of adoption employed in cases where the adoptee was *not* under the *patria potestas* of another.

The primary problem with *adrogatio* as a method of adoption was that, if a man was not under another's *patria potestas*, then, "if he were adopted, his family would at once die out and there would be no one to continue the family's religious rites."[8] Thus, the law developed certain prerequisites to *adrogatio*. First, the prospective adopter had to be childless. He had to be unable to father children. In the absence of any extenuating circumstances, he had to be at least sixty years old. He must at least have attempted to father children if possible. The pontiffs, themselves, conducted an investigation into these matters. Then if they approved, next, the *comitia curiata*[9] (using the appellation *comitia calata* for this process) had to vote to approve the adoption.

§ 14.04 Tutors

Boys and girls who had not reached puberty and who, for one reason or another, were not under the power of a *paterfamilias* were legally required to have a tutor to look after them and their affairs. A tutor managed his ward's affairs in the best interests of the ward. A tutor was obligated to serve at least until the ward reached puberty. Even after a girl had reached puberty and had grown to womanhood, she was legally required to have a tutor if she was *sui iuris*. Such women, however, had a certain degree of flexibility and freedom of action not possessed by their pre-pubescent analogues.

There were four ways of creating a tutor, and several had specific formalities: 1) by will; 2) by law; 3) by public official; and, 4) temporary tutor. The establishment of a tutor by a will was known as a *tutor testamentarius*. There were fairly rigid formulae necessary for setting up a tutor by will. The testator was required to use specific language. A tutor could be appointed by operation of law when there was no testamentary appointment (*tutor legitimus*). This method of appointment was part of the Twelve Tables. The law favored appointment of a tutor by agnatic relationship (*i.e.,* relationship connected through

---

8. WATSON, ROMAN LAW & COMPARATIVE LAW 34.
9. *See supra* § 11.02[B].

men).[10] In some cases, public officials (usually a praetor and a majority of the tribunes of the plebs) could appoint a tutor. This type of tutor was called a *tutor dativus*. The appointment of a temporary tutor was a very old form used during the pendency of a dispute between the ward and the person who was his regular tutor. This may have fallen into disuse by the time of Gaius (*i.e.*, the great jurist who wrote the *Institutes* about 161 A.D.).[11]

Roman law considered tutorship a serious obligation. If appointed as a tutor, the appointee was required to fulfill his obligation to serve. There were exceptions for disqualification or for certain exemptions. But the laws regarding exemptions were long and complicated. There were a number of legal actions that a ward could bring against his tutor if he (*i.e.*, the ward) believed that the tutor had been remiss in his duties. The precise forms and remedies for these legal actions varied depending upon factors such as whether the tutor had been appointed by will or by operation of law, whether the ward was still under the tutor's protection, and whether the conduct complained of was alleged to have been intentional or merely negligent.

§ 14.05 Curators

Under the Twelve Tables, persons who were mentally incompetent had to be cared for by their closest agnatic relative, who served as a curator. The Twelve Tables also reiterated an old law that provided that a magistrate could appoint a curator for a prodigal/spendthrift who had squandered his inheritance. This law originally applied only to an inheritance by intestacy but was later amended to include a prodigal who squandered his testamentary inheritance as well. By the later Republic, youth between age fourteen (*i.e.*, the time when the tutorship over them expired) and age twenty-five were required to have a curator who managed their affairs and helped to ensure that others would not take advantage of them.

§ 14.06 Chapter Summary

In a Roman family, one individual was the *paterfamilias* (typically the father/husband) who controlled the legal rights and affairs of his family members. A Roman *paterfamilias* held the *patria potestas* (father's power) over all

---

10. For more on agnatic relationships, *see infra* § 15.02.
11. *See supra* § 10.04[A].

his subordinate family members. *Patria potestas* gave a father/*paterfamilias* tremendous control over the lives of his subordinates. Augustus granted a limited degree of freedom to sons who were in the army; permitting them to control the assets that they obtained through military service (*peculium castrense*).

Before the Empire, it was usually the *paterfamilias* of the groom and the *paterfamilias* of the bride who fashioned an agreement for marriage. The bride's family customarily contributed a dowry (*dos*) and the groom's family contributed marriage gifts of an equivalent amount. The offspring of a valid marriage between Roman citizens were considered both legitimate and Roman citizens as well. As a rule, girls had to be at least twelve to marry and boys had to be at least fourteen. Roman law did prohibit marriage between close relatives, but the proximity of the barred relationships varied throughout Roman history.

The two recognized, legal types of marriage were *matrimonium cum manu* (marriage with power), the older of the two, and *matrimonium sine manu* (marriage without power). When a woman married *cum manu*, she legally became subject to her husband's authority, having essentially the same legal status as a daughter. There were three principal kinds of marriage *cum manu*: 1) *confarreatio* (involving a religious ceremony); 2) *coemptio* (fundamentally an old ritualistic form of sale); and, 3) *usus* (resulting from continuous cohabitation for a year). By the Empire, marriage *sine manu*, allowing a wife to retain independent legal status, became the more common type of civil marriage.

During the Monarchy (753–509 B.C.), a husband was entitled to divorce his wife, with impunity, if she committed adultery, "tampered with the keys," or poisoned a child. The most common means of divorce was a rather simple repudiation (*repudium*), which did not even require mutual consent. Although in early Roman law a husband or wife could be penalized for initiating divorce without cause, as the law evolved, divorce without cause became common and legally accepted without penalty. As a rule, upon divorce a husband had to return most of the dowry.

Adoptio was the form of adoption that Romans used when the adoptee was still under the *patria potestas* of his *paterfamilias*. *Adoptio* employed the machinery of an artificial triple sale to make the adoption possible. *Adrogatio* was the procedure reserved for adoptees not under *patria potestas*. Because of the likelihood of extinguishing an entire family, the pontiffs and the *comitia curiata* had to approve any adoption done through *adrogatio*. A person had to be both childless and also incapable of fathering children in order even to be considered eligible to adopt by *adrogatio*.

Boys and girls who had no *paterfamilias*, and who had not yet reached puberty, were required to have a tutor to take care of them and to manage their affairs. A tutor could be appointed by a will, by a public official, or one could be appointed as a temporary tutor. A ward could bring legal action against a tutor who mismanaged his duties. Curators were appointed both for the mentally incompetent as well as for prodigals who squandered their inheritance.

CHAPTER 15

INHERITANCE AND SUCCESSION

§ 15.01 Introduction

Justinian's *Digest* has 50 books, and eleven of them deal with succession. The law of succession is related both to property and the methods of acquiring property. In Roman law, an heir became the owner, creditor, and debtor of a deceased's estate. As is common in modern legal systems, the ancient Romans appreciated two basic types of succession: 1) *intestate* (without a will; thereby forcing property to pass to persons and in proportions established by law); and, 2) *testate* (with a will indicating who should receive property and in what proportions). Intestate succession rules controlled long before the law recognized a person's ability to control the allocation of property by means of a will.

§ 15.02 Intestate Succession

In order to comprehend the workings of Roman intestate succession, it is first important to understand the distinction between two groups: the *cognati* and the *agnati*. The *cognati* were those relatives who were related by blood. The *agnati* were those relatives who were related through a male ancestor. The distinction between the concepts of *cognatio* and *agnatio* was central in determining inheritance. *Cognatio* distinguishes between direct linear and indirect linear descendants. Direct linear descendants are those on a direct originating line with one another (*e.g.*, grandparents and grandchildren). Relatives on a direct linear line are the most favored for inheritance based on *cognatio*. Indirect linear descendants are those with a common ancestor (*e.g.*, brother and sister). In an inheritance system based on *cognatio*, indirect linear descendants have fewer rights than direct descendants (sometimes they get no inheritance at all).

In terms of inheritance in the absence of a will, the Twelve Tables showed a preference for agnates, those related to a deceased through males. Roman succession law slowly, step-by-step, evolved towards a system based on blood relationship (*i.e.*, as opposed to agnatic relationships). Praetors' edicts amended the law as did statutes in the mid-2nd century A.D. Under Justinian's *Novellae* (which superseded the *Institutes*—which had retained some of the agnatic elements of the Twelve Tables and other prior law), blood relationship became the cornerstone of intestate succession. Thus, although early in the Roman legal development of succession, the laws preferred the *agnati*, later, the law shifted to prefer *cognati*.

As part of their law of inheritance,[1] the Romans also developed the notion of degree of kinship. In order to determine degrees of kinship, one must simply count the number of births necessary to get from one person to the other. For example, a mother and child are in the "first degree"—because they are only one birth (or "step") removed from one another in descent. A grandfather and grandchild are in the "second degree" because they are two births (or "steps") removed. In the examples just given, it only takes one birth to get from a mother to her child (the child's birth), but two births are required in order to get from a grandparent to a grandchild (the birth of the grandparent's immediate offspring—a son or daughter—and then the birth of his or her child—the grandchild).

By the time of Justinian in the 6th century A.D., the laws of the praetor (*i.e.*, the praetorian order of succession) established a fixed order of preference for inheritance. Most modern legal systems today (except Muslim) use basically the same scheme. In the *Corpus Iuris Civilis*, the order of intestate succession was as follows. The first rank in line to inherit were the *liberi* (literally "children"). These ordinarily were the children and grandchildren. Typically, children inherited equal shares (*per capita*) and the grandchildren inherited on the basis of *ius representationis*, the right of representation, from their parents (also known as *per stirpes*, "through the stem"). For example, if a *paterfamilias* had three sons at the time of his death, each son took one-third of his father's estate (*per capita*). But, now assume that each son himself had two sons as well (*i.e.*, that would make a total of six grandsons). If each of the original three sons was alive when the *paterfamilias* died, the grandchildren took nothing at that time. But, if, for example, before the *paterfamilias* died, one of his three sons had predeceased him, then each of the dead son's surviving sons (*i.e.*, the *paterfamilias'* grandchildren by his deceased son) would take one-half of the one-third to which his father would have been entitled, had he lived. In such a case, then, each of those two grandsons would take one-sixth of the *paterfamilias'* estate by *ius representationis* (*per stirpes*). This principle still operates

---

1. This was also relevant for marriage law. *See supra* § 14.02[A].

today in many legal systems (*e.g.,* French and German law). Second in line were the *legitimi*. These were usually the parents, grandparents, brothers, and sisters (in that order). These were the closest relatives, who excluded the remoter relatives in succession. The parents were deemed closer relatives than grandparents and also closer than brothers and sisters. Third were the *cognati*. In particular, this group consisted of any other blood relatives who were not included in the *legitimi* (*e.g.,* any half-brothers or half-sisters). The fourth rank of heirs was the husband or wife of the deceased—last in line to inherit. To summarize, then, in Justinian's *Novellae*, the order of intestate succession is as follows: 1) male and female descendants (offspring taking their deceased parent's share); 2) ascendants (*e.g.,* parents and grandparents); 3) full brothers and sisters; 4) if there were no full siblings, half-brothers and half-sisters; 5) all other blood relatives. Husbands and wives succeeded one another. If all else failed, the deceased's property escheated to the State.

§ 15.03 Testate Succession

The Twelve Tables make it clear that wills were an accepted means for transferring property to heirs even in the 5th century B.C. In early law, there were two distinct types of wills. The *testamentum comitiis calatis* required public approval by the *comitia calata,*[2] and could only be made on either March 24 or May 24. The *testamentum in procinctu* was the type of will that a soldier could make when he was part of an army that was prepared to march. A *testamentum in procinctu* could be made orally and did not require any specific formalities. Soldiers' wills enjoyed a number of legal exceptions. For example, a soldier was permitted to name foreigners as heirs and legatees. But a soldier's will was only valid for one year after discharge. The Twelve Tables mention a later form of will known as *testamentum per aes et libram* ("will by means of bronze and a scale"). This type of will clearly is adapted from sale of *res mancipi* by *mancipatio.*[3] It was the conventional will in the late Republic and then throughout the Empire. There were certain requisite elements: 1) five witnesses; 2) another person to hold the scale; 3) the presence of the *familiae emptor* ("buyer of the family", *i.e.,* the person to whom the estate would eventually be transferred); and, 4) specific prescribed declarations of transfer made by both the testator and the *familiae emptor*. Ordinarily the witnesses, scale holder,

---

2. *See supra* § 11.02[B].
3. *See supra* §§ 13.01 and 13.04[A].

and *familiae emptor* affixed their seals to the document. Augustus (27 B.C.–14 A.D.) made codicils, "informal additions to wills," enforceable. And, finally, in the 5th century A.D., the "tripartite will" became popular. The three "parts" were: 1) there had to be seven witnesses; 2) each witness had to affix his seal to the document; and, 3) the testator had to sign the document.

A person had to have capacity to make a will (*testamenti factio*) in order for his will to be considered valid and effective. Males had to be at least fourteen years old and females had to be twelve.[4] Generally speaking, a testator was required to be a Roman citizen who was *sui iuris* (*i.e.*, not under the *patria potestas* of another).[5] Until the mid-2nd century A.D., there were complicated restrictions on the ability of women to make wills. After that time, a woman could be a valid testatrix with the consent of her *tutor*.[6]

There are certain elements commonly found in ancient Roman wills. To be a valid will, the document had to name an heir and the heir had to be a Roman citizen, unless the heir was a slave, in which case the will's provisions had to free the slave. Roman law required precise language in a will to create an heir. There were two acceptable patterns. If the testator, for example, wanted someone named Marcus to be his heir, in order to be valid, the will had to state either, "Let Marcus be my heir" or "I order Marcus to be my heir." The clause creating the heir usually came first in the will because anything that preceded it was deemed invalid. The *lex Voconia* (169 B.C.) established that the wealthiest class of Romans could not appoint a woman as heir. By the Empire (27 B.C.–mid-5th century A.D.), *fideicommissa* (trusts)—which from the time of Augustus forward gained increasing validity—provided effective mechanisms to obviate the *lex Voconia*. Trusts also gave a testator a way to leave property to a foreigner. Occasionally an heir would have predeceased the testator or would refuse his inheritance. Whether an heir could legally refuse an inheritance was an important issue, because heirs inherited the debts of the testator as well as his assets. Thus, Roman testators often included in their wills several persons designated as *substitutii* (*i.e.*, substitute heirs). The *substitutii* were added to take an inheritance in the event that heirs named either refused or had predeceased the testator. Although there were some restrictions, it was, as a rule, possible to disinherit sons, daughters, and other descendants in one's will. A Roman testator could disinherit persons who otherwise would have been heirs, and it was common for a will to include a clause saying "and let all others be

---

4. These were the same ages required prior to marriage. *See supra* § 14.02[A].
5. *See supra* § 14.01.
6. See *supra* § 14.04.

disinherited." But eventually, by the early Empire, a person who was disinherited could contest the will on grounds that s/he had been disinherited by an undutiful (*inofficiosi*) will. These cases were tried by the *centumviri*.[7] If the plaintiff won, s/he received that which would have been his/her intestate portion of the decedent's estate. Other clauses commonly found in Roman wills relate to: 1) the manumission of slaves; 2) the appointment of tutors for children; 3) the creation of legacies (*i.e.*, bequests of specific property or specific rights to individuals); and, 4) the establishment of trusts (*fideicommissa*).

There were three categories of heirs under Roman law: 1) *necessarii* (slaves who were not allowed to refuse their inheritance); 2) *sui et necessarii* (persons who passed from the *potestas* of the testator to their own [*i.e.*, they gained their legal independence] upon the testator's death, *e.g.*, the testator's sons,); and, 3) *extranei* (all others). The *heredes necessarii* were the testator's slaves who were manumitted by the will. They were obliged to accept what was given to them; they could not refuse acceptance. The *sui et necessarii heredes* were those who had been under the testator's *potestas* (power) at the time of his death. For example, children, grandchildren, and wives (*in manu*). The third type of heir, the *extraneus heres*, was one who, in order to accept his legacy, had to do so in the presence of a Roman magistrate.

Roman inheritance involved the acceptance of both rights and also duties. Heirs were required to pay the debts of the deceased even if the property of the deceased was insufficient to cover those debts. Thus, creditors of the testator became creditors of the heirs. Because an heir would inherit debts, Justinian's approach was to grant the named heir (*i.e.*, an *extraneus* not a *necessarius*)—before deciding whether to accept or decline as heir—the opportunity to request an inventory of the testator's estate. In that way, before making a commitment, an heir could ascertain whether there would be sufficient funds to pay the testator's debts.[8] In one sense, then, since a potential heir was unlikely to accept an inheritance in a case where a testator's property was insufficient to cover his outstanding debts, the practical result was that a deceased's debt liability was limited to the value of his property.

A legatee had to be a Roman citizen. In early Roman law, specific language was necessary to create a valid legacy. The *senatus consultum Neronianum* (64 A.D.) significantly relaxed the interpretation for legacies. Justinian tore down the remaining barriers, in effect, lending validity to virtually any form of legacy.

---

7. *See supra* § 11.03[B].
8. The heir had to begin the inventory within 30 days and had to complete it within 90.

§ 15.04 Chapter Summary

Roman law acknowledged two basic types of succession: 1) intestate (without a will; thereby forcing property to pass to persons and in proportions established by law); and, 2) testate (with a will indicating who should receive property and in what proportions). Roman inheritance law depended, to a great degree, on the distinction between cognatic relationships (family related by blood) *versus* agnatic relationships (family related through a male ancestor). Although the earliest laws of intestate succession (*i.e.,* principles established in the Twelve Tables) favored agnatic relationships, in time laws gradually came to favor cognatic ones. Intestate succession generally preferred relatives who were close in terms of degrees (*i.e.,* in terms of the number of births necessary to go from one person—ordinarily the deceased—to another—ordinarily the putative heir). As established under Justinian, the order of intestate succession was as follows: 1) children and grandchildren (*liberi*); 2) parents, grandparents, brothers and sisters (*legitimi*); 3) any other blood relatives who were not included among the *legitimi* (*cognati*); and, 4) the spouse of the deceased.

Roman law admitted a number of different forms of wills: 1) *testamentum comitiis calatis* (requiring public approval on specified days); 2) *testamentum in procinctu* (an oral will made by a soldier preparing for battle); 3) *testamentum per aes et libram* (the conventional will of the late Republic and Empire, requiring certain formalities, such as witnesses, scales, and a "buyer"); 4) the tripartite will (requiring seven witnesses, seals, and the testator's/testatrix's signature). A girl, by age twelve, and a boy, by age fourteen, could make a valid will provided that s/he was a Roman citizen and not under the *patria potestas* of another. Provisions commonly found in a Roman's will are: 1) appointment of an heir (using very precise wording); 2) appointment of *substitutii* (in the event that the named heir could not or would not serve); 3) disinheritance; 4) manumission of slaves; 5) appointment of a tutor; 6) creation of a legacy; and, 7) establishment of a trust.

There were three categories of heirs under Roman law: 1) *necessarii* (slaves, who were not allowed to refuse their inheritance); 2) *sui et necessarii* (persons who passed from the *potestas* of the testator to their own [*i.e.,* they gained their independence upon the testator's death]); and, 3) *extraneii* (all others). Because a testator's heirs inherited his debts along with his assets, Justinian's laws permitted an *extraneus* to take an inventory prior to deciding whether to accept or decline an inheritance (*i.e.,* giving him the opportunity to determine whether the estate had funds sufficient to pay the testator's debts). Early laws rigidly controlled the means by which a testator could create a legacy, but later laws under Nero and Justinian relaxed these restrictions.

Law in Literature: Caesar's *De Bello Gallico*

Introduction

Although scholars have examined many aspects of Julius Caesar's life, little scholarship has considered his perceptions about the role of law in society. However, an examination of Caesar's early life reveals that he possessed substantial academic and practical legal experience. Moreover, a careful reading of his great historical work, *De Bello Gallico*, illuminates various concepts of justice that appear to be of significant interest to Caesar. When these two sources are studied together and viewed in their totality, it becomes evident that certain fundamental principles of basic fairness served as a foundation for Caesar's understanding and application of the law.

I. Caesar's Background in Law

Although Caesar became a powerful general and shrewd politician, he served in a variety of capacities that required legal training. He was a litigator, judge, consul, and governor. These positions directly related to the practice of law and required that he understand and apply legal concepts daily.

During his twenties, he successfully prosecuted at least three cases involving extortion. These experiences undoubtedly refined Caesar's skills in rhetoric and advocacy. To develop his skills as an advocate, in 75 B.C. Caesar sailed to Rhodes to study rhetoric under Apollonius Molon, who at the time was considered the "best living exponent of the art."

After returning from Rhodes at the age of twenty-seven, Caesar was elected Pontifex Maximus. As part of the college of pontiffs, he interpreted and judged a variety of religious matters and issued opinions regarding the appropriate penalties for "infringements." This position provided an opportunity to influence the political climate. Perhaps this experience taught him about the relationship between law and politics.

In his early thirties, Caesar served in a number of judicial capacities. As quaestor in Western Spain, he acted as a circuit judge and heard disputes throughout the region. Subsequently in 65 B.C., he served as curule aedile, an office whose "function was police control of market trade and generally the supervision of public order in the streets and squares." (MATTHIAS GELZER, CAESAR: POLITICIAN AND STATESMAN 42 (Peter Needham trans. 1968)). Next Caesar was a judge in a court that reviewed various criminal matters including murder. These experiences forced him to ponder serious legal questions and acquaint himself with both procedural and substantive law.

In addition to his roles as litigator and judge, Caesar's offices frequently involved executive decision making. While governor of Western Spain, he confronted issues that related to law daily. As consul, he amended specific laws relating to the debt of Roman tax farmers in the province of Asia and laws relating to financial abuse by provincial governors. However it was during this period that Caesar began to push the boundaries of legal tradition and interpretation. Most notably, he by-passed the Senate and used the popular assembly to ratify certain treaties; a maneuver that was in flagrant disregard of traditional practice. Furthermore, Caesar utilized his dual positions as Consul and Pontifex Maximus to permit a political ally to become a plebian through adoption. Scholars have noted that this action was legally invalid under the existing law at the time. (GELZER, *supra* at 77) As a result of the questionable means Caesar employed while Consul, a group of senators threatened legal action against him. Tension further increased when he refused to accept a compromise offered by the senators. After being appointed governor of Gaul, his opponents in the senate feared that he would become too powerful. The group of senators, therefore, initiated criminal charges against him. In order to avoid prosecution, Caesar quickly left Rome to assume his post in Gaul.

As the proconsular governor of Gaul for eight years, Caesar possessed immense authority and enacted significant change. Julius Caesar had a firm foundation in law and was well qualified to interpret and apply complex legal concepts. As his knowledge and command of the legal system expanded, so did his ability to stretch and perhaps manipulate it. These manipulations promoted hostility between Caesar and other factions, eventually culminating in the Civil War. Then when he returned to power in Rome at the end of the Civil War, he planned to initiate legal reforms such as strengthening criminal penalties and condensing the Civil Code into volumes in order to make it more usable. However as was the case during his consulship before leaving for Gaul, a number of senators questioned the legality of Caesar's actions while serving in Gaul. In particular, many of his opponents believed that his declarations of war in Gaul violated "conventional standards" and defied "the rules of international law." (CHRISTIAN MEIER, CAESAR: A BIOGRAPHY 236–37 (David McLintock trans. 1995)).

II. Foreign Laws and Justice

In 59 B.C. Caesar moved to Gaul as the proconsular governor where he observed and analyzed how foreigners organized their legal systems, and he compared their notions of justice with his own. Caesar focused his observations regarding these foreign legal systems on their methods of selecting judges and leaders, how marital property and marital relationships were governed, and the various legal methods used to provide safety and security for their communities.

A. Judges & Legal Procedure

He recognized that the Gauls were not merely barbarians; rather they had established judges and legal procedure. He noted that the Gauls had specific persons with authority to resolve legal disputes. Caesar emphasized that this was significant because, in his view, the purpose of having individuals identified as judges was to protect the interests of the lower class. According to Caesar, the purpose of law is to protect the weak. And the presence of judges and procedure prevents the more powerful from oppressing the weak.

In Gallic society, leadership was divided into two classes, Druids and Knights. The Druids held the distinguished positions and acted as both religious officials and judges. The Druids acted as judges in almost all disputes, including instances when crimes were committed or when a dispute arose relating to an inheritance or a boundary. The Druids adjudicated these matters and decided the appropriate compensation to be paid or received by the parties concerned. Those who failed to comply with the Druids' decisions were treated as outcasts and criminals.

The Gauls had put a system in place for selecting a chief justice of the Druids. The chief justice retained his position for life. Upon his death, the Druid with the highest rank became the new chief justice. However, if more than one Druid held the next highest rank, the others then voted for the next chief justice. Caesar also noted that, in some extreme instances, the Druids held a contest of arms between the eligible judges for the chief justice position. Caesar implied that it was better to have a system of succession based either on rank or a voting process as opposed to violence.

B. Marriage & Family

A Gaul who planned to marry was required to add a portion of his own property to his wife's dowry. The common English term for this portion of property contributed by the husband's family is "bridewealth." The dowry and bridewealth together were invested to earn for both the husband and wife together. If either spouse died, the survivor received the dowry and bridewealth plus any profits accumulated since the beginning of the marriage. This system provided a measure of financial security similar to today's modern rights to an estate possessed by a surviving spouse.

Caesar compared the legal power of a Gallic husband and father to that of the Roman *paterfamilias*. Gallic husbands had the power of life and death over their wives and children. Upon death, a Gallic husband's relatives assembled. If the circumstances of his death were suspicious, they examined his widow under torture to determine whether she had a hand in her husband's death. If found guilty, she was burned to death. Considering the severity of the punishment, the Gauls obviously deemed a wife's involvement with a husband's death an extremely serious crime.

C. Safety & Security for the Community

Caesar wrote about foreign laws that promoted safety and security for the community. One such Gallic law prohibited public discussion of politics outside of an assembly. The law provided that when a citizen overheard any rumor or news concerning the State, he was required to communicate it to a magistrate, without speaking to anyone else. The law provided safety by limiting false reports that had the potential to incite chaos among the public. Of course this law also had the effect of silencing dissenters and limiting freedom of speech.

Caesar mentions another law that promoted public safety; a Gallic law requiring a prompt "call to arms." All men were required to answer the call to arms but the last man to arrive was tortured and executed. The law promoted safety by encouraging prompt arrival in preparation for battle and by fostering efficient troop organization. The law also illustrates the importance that the Gauls placed on serving in the military for the public defense.

Another Gallic law combined aspects of military law and property law. This provision mandated that individuals relocate from one parcel of land to another on an annual basis. Caesar maintained that the law's purpose was for men to sharpen their warlike edge and turn them into better fighters. By preventing them from becoming accustomed a sedentary lifestyle, this law ensured that they would not "lose their warlike enthusiasm, and take up agriculture instead." Similarly, the Suebi, the most bellicose of the German nations, created a law that promoted enthusiasm for warfare. The Suebi law required a mid-year rotation of lifestyle and duties. Men spent half the year as soldiers in the military and the other half as farmers at home, growing crops to support those serving in the military. Both the Gallic law and the Suebi law shared a common purpose: to prevent men from becoming complacent by requiring them routinely to change their circumstances.

Caesar concludes his analysis of foreign laws with the Aeduans' rules and procedures regarding the transfer of magisterial power. Aedan law prohibited a chief magistrate from leaving the country. This law promoted continued governmental stability by requiring that the head of State always be on hand to maintain control even during times of war when other men were absent. Caesar also mentions an Aeduan election law requiring that all elections be held openly and at a specific time and place. Fair notice to the public about where and when an election was going to occur promoted a fair and peaceful process in electing new leaders.

III. Principles of Caesar's Jurisprudence

Introduction

The principles of justice that stand out most prominently in *De Bello Gallico* are similar in many respects to basic principles of modern American justice. However, although these principles may bear some similarities to today's moral standards, the interplay between each of Caesar's concepts of justice and the manner in which he saw these principles manifest were premised on the harsh lifestyle of one groomed in warfare. Seven concepts of justice featured most prominently in Caesar's writing are as follows:

1) It is just to repay kindness;
2) It is just to punish wrongs simply for the sake of vengeance and/or teaching the wrongdoer a lesson;
3) It is just to use punishment as a normative device in order to deter others from committing wrongs;
4) It is just for the needs of many to supersede those of the few;
5) It is just that one who occupies property first should have rights superior to a second-comer;
6) It is just to provide compensation for victims who have incurred damage; and
7) It is just to be forgiving.

1. *It is just to repay kindness*

Caesar used this principle to his advantage during his campaign in Gaul. He reminded the Aedui that they owed him aid precisely because he was working for their benefit. Caesar frequently portrayed himself as occupying a position of virtue, and using guilt as leverage, he used that image to manipulate his allies so that they might provide him with what he thought he deserved. Despite his ability to use such a principle to his advantage, he appears honestly to have believed in this concept. He was well-known for his steadfast loyalty and his belief that such a concept of justice should be universal. Superficially, Caesar's belief that repaying kindness should entail obligatory reciprocity may seem more a restatement of the notion of *quid pro quo* rather than of doing what is right for the sake of justice itself. But human nature may be universal in some regards. Throughout history people have tended to be more comfortable asking for favors when they have provided favors in the past. Similarly, a person may feel betrayed if he or she constantly provides kindnesses to another and yet that person fails to do anything in return.

2. It is just to punish wrongs simply for the sake of vengeance and/or teaching the wrongdoer a lesson

The next two principles of justice—punishing for the sake of vengeance and/or teaching a lesson, and using punishment to deter others—are central, though often competing, goals of the modern American criminal justice system. In modern jurisprudence, we typically refer to these concepts as 1) retribution (or specific deterrence), and 2) general deterrence. Though the names are different, the concepts have remained the same for over 2,000 years.

Punishment for the sake of vengeance is essentially the converse of the principle that justice requires the repayment of kindness. Justice requires the repayment of injury as well. While vengeance might seem to contradict forgiveness, both of these principles are prevalent in modern jurisprudence. And, although most would teach that it is better to forgive than to seek vengeance, the desire to hurt those who have hurt us is a basic human instinct.

3. It is just to use punishment as a normative device in order to deter others from committing wrongs

Caesar's severe treatment of military deserters serves as a prime example of his belief that it is just to use punishment to deter others. His goal was to deter other soldiers from making similar choices. Of the three justifications for punishment—vengeance, deterring individuals, and deterring others—Caesar appears to have believed that deterring others was the most important.

4. It is just for the needs of many to supersede those of the few

In 52 B.C., Caesar suspended his siege plans when he realized how many men would lose their lives in support of his goals if he were to move forward with the attack. Indeed, Caesar claimed "he would be guilty of the grossest injustice if he did not consider [his soldiers'] lives before his own interests." (CAESAR, THE CONQUEST OF GAUL 190 (S.A. Handford trans. 1951)). However, Caesar seems to have forgotten this principle when he started a civil war—a certain death sentence for thousands—so that he could avoid a personal prosecution.

5. *It is just that one who occupies property first should have rights superior to a second-comer*

Today we often use the phrase "first in time, first in right." This fundamental principle of property law has changed little in the past 2,000 years. Both Caesar and the Gallic leader, Ariovistus, argued over whether the Romans or Gauls had controlled a certain territory in Gaul first. But they agreed that the principle of "first in time" was the rule that governed. Thus, both foreigners and Romans shared this property concept.

6. *It is just to provide compensation for victims who have incurred damage*

Caesar's view that it is just to provide compensation for victims who have incurred damage is echoed today as one of the foundational principles of American tort law. However, like most examples discussed thus far, Caesar applied the principle to military life. Caesar declared that he would make peace with an enemy, the Helvetii, but only if the Helvetti agreed to "recompense [Caesar's allies] for the injury you have done them." (HANDFORD, *supra* at 46).

7. *It is just to repay kindness*

Caesar "was famed for his clemency and compassion" and "won fame through giving, helping, and forgiving." Thus, it is not surprising that we should find Caesar suggesting that one aspect of justice is to be forgiving. In 54 B.C., the Nervii attacked Cicero's winter camp. When several Nervian leaders approached him to discuss the situation, one of the things that Cicero said (of course these are words that Caesar puts into Cicero's mouth) was that perhaps Caesar would forgive them: *sperare pro eius iustitia.*

By way of reply [to the Nervii], Cicero contented himself with saying that it was not the habit of the Roman people to accept any terms from an armed enemy. If they would lay down their arms, and send an embassy to Caesar to ask for terms, he would support their request, and hoped that Caesar in his justice would grant it.

Conclusion

Caesar's sense of justice contributed to his military successes, both in making him a more effective leader of his own men and in subduing the Gallic tribes, but at the same time led to his political downfall. With respect to the Gallic tribes, his ability to adapt and to relate concepts of justice helped him gain the respect of those tribes and ally them with the Roman cause. With respect to Roman affairs, his manipulation of the law, as well as his sometime disrespect for it, along with his appeals to justice, made him popular with the people, while at the same time infuriating his political enemies and forcing them ultimately to assassinate him. Indeed, Caesar's personal view of law and justice was integral both to his rise and his fall.

He rose as a military and political leader in large part because of his sense of justice and his ability to manipulate law. But his disregard for the law in the end caused his downfall. Perhaps he was simply too good at using the law for his own purposes. Caesar's legal manipulation and lawlessness forced others first to attempt to manipulate the law against him and then, when that failed, to take (at least arguably) lawless measures (assassination being the most dramatic example).

Few individuals have had as great an impact upon world events as Julius Caesar. Caesar shaped the last quarter century of the Roman Republic, and in so doing, profoundly influenced the creation of the Roman Empire and Western Civilization. This Study in Law in Literature has trained our attention on one significant thread of his complex life and legacy: law. Because of his legal education, training, and practical experience, it is certain that he was intimately familiar with the substantive, procedural, and jurisprudential aspects of Roman law. Because of his political life, legal issues and legal questions affected the course of his life and many of his most important decisions. Hence, it comes as no surprise that his own writing reveals a rich and broad understanding of law and legal principles. His commentaries on the Gallic War, *De Bello Gallico*, contain hundreds of direct and indirect references to law and legal institutions. This Study in Law in Literature has confined its focus to only two types of those references: 1) remarks concerning foreign laws; and, 2) remarks that reflect Caesar's viewpoint of justice as an abstract principle.

In discussing and describing the laws and legal institutions of foreigners such as the Gauls and Germans, Caesar indirectly reveals something about his own thinking about law. Arguably, he only chose to discuss those aspects of foreign laws that he considered interesting or significant. Thus, he noted the following: 1) it is important for a legal system to have judges and legal procedure; 2) it is important for a legal system to have an organized process for selecting judges and leaders; 3) it is important for a legal system to establish mechanisms for governing marital property and marital relations; and, 4) it is important for a legal system to provide safety and security for the community.

His isolated discussions of justice in the abstract show an appreciation of at least seven distinct tenets: 1) it is just to repay kindness; 2) it is just to punish wrongs simply for the sake of vengeance and/or teaching the wrongdoer a lesson; 3) it is just to use punishment as a normative device in order to deter others from committing wrongs; 4) it is just for the needs of many to supersede those of the few; 5) it is just that one who occupies property first should have rights superior to a second-comer; 6) it is just to provide compensation for victims who have incurred damage; and, 7) it is just to be forgiving.

By gaining a better understanding of the role that law played in Caesar's life and his perceptions of law, perhaps we can better understand who he was, why he did the things that he did, and how those things, in turn, combined to affect the world that evolved after his death. To some degree, because Caesar's actions affected the shape of Rome's Empire and the whole of the Western World, those actions also affected the shape of the world in which we live today. The role that law and legal issues played in his life, then, continues to influence our modern world.

CHAPTER 16

CRIMINAL LAW

§ 16.01 Criminal Liability & Elements of Crime

Dolus (criminal intent) was ordinarily a required element of any crime. Modern legal systems typically refer to this element as *mens rea* (a guilty mind). Roman law considered that children under the age of seven were incapable of conceiving *dolus*. Therefore, they could not be criminally liable. Similarly, between age seven and puberty, Roman law considered a child's inability to conceive of *dolus* as a rebuttable presumption. In like manner, the insane were treated as incapable of being criminally liable. Roman magistrates with *imperium* were insulated from criminal liability while they were in office.

In addition to *dolus*, an *actus reus* (criminal act) was an essential element for a crime in Roman law. An *attempt* to commit a criminal act could also constitute an *actus reus*. Treasonous speech could constitute an *actus reus,* as could defamatory speech and certain other false communications (such as perjury, forgery, and false pleadings). Women, minors, and those who lived in the country were usually held to a lesser standard than others. The law presumed that they simply could not conform their conduct to the higher standards of adult men who lived in Rome. The jurists Labeo and Paul explained that accomplices (*socii*) could be liable for criminal acts along with the principal who actually committed a crime. Accomplices ordinarily received the same punishment as actual perpetrators.

§ 16.02 Homicide

Prior to the Twelve Tables (451/450 B.C.), there may have been a very old rule regarding homicide which stated that if the killing was accidental, the killer was required to perform some sort of religious atonement but could not receive the death penalty. In order to effectuate this rule, special magistrates, called *quaestiones paricidii*, were appointed to determine whether a death was caused intentionally or accidentally. Supposedly the king Numa Pompilius (the legendary second king of Rome, *c.* 715–673 B.C.) enacted that death was the penalty for premeditated homicide. In the Republic the death penalty was usually inflicted by decapitation by axe or later by sword.

In 81 B.C., Sulla's *lex Cornelia de sicariis et veneficis* (Cornelian law regarding murderers and poisoners) established a *quaestio perpetua* (*i.e.,* permanent court) designed to handle murder trials. The praetor, or judge, supervised the jury in cases involving a murder that had been committed within one mile of Rome. The law also criminalized the act of carrying weapons with the intent to kill or steal. The *lex Cornelia de sicariis et veneficis* could be used as both a peacekeeping measure and a statutory basis for prosecuting murder. But throughout the Republic, Roman law ordinarily treated murder as a matter to be addressed by the victim's *paterfamilias* not necessarily by the State. Presumably, the victim's *paterfamilias* did his best to track down the murderer and then accused him. The most probable person to accuse another of murder (*i.e.,* to serve as prosecutor) was the victim's father, husband, or brother. As a general rule, only male citizens could instigate murder charges. The most common exception to this rule existed for a woman when the victim was her parent or child. But in any case the action was, by and large, originally private.

According to the jurist Paul, the *lex Cornelia*, in addition, punished those who possessed, sold, or made a poison with intent to murder, and also punished anyone whose false testimony caused another's death. Paul wrote: "A murderer is someone who kills a man with any kind of weapon or causes death."[1] Before long, the *lex Cornelia* was applied to common murder—not only murder associated with public violence. Generally speaking, however, suicide was not a criminal act. Those from the upper classes who were convicted under this law, received capital punishment. Death by crucifixion or being thrown to wild animals was the punishment for the lower classes.

One of the essential elements of murder was intent. Thus, neither the insane nor minors could be guilty of murder since the law presumed them incapable of having legal intent. But there was a distinction between intent and even "gross carelessness." An absence of premeditation might serve as a mitigating circumstance.

The *lex Pompeia* (55 B.C.) was the first statute that criminalized parricide (murder of close relatives) as an offense distinct from ordinary murder. This law defined the relationships that encompassed parricide. In addition to the obvious—killing one's parent—the Romans also treated the murder of a grandparent, sibling, cousin, aunt or uncle, and patron as parricide. The punishment

---

1. ROBINSON, CRIMINAL LAW 42–43 (Citing and quoting Paul's *Sententiae* 5.23.1-2).

for parricide was usually either death or banishment. It was also common for a person convicted of parricide to forfeit his property. There was a particularly cruel punishment, called the sack (*culleus*), that was sometimes administered in the case of someone who murdered either a parent or grandparent. By the end of the 3rd century A.D., burning alive or mauling by wild animals was used instead. Much later in the Empire (*i.e.,* in the time of the Christian emperors), the *culleus* again became fashionable. And, in fact, to increase the suffering of the convicted parricide, assorted deadly animals were inserted into the sack along with the convicted criminal.

Abortion was treated as a crime insofar as the death of the fetus was considered a crime against the woman's husband. The law presumed that a married woman might take poison to induce abortion, hoping to hide an adultery or to deprive her husband of an heir. The punishment was exile. Since abortion was, therefore, deemed a violation against the husband, it was, apparently, legal for an unwed woman to induce abortion.

Because slaves were considered property, in early Roman law, murder did not apply to the killing of a slave. At some point, possibly in the late Republic, murder of a slave became cognizable. Ultimately, in the Empire, even the killing of one's own slave was criminalized.

Roman law validated certain affirmative defenses to murder. For example, self-defense and defense of a family member (even from sexual assault) were legitimate excuses. In addition, killing a military deserter was considered justifiable homicide. A father was barred from killing a son unless he first accused him and had a hearing with the Urban Prefect.

§ 16.03 Theft Crimes

The Twelve Tables punished the cutting of another's fruiting trees as a kind of crime. Forced labor was the penalty for the less privileged citizens, while the *honestiores* (*e.g.,* army veterans) merely paid a fine. Also in the Twelve Tables, the death penalty was imposed both for arson and for theft of crops at night (burglary). It was during the Empire that Romans began treating theft in general more as a crime than as a tort. During the Empire (27 B.C.–mid-5th century A.D.), ordinarily a victim of theft had a choice of bringing either a criminal action or a civil action. In Republican Rome (509–27 B.C.), the *tresviri capitales* routinely handled cases involving theft, and in the Empire, it was the Prefect of the Night Watch (*Praefectus Vigilum*).

Abigeatus (rustling) was a specific subspecies of theft. Both the type of animal stolen and the number of animals stolen were factors that could turn simple theft into *abigeatus*. According to Paul, the theft of one stallion, or two mares or oxen, or ten sheep or goats, or five pigs constituted rustling. Forced labor was a common penalty. But a rustler could receive a more harsh penalty— such as work in the mines or even death—if he acted as part of a hired band, was armed, or was a recidivist. The Emperor Hadrian (117–138 A.D.) made *abigeatus* a capital offense in Spain.

The *Praefectus Vigilum* had charge of burglary, arson, mugging, theft, and the resale of stolen goods on the black market. Roman law had special names for certain types of thieves. For example, *effractores* were burglars who broke into apartments, and *saccularii* were thieves who slit pockets and purses to empty their contents. Particular thieves, called *expilatores,* who ransacked homes in the countryside, were considered especially blameworthy. These thieves usually were punished with forced labor. According to the jurist Paul, thieves often received forced labor as a penalty. Some were beaten first. Convicted burglars frequently were beaten and then also sent to the mines. A praetor's edict established the delict *rapina* (*vi bonorum raptorum*), theft with violence. *Rapina* was, in a number of respects, treated as a crime. For *rapina* a thief had to pay multiple damages, four-times the amount stolen.[2]

Roman law had an action for conduct that was, essentially, looting in the wake of a natural disaster like fire, shipwreck, or a collapsed building (*de incendio ruina naufragio rate nave expugnata*). If a complainant brought his action within one year, the criminal was liable for four-times the value of what he stole or damaged. For a suit brought after one year, the fine was only the value of the stolen or damaged property. If, on the other hand, the culprit, instead of merely being opportunistic, deliberately set a fire as a stratagem for stealing goods, he faced capital punishment if his crime was in the city, and faced work in the mines, forced labor, or banishment if he had targeted a rural farm or villa.

Those who bought or otherwise received stolen goods, knowing them to have been stolen ("fencing"), were treated just the same as thieves. Harboring thieves was also a criminal offense. Interestingly, Roman law considered that a person who harbored a relative who was a thief should not be treated as harshly. The relationship, therefore, served as a mitigating circumstance.

§ 16.04 *Vis*

The Romans treated *vis* ("force/violence") as a special kind of crime. *Vis* included conduct such as armed robbery, battery, and sedition. Late in the

---

2. *See also infra* § 17.02[C].

Classical period (*i.e.*, 3rd century A.D.), two separate kinds of *vis* were recognized, public and private. Public *vis* included offenses committed by public officials (*e.g.*, killing, torturing, or beating a citizen), and private *vis* involved violent crimes perpetrated by private individuals. Brandishing a weapon in a threatening manner could constitute *vis* in certain social contexts. Although the penalty for *vis* was usually capital punishment or exile, there were a number of instances in which lesser punishments were applied instead. If the *vis* involved abduction of a freeborn woman, in addition to a death penalty, the offender's property was confiscated. Roman law used the concept of *vis* in a very broad sense to include many kinds of criminal conduct. But, in particular, physical and sexual assault (including abduction)—motivated either by political advancement, sexual desire, or profit—were also considered forms of criminal *vis*.

§ 16.05 Sexual Conduct

A. Adultery & *Stuprum*

Before the time of Augustus (27 B.C.–14 A.D.) Roman law treated adultery basically as a private matter. In the Republic (509–27 B.C.), it was considered justifiable for a husband to kill or beat his wife's paramour when caught in *flagrante delicto*. Republican law provided that the husband would divorce his wife and that he would keep the dowry. In about 18 B.C., Augustus spearheaded legislation that functionally criminalized adultery. The *lex Iulia de adulteriis coercendis* (Julian law regarding forced adultery) established a permanent court, the *quaestio perpetua de adulteriis*. In order for adultery to occur, the female involved had to be a "respectable married woman" and the man had to be someone who was not her husband. According to Ulpian, to be found guilty, the accused must have acted *sciens dolo malo* ("knowingly and with malicious intent").

The crime of *stuprum* occurred when a man, acting *sciens dolo malo*, had sexual relations with a "respectable" unmarried girl or woman, or a respectable man or boy. Under the *lex Iulia*, both abduction and rape fell within the scope of criminal *stuprum*, and both were punished with death. Justinian's Code makes it clear that an unwilling victim was not guilty of either adultery or *stuprum*.

Schoolbooks often make much of the paterfamilias' *ius occidendi* ("the right of killing"). Technically, a *paterfamilias* was entitled to put family members to death at his discretion.[3] But even by the late Republic, ordinarily fathers only

---

3. *See supra* § 14.01.

used the *ius occidendi* just after a child was born (*i.e.*, his decision to accept or reject the child). Augustus' *lex Iulia*, however, granted a *paterfamilias* authority to kill his own daughter if she were caught committing adultery *in flagrante delicto* either in his house or the house of his son-in-law. It was considered homicide if the *paterfamilias* killed the lover but not his daughter. The law made divorce compulsory when a wife was caught in the act. The husband was also obligated to initiate criminal charges against his wife.

Even though a man was capable of committing adultery (*e.g.*, when a married man had sex with a married "respectable" woman), the *lex Iulia* did not give the man's wife authority to charge him with adultery. She could, however, initiate divorce proceedings against him.

When charges were brought for adultery, slaves were usually questioned as part of the evidence taken against the accused. The *lex Iulia* provided extraordinarily harsh financial penalties for adultery. A woman's paramour paid a fine amounting to one-half of his patrimony and he was thereafter no longer able either to make a will or to take anything pursuant to someone else's will. An adulteress paid a fine of one-third of her patrimony and also forfeited one-half of her dowry. In addition to these fines, a later version of the law confined adulterous lovers to different islands.

B. Incest

Not only were sexual relations between a parent and a child considered incest but also marriage between persons whose family relationship was considered too close (*i.e.*, marriage was permitted by persons no more closely related than first cousins — the fourth degree).[4] The Emperor Claudius (41–54 A.D.) had special legislation passed that permitted him to marry his brother's daughter (*i.e.*, his niece). Even a marriage between tutor and pupil was considered incest. There were various penalties possible for incest, ranging from death by crucifixion and banishment to more moderate punishments.

C. *Lenocinium*, Prostitution, & Homosexual Activity

The *lex Iulia* also created a statutory basis for the crime known as *lenocinium*. In simple terms, *lenocinium* was any conduct that facilitated sexual crime (*e.g.*, adultery and *stuprum*). For example, a husband who was aware of his wife's adultery but failed to divorce her or to take appropriate legal steps was, himself,

---

4. *See supra* § 14.02.

guilty of *lenocinium*. Friends of adulterous lovers who kept the secret were also culpable under this law. This was especially true if the friends secured money or gifts as "hush money." Interestingly, *lenocinium* even applied to a man who married a woman who had, at some earlier date, been convicted of adultery or *stuprum*. Organized prostitution was, literally speaking, *lenocinium* under the *lex Iulia*. However, ordinarily the *leno* ("pimp") was punished with only infamy (*infamia*—*i.e.*, a formal loss of reputation and certain rights[5]).

Roman law treated homosexual conduct as criminal only in narrowly defined circumstances. If a man raped or seduced another male (adult or minor) he was guilty of *stuprum*. In order for the act to be considered criminal, the victim must have been "freeborn" (*i.e.*, neither a slave nor a freedman). Otherwise, sex between a man and a male slave or a male prostitute was not criminal. Roman law did not treat lesbian sex as wrongful in any manner. In the Classical period (1st century B.C.–3rd century A.D.), convicted homosexual rapists received death sentences. A willing, passive partner paid one-half of his property as a fine, and any will that he made was declared invalid. Justinian's *Institutes* assigns death as the penalty for homosexual *stuprum*.

§ 16.06 *Iniuria*

It is possible that Sulla was responsible for establishing a permanent court regarding *iniuria* but we cannot be certain. Sulla enacted the *lex Cornelia de iniuriis*, a law that created what amounted to a criminal cause of action against persons for hitting others or for forcefully breaking into another's home. Roman law also treated *iniuria* as a kind of tort (delict).[6] We really are uncertain of the subtle distinctions that differentiated criminal *iniuria* from *iniuria* as an *obligatio ex delicto*. From our ancient sources (*e.g.*, Gaius) it appears that the two operated in a parallel, non-exclusive fashion.

Any injury to one's reputation, dignity, honor, or bodily integrity was classified under *iniuria*. *Iniuria* applied to a variety of offensive conduct. For example, daubing excrement on a person and the deliberate contamination of a water supply were considered types of *iniuria* that warranted severe penalties. If an alleged defamatory statement were proved true, that truth operated as a defense to *iniuria*. Fines, beating, and flogging were common punishments imposed for *iniuria*. Apparently, the severity depended, in part, upon the status of the perpetrator, and, in part, upon the perceived outrageousness of the conduct involved.

---

5. *See* J.A. CROOK, Law and Life of Rome, 90 B.C.–A.D. 212 83–85 (1967).
6. For more about torts and delicts, *see infra* Chapter 17.

§ 16.07 Crimes Against the State

A. *Perduellio* & *Maiestas*

In the Classical period (1st century B.C.–3rd century A.D.), the most commonly used term for treason was *maiestas* (short for *crimen laesae maiestatis*). *Perduellio* is a term that also refers to treasonous conduct, but it was a term used more in the earlier Republic. Clearly one could be guilty of *vis, res repetundae* (extortion),[7] and *maiestas* for the same act. According to the jurist Paul, *maiestas* included a number of illegal activities: armed assault on the State; gathering soldiers or conducting warfare without the State's permission; and, desertion. The giving of any assistance to an enemy (*e.g.*, supplying information, selling goods, providing shelter) constituted treason as well. Ulpian says that conspiring to kill a magistrate or other public official was treasonous. In 103 B.C., the *lex Appuleia* established the first permanent court dedicated to accusations related to treason. As part of his court revamping, Sulla (82/81 B.C.) appended additional measures to address *maiestas* in the provinces. The most common penalties for *perduellio* during the Republic were death or exile. In the Classical period, although it was possible to receive a milder punishment if the circumstances warranted it, *maiestas* was routinely punished with the combination of execution (often by crucifixion) and forfeiture of one's property to the State.

B. *Res Repetundae*

The *lex Calpurnia* (149 B.C.) criminalized *res repetundae* (extortion) by provincial governors. Other legislation, probably passed in the latter half of the 2nd century B.C., broadened the definition of extortion to include losses not only by Roman citizens but losses suffered by allies and foreigners as well. In time, in addition to treating improper gain by provincial governors themselves as *res repetundae*, Roman law also punished others working for or in association with provincial governors for extortion (even the wives of provincial governors). *Res repetundae* included within its scope a variety of activities, such as accepting bribes or special favors, trading for personal profit, and any other conduct that allowed a person to reap individual gain by virtue of his office. By the last century of the Republic, banishment was the most common punishment for *res repetundae*. In the Empire both banishment and execution are attested as penalties.

---

7. *See infra* § 16.07[B].

C. *Peculatus* & *De Residuis*

Paul describes the crime *peculatus* (a kind of embezzlement), as defined by the *lex Iulia*, as any wrongful appropriation, diversion, or conversion of sacred, religious, or public funds. *Peculatus* included taking the spoils of war, since such plunder technically belonged to the Roman people. What we ordinarily think of as embezzlement (*i.e.,* the unlawful appropriation of money that has been entrusted) is closer to the Roman crime of *de residuis.* Another fundamental difference is that in *peculatus* the embezzler never has the right to possession of the money (or property) whereas in *de residuis* he did, at one point at least, have lawful possession. The punishment for *peculatus* was usually banishment and, in the Empire, confiscation of the offender's property. The customary penalty for *de residuis* was payment of a fine.

D. *Ambitus*

Ambitus was criminal conduct related to elections, such as bribery and other types of electoral corruption. *Ambitus* is well attested as a crime even in the early Republic, and we know of trials in the *quaestio de ambitu* in the late 2nd century B.C. There was quite a bit of legislation concerning *ambitus* in the last half century of the Republic. As the law developed, even activities such as staging gladiatorial contests and giving lavish banquets were considered to come within the scope of *ambitus.* The commonest punishments for *ambitus* were fines and a loss of status (*e.g.,* expulsion from the Senate).

E. Counterfeiting & Forgery

Sulla's legislation (82/81 B.C.) created a permanent court that dealt with forgery of money and forgery of wills (*falsum*). In the Empire (27 B.C.–mid-5th century A.D.), the *cognitio* procedure saw to it that the concept of forgery was broadened.[8] Eventually any intentional alteration of a formal document was considered forgery. Sulla enacted the *lex Cornelia nummaria*, the earliest Roman statute to criminalize the counterfeiting of money. Ulpian says that Sulla's law prohibited the unsanctioned manufacture of silver coins as well as the purchase or sale of coins that were made to look like silver, but which were, in truth, some cheaper metal substitute. By the early 4th century A.D., the Romans had passed legislation that expanded counterfeiting to include copper

---

8. See *supra* § 11.03[C] regarding *cognitio* procedure.

money as well as silver. Paul specifically notes that coins might be "counterfeited" in a number of creative ways: *lavaverit* ("washed"), *conflaverit* ("melted"), *raserit* ("shaved"), *corruperit* ("sheared"), *vitiavert* ("adulterated"). Ulpian explains that counterfeiters tried to simulate gold coins by rubbing or washing fakes with an artificial gold color or they attempted to shave traces of metal from otherwise legitimate gold coins.

The penalties for counterfeiting silver or copper coinage depended, to a great extent, on the counterfeiter's social class. Free men were usually banished (to distant islands during the Empire) and forfeited their property. Lower classes were either condemned to work in the mines or crucified, and slaves were executed. If, on the other hand, the counterfeiting involved gold coins, even upper class citizens could be sent to die by wild animals or, in special circumstances, burning, and slaves were executed by either burning or crucifixion.

§ 16.08 Miscellaneous Crimes

A. *Stellionatus*

One of the more interesting crimes was *stellionatus* (acting like a lizard). There do not appear to have been specific elements necessary for proof of *stellionatus*. Rather, it seems to have been a general concept that was related to fraud. According to Paul, it involved one person convincing another to give him property. For example, pledging property that belonged to someone else was *stellionatus*. Also, an imposter who posed as another person (and thereby profited) was guilty of *stellionatus*. Presumably, any conduct that was dishonest or fraudulent (but that did not fit neatly into another defined criminal category) could be dealt with as *stellionatus*.

B. Kidnapping

Kidnapping (*plagium*) was treated as a crime. A late Republican statute, the *lex Fabia* (63 B.C.), criminalized the sale of a Roman citizen, freedman, or slave who belonged to someone else. Indeed, this was simply a kind of kidnapping. If the buyer knew that the object of the sale was actually a free citizen, he also was liable as a criminal for kidnapping. On the other hand, a good faith purchaser of someone else's slave could not be criminally liable. Depending on the individual factors present in a kidnapping case (and the particular period of legal history), the penalty might be death. But we know that not all kidnappings were punished by death. Some kidnappers were fined. In the Empire, members of the upper classes were fined as much as half of their property. Lower classes guilty of kidnapping were sometimes crucified and sometimes sent to work in the mines.

C. Sale of Runaway Slaves

Criminals guilty of trading in runaway slaves were usually punished with fines. Near the end of the Republic, one of the praetor's edicts transformed the delict of slave corruption into a criminal act as well.[9] The criminal penalty for slave corruption was twice the value of the slave. Nevertheless, the civil aspects of this wrong continued to dominate.

D. Castration & Circumcision

A person guilty of castrating another received capital punishment. Slaves were the most common victims. Interestingly, the Emperor Hadrian (117–138 A.D.) broadened the ban on castration to include circumcision within its scope as well. Later, the Emperor Antoninus Pius (138–161 A.D.) made an exception regarding circumcision for the Jews.

E. Gambling

Certain Republican laws prohibited gambling, at least outside of the family. Even the Senate resolved to forbid gambling but, in the same way that office pools thrive during NCAA March Madness in the United States, a fair amount of informal wagering prospered in ancient Rome as well.

F. Crimes Related to Religion

Although the Romans resisted the infiltration of foreign religions, legally, at least, they were reasonably tolerant. They drew the line, however, at the human sacrifice involved in Druidism. The extent to which Christianity was illegal is the subject of robust historical debate. Clearly there were persecutions under Nero (54–68 A.D.) and other emperors in the early Empire. But it is doubtful that Christianity was "illegal" *per se* under Roman criminal law.

Roman law did treat circumcision of non-Jews as a criminal offense,[10] but Imperial Roman law dealt with Jews and Jewish religion itself with a consid-

---

9. *See infra* § 17.02[F].
10. *See supra* § 16.08[D].

erable degree of tolerance. For example, Jews were allowed to worship on their Sabbath and they did not have to sacrifice to the State gods of Rome. But Christians were prohibited from converting to Judaism and Christians and Jews were not allowed to intermarry.

§ 16.09 Chapter Summary

Roman law assumed that infants and insane persons were incapable of possessing criminal intent (*dolus*). Both criminal intent and a criminal act (*actus reus*) were considered standard, essential elements of any crime. Some evidence suggests, before the Twelve Tables, that an accidental homicide was punished by religious atonement, not the death penalty. In 81 B.C., Sulla established a permanent court to hear homicide cases, but the responsibility for prosecuting such a case continued to fall upon the victim's *paterfamilias*, not the State. Sulla's law, the *lex Cornelia*, brought within its scope both murder by poison and murder by means of a weapon. But intent was an element necessary to convict for murder, and absence of premeditation could serve as a mitigating circumstance. The *lex Pompeia* (55 B.C.) addressed parricide (murder of a close relative), which resulted in severe punishments such as forfeiture of property, banishment, and/or death by burning, by wild animal, or by enclosure in a sack (*culleus*). Abortion was considered a crime against a woman's husband (*i.e.*, either as a means to conceal an adultery or as a way to deprive the husband of an heir). Although early Roman law did not consider the killing of one's slave as murder (because a slave was considered mere property), by the Empire such an act was criminalized as murder. Self defense, defense of a family member, and the killing of a military deserter were all considered justifiable excuses that absolved a slayer of murder charges.

The Twelve Tables punished certain types of theft with forced labor or fines, but inflicted the death penalty in the case of arson and burglary of crops. *Abigeatus* (rustling) was treated as an extremely serious offense. During the Republic the *tresviri capitales* ordinarily adjudicated theft cases, while in the Empire it was the Prefect of the Night Watch. In addition to the garden variety thief, officials brought to justice a variety of thieves who had distinctive names: apartment burglars (*effractores*); purse cutters (*saccularii*); and those who ransacked country homes (*expilatores*). Romans usually punished thieves with forced labor in the mines and/or beatings. Special theft laws punished looters, persons who knowingly bought or otherwise received stolen goods, and persons who harbored thieves.

Vis—both public and private—was considered a unique kind of crime that encompassed a vast array of criminal conduct, typically characterized by threats, force, and violence. Acts such as armed robbery, battery, sedition, violent threats, and certain kinds of sexual assault constituted forms of *vis*.

Early Roman law treated adultery as a private matter which a husband vindicated, but Augustus (27 B.C.–14 A.D.) made it a crime and established a permanent court to hear adultery cases only. Roman law imposed severe financial penalties for adultery. Both conduct that we today would classify as seduction and conduct that we would classify as rape (*i.e.*, sex without consent involving an unmarried victim) the Romans called by the name *stuprum*. Under Augustus' law, a father was given legal authority to kill his own daughter if she were caught *in flagrante delicto* either in his house or in the house of his son-in-law. Not only were sexual relations between a parent and a child considered incest but also marriage between persons whose family relationship was considered too close (*e.g.*, marriage was permitted by persons no more closely related than first cousins—the fourth degree). The crime of *lenocinium* was any conduct that facilitated a sexual crime, such as adultery or *stuprum* (*e.g.*, knowing about but not disclosing an adultery). Homosexual relations between men were considered criminal (*i.e.*, *stuprum*) only in cases were the victim was "freeborn".

Sulla's *lex Cornelia de iniuriis* created what was essentially a criminal cause of action against persons for hitting others or for forcefully breaking into another's home. Other types of *iniuria* that, in context, strike modern readers as having more in common with crimes than torts include: 1) an injury to reputation, honor, or bodily integrity; 2) defiling another with excrement; and, 3) deliberate contamination of a water supply.

Roman law recognized several crimes that were committed against the State. *Perduellio* and *maiestas* are the terms used by the Romans of the Republic and Empire, respectively, to refer to various acts that constituted treason (*e.g.*, armed assault on the State, assisting an enemy, conspiracy to murder a public official). The Romans usually punished *res repetundae* (extortion) by provincial governors and their accomplices with banishment. Banishment was also the normal punishment for *peculatus*, embezzlement of State-owned funds. Persons found guilty of *ambitus* (*i.e.*, criminal conduct related to elections, such as bribery and other types of electoral corruption) were usually disciplined with fines and a loss of status. Roman law punished counterfeiting and forgery severely (*e.g.*, with banishment, forced labor, crucifixion, burning, mauling by wild animals).

Criminal law also penalized a number of acts which do not fit neatly into other categories. For example, *stellionatus* was a crime associated with several kinds of ill-defined fraudulent practices. *Plagium* was the Roman crime analogous to kidnapping. And it was illegal to sell a runaway slave. As a rule, castration was a crime and, by the time of Hadrian (117–138 A.D.), circumcision also was forbidden. Laws designed to curb gambling existed but were not as effective as the senate had intended. The Romans, and to a limited extent Roman law, treated Druidism and Christianity rather harshly. They dealt with Judaism, on the other hand, with comparative leniency; allowing Jews, for example, to practice circumcision and to worship on the Sabbath.

CHAPTER 17

TORTS: *OBLIGATIONES EX DELICTO* AND *OBLIGATIONES QUASI EX DELICTO*

§ 17.01 Classification: The Law of Obligations

In a very basic sense, there were essentially two methods of acquiring things in Roman law: 1) by succession; and, more importantly, 2) by an *obligatio*. Although the law of *obligationes* (obligations) is not commonly used in the terminology of English Common Law, it is still conventional in the Civil Law countries of continental Europe. In the United States lawyers speak of torts and contracts, but in most European legal systems, these are lumped together in the law of "obligations."

Generally speaking, an *obligatio* in Roman law entailed some relationship between two persons in which one was a creditor and the other a debtor. Legal relationships that gave one person the right to require any performance of any sort from the other were *obligationes*. According to one definition in Justinian's *Digest*, a creditor had the right to require a debtor to perform any one of three tasks: 1) *dare* (to give); 2) *facere* (to make or do); and, 3) *praestare* (to give to the creditor that which the debtor has produced).[1]

The Roman jurists who compiled Justinian's *Institutes* categorized *obligationes* into four groups: 1) *obligationes ex contractu* (obligations arising from contract); 2) *obligationes ex delicto* (obligations arising from delict); 3) *obligationes quasi ex contractu* (obligations as if arising from contract); and, 4) *obligationes quasi ex delicto* (obligations as if arising from delict). For purposes of our study, we will consider *obligationes ex delicto* and *obligationes quasi ex*

---

1. For example, this would occur when a publisher contracts with an author to write a book and then transfer the manuscript to the publisher.

delicto as part of the body of tort law.[2] Similarly, we will consider *obligationes ex contractu* and *obligationes quasi ex contractu* as part of the law of contracts.[3]

§ 17.02 *Obligationes ex Delicto* (Delicta)

A. Introduction

Although the Roman law of delict is analogous in some respects to modern tort law, (*i.e.*, civil wrongs), merely translating the Latin term *delictum* as a "tort" is, strictly speaking, unsatisfactory. In many respects Roman *delictum* was closer to either crime or an intentional tort. Damages for delicts were usually punitive. The Romans thought of a delict as any violation of legal prohibitions that caused a negative result. As is true with tort law today, however, there is no one, all-encompassing definition for delict. Rather, there are distinct types, individual delicts. Gaius and Justinian, in their *Institutes*, address four delicts: 1) *furtum* (theft); 2) *rapina* (robbery with violence); 3) *damnum iniuria datum* (property damage); and 4) *iniuria* (personal injury).

B. *Furtum* (Theft)

The Twelve Tables differentiated between *furtum manifestum* and *furtum nec manifestum*. This distinction is basically the difference between whether a thief is caught in the act or not. The penalty for *furtum manifestum* was to be beaten and then the perpetrator was handed over to the victim of the theft as a slave or bondsman. In addition, the thief was required to pay quadruple damages (*i.e.*, four-times the value of the objects that he had attempted to steal). A slave who was found guilty of *furtum manifestum* was first beaten and then executed by hurling him from the famous Tarpeian Rock. According to the Twelve Tables, when someone discovered a thief red-handed at night, he was entitled to kill him on the spot. By the time of Hadrian (117–138 A.D.), summary execution in this manner was considered illegal only if the death was later deemed unwarranted.

The Twelve Tables permitted someone who accused another of *furtum* to search the accused's house to look for the stolen property. The accuser was required to search practically naked (save for a plate tied around the waist with a string to hide one's genitalia) so that he, himself, could not later be accused

---

2. This not because the analogy is perfect, but because it is adequate for our purposes.
3. *See infra* Chapter 18.

of planting the allegedly stolen property by hiding it under a garment. This ritualistic search was called *lance et licio* ("with plate and string"). If the accuser discovered stolen property in this manner, the theft was considered *manifestum*. If the accused refused to permit the *lance et licio*, his penalty was to pay quadruple the value of the goods alleged to have been stolen.

Roman jurists debated the nature of the *actus reus* ("wrongful conduct") that was necessary as an element of *furtum*. Did a person have to actually remove the thing (*res*) or was merely touching the *res* sufficient to constitute the requisite *actus reus*? This, in turn, sparked a debate as to whether the taking of only a small portion of a bulk constituted a theft of the whole or whether it really should be considered merely a theft of that portion taken. For example, was the taking of a few sips of wine or a few grains of wheat the taking of the entire cask or bushel? The debate was lively but never satisfactorily resolved by the jurists.

C. *Rapina* (Robbery with Violence)

Rapina was identified as a separate wrong about 76 B.C., after the civil war. As a penalty, a convicted robber paid his victim quadruple damages. Oddly, most scholars believe, however, that the victim was not also entitled to have his property returned to him.

D. *Damnum Iniuria Datum* (Property Damage)

In 287 B.C., the *concilium plebis* enacted the *lex Aquilia*, the principal Republican statute that dealt with property damage. There were three main sections, or chapters, of the *lex Aquilia*: 1) relating to the killing of slaves and herd animals; 2) relating to debtors who defrauded their creditors; and, 3) relating to other general property damage.

In chapter one, the law addressed situations where a person intentionally or negligently killed either a slave or herd animal. Some of the animals that came within this statute were horses, mules, sheep, goats, and pigs. In order for a cause of action to be viable, the death had to have been the result of a direct cause. For example, if A's cart ran over B's pig, A would be liable. But if an axe fell off of A's cart and B's pig came along later and tripped over it resulting in the swine's death, A would not be liable, because the death was indirect. Nevertheless, a praetor could interpret this rule broadly if he felt that justice would be served in any given case. If found liable, a defendant had to pay the owner the highest value of the slave or animal during the previous year.

Chapter two was intended to deal with special situations involving fraud in a creditor-debtor relationship. Later, the contract known as *mandatum*[4] rendered this section obsolete.

In chapter three, the law dealt with property damage that was: 1) direct (like the damage in chapter one); 2) intentional or negligent; and, 3) caused by burning, snapping, or breaking (*urere, frangere, rumpere*). If found liable, the defendant had to pay the amount of damage incurred as assessed up to thirty days after the incident.

E. *Iniuria* (Personal Injury)

The Twelve Tables had three provisions that dealt with *iniuria*. The first established that, if a person's limb were actually destroyed, the injured party and the wrongdoer should try to reach a monetary settlement; but if they could not, the injured party was entitled to seek revenge. The second provided that when a person suffered a broken bone as a result of another's wrongdoing, the injured party was entitled to 300 asses[5] if he was a free man and 150 asses if he was a slave. The third provision gave an action for 25 asses for all lesser injuries. Aulus Gellius (*c.* 130–180 A.D.) tells the story of a wealthy Roman who used to walk around town accompanied by a slave who held a bag of coins. The man simply smacked any person whom he pleased and then instructed the slave to give his victim 25 asses. If a plaintiff sued for *iniuria* and lost, he had to pay the defendant 10% of the value of the claim. Presumably, this rule discouraged the bringing of frivolous lawsuits.

In the 3rd century B.C., praetors included a law of *iniuria* in their edicts and gradually transformed the law. Under the praetors' edicts, judges determined damages on a case by case basis rather than having damages that were fixed by statute. In addition, praetors expanded the law of *iniuria* to include intangible as well as tangible injuries. For example, certain insults and verbal abuse intended to disgrace or dishonor others were interpreted as forms of *iniuria*.

F. Miscellaneous Delicts

Other major delicts included the following:

1) About 80 B.C. the praetor named Octavius issued an edict that dealt with extortion.

---

4. *See infra* § 18.05.
5. An *as* was the principal bronze coin and monetary unit in the Republic.

2) In 66 B.C. Aquillius Gallus issued an edict on fraud that actually related to fraud in a contract context only. In the Empire, Labeo redefined fraud more broadly to include non-contractual fraud as well.

3) Another edict created an action known as *actio servi corrupti*. This action concerned situations where a person influenced another's slave in a negative manner.

4) There were a number of other miscellaneous actions that dealt with the use of and damage to agricultural property.

§ 17.03 Noxal Liability & Liability for Damage Caused by Animals

The concept of noxal liability operated to limit liability for a father or a slave owner—for injuries caused by a son or slave—to the amount of the value of the son or slave. If a son or slave caused damage to another, the father/master retained the option of paying the claim up to the value of the son/slave. If the claim was worth more than the son/slave, the father/master, then, had the option of merely turning the son/slave over to the victim, as full payment.

Under the Twelve Tables, an animal's owner was liable for damage caused by the animal. The owner, though, was not liable in cases where someone provoked the animal. If, however, the amount of damage was greater than the beast's value, then the owner could opt, instead, simply to turn over the animal. Aediles issued special edicts regarding damage done by wild animals that were being kept near a road in preparation for gladiatorial combat.

§ 17.04 *Obligationes Quasi ex Delicto* (Quasi Delicts)

Justinian, but not Gaius, categorized four separate actions that he labeled as *quasi ex delicto* (as if arising from delict). It is difficult to isolate a common thread that unites the *obligationes quasi ex delicto*. In certain respects these quasi delicts—at least three of the four—are similar to some modern torts in which American law imposes liability as a matter of vicarious liability (*e.g.,* liability imposed on employers due to injuries caused by employees). But the oldest, "the judge who made the case his own" (*iudex qui litem suam fecit*), does not involve the principle of vicarious liability. One common characteristic, however, may be that each quasi delict, apparently, imposed liability without reference to fault. In other words, Roman law concerning *obligationes quasi ex delicto* imposed liability in circumstances where modern law imposes strict liability (*i.e.*, liability imposed without regard to "fault"). The following were the four most prominent quasi delicts: 1) *actio de rebus effusis vel deiectis* ("an action relating to things which have been poured out or thrown out"); 2) *actio de posito et suspenso* ("an action relating to something that has been placed or hung out"); 3) *iudex qui litem suam fecit* ("a judge who has made a case his own"); and lastly, 4) an action relating to *nauta, caupo, stabularius* (for owners of a ship, inn, or stable).

1) *Actio de rebus effusis vel deiectis* was an action against the owner of premises from which things were thrown or poured onto a street. This action gave passers-by redress for damage caused by the things that were thrown or poured from a structure.

2) *Actio de posito et suspenso* was an action against the owner of a structure when an obstruction was suspended or otherwise placed in such a way that it injured passers-by.

3) *Iudex qui litem suam fecit* occurred when a judge rendered an incorrect decision or otherwise wrongfully damaged a litigant (*e.g.*, if the judge imposed damages outside of the scope of those provided in the praetor's formula).

4) There was also strict liability imposed on those in charge of a ship, inn, or stable for damages caused to persons or their property on the ship, at the inn, or in the stable.

§ 17.05 Chapter Summary

The civil law countries of continental Europe have adopted the Roman law classification that includes the law of obligations, roughly equivalent to what Anglo-American lawyers refer to as both contracts and torts. An *obligatio* (obligation) in Roman law created a legal relationship that made one person a debtor and the other a creditor. Justinian's *Institutes* classify obligations into four groups: two that are analogous to categories of modern contract law and two that are analogous to modern tort law.

The closest Roman law classification to what American lawyers call torts was the group called *obligationes ex delicto* (delicts). But to be more precise this group bears strong similarities to intentional torts and some crimes (theft, violent robbery, property damage, personal injury). The Romans subdivided theft (*furtum*) into *furtum manifestum* (caught in the act) and *furtum nec manifestum* (all other thefts). The Twelve Tables permitted an accuser to search an accused thief's home, looking for stolen goods (*lance et licio*). Roman jurists debated the philosophical distinctions of the requisite *actus reus* for theft, without ever reaching any definitive conclusions. Violent robbery (*rapina*) was identified as a distinct kind of theft around 76 B.C. The *lex Aquilia* of 287 B.C. contained three principal sections: 1) laws relating the killing of slaves and herd animals (only direct not indirect); 2) laws relating to debtors who defrauded their creditors; and, 3) laws relating to other general property damage (direct, negligent, intentional, burning, snapping, breaking). The laws governing personal injury (*iniuria*) awarded money damages to victims. The Twelve Tables, generally speaking, established fixed damage amounts, whereas the praetors later modified *iniuria* to provide damages on a case by case basis, including cases involving intangible injuries such as insults. Roman law also recognized delicts dealing with matters such as extortion, fraud, corruption of slaves, and injuries to agricultural property. Although a father was generally liable for damage caused by his son, a master was generally liable for damage caused by his slave, and an owner was generally liable for damage caused by his animal, the concept of noxal liability allowed that if the amount of liability exceeded the value of the son, slave, or animal, then the father, master, or owner could merely surrender the son, slave, or animal instead of paying. Generally speaking, both vicarious liability and strict liability appear to have been common features of the actions that the Romans called *obligationes quasi ex delicto*: 1) an action relating to things which have been poured out or thrown out; 2) an action relating to something that has been placed or hung out; 3) a judge who has made a case his own; and, 4) an action relating to a ship, inn, or stable.

CHAPTER 18

Trade, Contracts, and Commercial Law

§ 18.01 Introduction

All school children are familiar with the vast extent of the Roman Empire. Its size and importance are well known. Sophisticated laws of contract and commercial law were necessary for the economic growth of such an empire. Even as early as the Etruscan period in the 6th century B.C., Rome was known for its vibrant trade and commerce.

As was noted, the Roman law relating to contracts, *obligationes ex contractu*, was actually a sub-part of the Roman law of *obligationes*.[1] A contract to an ancient Roman was altogether a different notion from what it has become in Anglo-American Common Law. A Roman contract was any agreement expressed in the appropriate form (of course there also had to be some cause or purpose). In early Roman law, without the proper form, there was no contract. Unlike modern legal systems, Roman contract law was not based upon a general, abstract theory of contract. Instead, the Romans recognized a number of types of individual contracts. In order to be valid, an agreement had to be fashioned using one of these types, employing either an established pattern of words and conduct or, in the alternative, relating to a specific purpose.

Both Gaius and Justinian arranged contracts into four categories: 1) real; 2) verbal; 3) literal; and, 4) consensual. We shall examine these in a slightly different order: 1) verbal; 2) literal; 3) real; and, 4) consensual. In addition, we shall consider a fifth group that has come to be known as "innominate."

---

1. *See supra* § 17.01.

§ 18.02 Verbal Contracts

Verbal contracts existed well before the end of the *legis actio* period[2] but had long since lost their prominence by the time of Justinian (482–565 A.D.). These contracts were those executed orally. But the law strictly delineated the precise words that were required. The parties had to say a scripted formula of words in order for a verbal contract to be valid. If the parties failed to utter the proper words in the proper sequence at the proper time, the contract was void. *Stipulatio* (also known as *sponsio*) is the earliest known of the verbal contracts in Roman Law. The Twelve Tables make it clear that *stipulatio* was enforceable. *Condictio* was the name of the cause of action that a plaintiff brought for breach of *stipulatio*. Originally, only Roman citizens could conclude a contract by *stipulatio*. It became available to foreigners, however, by the Empire (27 B.C.).

Stipulatio required a very rigid verbal formula. It demanded that both promisor and promisee meet face to face to create their contract by means of an oral exchange in a prescribed formulaic pattern of question and answer. The promisee had to begin by asking the promisor a question using the Latin verb (second person singular, present active indicative) *spondesne*? (*Spondesne* to do such and such?—"Do you promise on your oath to do such and such?"). The promisor, playing his role, had to respond to the promisee's question using the same verb, but in the first person singular, present active indicative, *spondeo* (*Spondeo* to do such and such—"I promise on my oath to do such and such"). As the law evolved, other verbs were eventually accepted as valid in addition to *spondere*. But the essence remained the same; the promisor's answer to the promisee's question had to be a mirror image in order to meet the strict rules of contract by *stipulatio*. In time, a number of the formal requirements slackened. Ultimately, although this was certainly not required, it became commonplace for parties to chronicle their *stipulatio* in written form (*i.e., cautio*).

One of the truly remarkable features of *stipulatio*—at least in early Roman law—was that once made, it was virtually indestructible. To be sure, there were some circumstances that would make a purported *stipulatio* void. For example an agreement to do something that was immoral, illegal, or impossible was invalid. In addition, a *stipulatio* promising performance either by or for a third party was similarly invalid. But, otherwise, even if a promise had been coerced by fraud or threats of violence, a contract of *stipulatio* was considered iron-clad.

---

2. This period of Roman legal procedure came to a close about the end of the 3rd century B.C. *See supra* § 11.03[A].

Eventually, praetors took measures to alleviate some of these injustices during the final half-century of the Republic. For example, the praetor Octavius (80 B.C.) granted a cause of action (*metus causa*) that exacted quadruple damages to the victims of *stipulatio* by extortion. Similarly, he granted such victims a valid affirmative defense (*exceptio metus*) in cases where they were sued for breach of contract. Aquillius Gallus (66 B.C.) took corresponding steps for persons who had been lured into a *stipulatio* by fraud. He provided a cause of action (*actio de dolo*) for which he allowed compensatory damages. And, as was the case with Octavius' measures for extortion, Gallus allowed an affirmative defense for contracting parties who had entered a *stipulatio* due to fraud (*exceptio doli*).

§ 18.03 Literal Contracts

The literal contract is curious, indeed. We have a number of these contracts from the ruins of Pompeii. The Roman head of the household kept an account book. By recording transactions in this ledger, a literal contract was presumed to have been made. In several respects, the literal contract appears to have been a type of memorandum that was meant to formalize and amend an already existing debt. The detailed steps necessary for the creation of a literal contract were as follows. The *paterfamilias*, the creditor, wrote two records in his ledger: 1) He fictitiously indicated that his debtor had paid a certain debt; and, 2) He fictitiously indicated that he had made a loan to his debtor. It is possible that this was similar to our modern concept of "novation". We can only assume that the debtor agreed to the literal contract in exchange for a different interest rate or a longer period in which to repay the debt.

§ 18.04 Real Contracts

Real contracts were agreements that entailed one person (call him A) delivering a *res* (hence the appellation "*real*" from the Latin word *res*, "thing") to another (call him B). In simple terms, then, the agreement became binding when one party transferred an object to another. Basically, the agreement in each real contract was that B promised to return to A either the *res* itself or an equivalent *res*, depending upon which particular type of real contract was used. There were four kinds of real contracts: 1) *mutuum*; 2) *commodatum*; 3) *depositum*; and, 4) *pignus*.

In a contract of *mutuum*, one party gave either money or fungible goods (*i.e.*, goods that may be substituted for one another without significant impact) to another. The recipient then used the money or goods. His obligation was to return the equivalent amount of money or goods (*i.e.*, not the same exact money or goods that were loaned at the outset). *Mutuum* was a unilateral contract that bound the person who borrowed the money or goods. In short, *mutuum* was a loan of one or more fungible goods. For example, *mutuum* was convenient when grain or money was the subject *res*. The creditor did not care whether he received the exact grain or money in return. He only cared that he receive its equivalent. The creditor in a *mutuum* actually transferred ownership (*i.e.*, *dominium*) of the *res* to the debtor. Thus, many legal historians characterize *mutuum* as a loan for consumption.

Commodatum was a gratuitous loan.[3] Unlike *mutuum* the debtor did not receive actual ownership of the subject *res*. He simply was given the right to use it (*i.e.*, *usus*)[4], not to consume it. Thus, *commodatum* was similar to *mutuuum* in some respects (*i.e.*, a loan of goods) but ordinarily the borrower was obligated to return the thing, itself, not merely its equivalent, at the end of the contract. So, only *res quae usu non consumatum*[5] could be the object property of a contract of *commodatum*. In modern law, we might characterize this as a bailment for the benefit of the bailee.

Depositum differed from *commodatum* in that it was a delivery intended to benefit the depositor (bailor), not the depositee (bailee). The depositee was not permitted to use the thing deposited. He merely kept it for the depositor and returned it. *Depositum*, therefore, was a gratuitous loan for safekeeping. Again, like *commodatum*, ownership did not pass from bailor to bailee.

Pignus was a very old type of real security (a pledge).[6] In *pignus* the debtor transferred merely possession (*i.e.*, *detentio*) of the collateral to his creditor and he (*i.e.*, the debtor) retained ownership (*i.e.*, *dominium*) of it.

§ 18.05 Consensual Contracts

The Roman consensual contracts exhibit the practical common-sensical penchant of the ancient Romans. There was no specific formula required (*e.g.*, as in the case of the *stipulatio*) for these contracts, no formalities. The good faith agreement of the parties was really all that was necessary. The four consensual

---

3. It was essential that it was gratuitous or else the contract would be considered a contract for the hire of a thing (*locatio conductio rei*). *See infra* § 18.05.

4. *See supra* § 13.05.

5. *See supra* § 13.02.

6. *See infra* § 18.09.

contracts that Roman law admitted were: 1) *emptio venditio* (purchase and sale); 2) *locatio conductio* (renting and hiring); 3) *societas* (partnership); and 4) *mandatum* (mandate: grant and acceptance of a gratuitous commission). We do not know what praetor or praetors first recognized consensual contracts as valid and binding agreements. But Roman commercial law greatly benefitted from this innovation.

Emptio venditio was a contract for purchase and sale. It occurred simply when a seller transferred something to a buyer for a sum of money. The two indispensable ingredients needed for a contract of *emptio venditio* were an agreement as to the subject matter (*res*) and a stipulated price. It was routine, though not a legal requirement, for the buyer and seller either to reduce their agreement to writing or to conclude the contract in the presence of witnesses. Justinian altered the contract of *emptio venditio* in the following manner. If the parties agreed to put their contract in writing, then either party was entitled to withdraw unless the buyer had given an *arra* (deposit/earnest money). If the buyer backed out after he had given the seller an *arra*, then he forfeited it. On the other hand, if the seller was the one who withdrew, then he was obligated to give the buyer double the amount of the *arra* that had been given. This particular rule was similar to our modern liquidated damages (*i.e.,* an amount of money stipulated in a contract that a party promises to pay in the event of breach).

If the parties were mistaken about the *res*, it was possible for one of the parties legally to avoid the contract. For example, suppose a buyer agreed to buy a statue on the assumption that it was made of gold. If it turned out to be bronze, instead, the mistake was probably sufficiently significant to permit him to avoid the purchase.

The majority view (the Proculian view in this case) was that the price for *emptio venditio* had to be paid in coined money in order to be valid. The Sabinian view allowed for a contract of sale when the parties actually contemplated an exchange of goods (barter). The price had to be certain, not dependent upon future events. For example, the price could not be next week's market price. In addition, the price had to be a real price, not merely a sham amount used to mask what would have otherwise been a gift.

Locatio conductio was a contract of renting and hiring for money. The parties had to agree on both the subject matter and the price. There were three types of *locatio conductio* contracts: 1) *locatio conductio rei* (which involved the rental of a thing or land);[7] 2) *locatio operis faciendi* (which involved contracting

---

7. This could also include the hiring and rental of slaves.

for completion of a job—*i.e.,* work to be done—or the creation of a designated outcome for a fee, *e.g.,* constructing a building, washing clothes, providing medical care); 3) *locatio conductio operarum* (which was rental of services, usually relatively menial tasks that involved little, if any, independent judgment).

Societas was the Roman partnership or joint venture. And *mandatuum* was a originally any gratuitous service performed in response to another's request.[8]

§ 18.06 Innominate Contracts

There was a separate group of Roman contracts that did not fit neatly into any of these four categories. These came to be known as *innominate* (*i.e.,* without a name). Nevertheless, the law recognized that they created binding relationships (and in fact some did have names). This ultimately became a very large group. Three innominate contracts (that actually had names) are worth mentioning: 1) *permutatio* (analogous to barter); 2) *aestimatum* (analogous to a conditional sale); and, 3) *transactio* (analogous to a settlement in lieu of legal process).

§ 18.07 Contract Damages

Some Roman contracts included a *sanctio* (sanction) actually written into the text. This was generally analogous to liquidated damages in modern contract law. Similarly, it will be recalled that the consensual contract *emptio venditio* imposed a type of liquidated damages when the buyer gave a deposit (*arra*).[9] Otherwise, a *sanctio* could result from non-performance or improper performance of a contract. If the parties themselves failed to include a *sanctio,* the Roman law of contract presumed that the breaching party would compensate the injured party for two types of damages: 1) *damnum emergens* (damage suffered as a consequence of breach, *e.g.,* expenses for the decreased value of the property); and, 2) *lucrum cessans* (lost profit). A breaching party had to pay both of these types of damages. But in order to recover damages, a plaintiff was required to prove that the defendant had breached (*i.e.,* that the defendant

---

8. In later Roman law, the person who performed the service was permitted to receive compensation.

9. *See supra* § 18.05.

was guilty, *culpa*). There were different degrees of *culpa*; for example, *culpa lata* (broad guilt) and *culpa levis* (slight guilt). Even *culpa levis* made a breaching party liable for *damnum emergens*. But if a breacher was found to be *culpa lata*, he was liable for both *damnum emergens* and *lucrum cessans*.

Culpa lata was, in some respects, similar to the modern "reasonable person" standard; disregard of the vigilance which would be observed by any *paterfamilias*. *Culpa levis*, however, was analogous in many respects to a "very careful person" standard; disregard of the vigilance which would be observed by a *diligentissimus paterfamilias* (a very careful *paterfamilias*).

§ 18.08 Obligationes Quasi ex Contractu

In Roman Law quasi contract bore certain similarities to the notion of quasi contract in English and American Common Law. Although Justinian's laws discuss six different varieties, two examples should suffice to give a sense of the principles involved.

1) *Condictio indebiti per errorem soluti* was an action available when a person lost ownership of something (usually money) under conditions where the law considered that it would be unjust for him to be incapable of recovering it or its value. Essentially this happened whenever something belonging to one person passed into the hands of another in circumstances in which the latter ought not to be able to retain it. We might say that the latter had been unjustly enriched and that the former should be entitled to have the value returned to him.

2) *Negotiorum gestio* occurred when one person provided a service to another, even though the beneficiary had neither requested nor authorized the service. If performed in appropriate circumstances and in good faith, the party who conferred the benefit was entitled to reasonable compensation. A standard example of *negotiorum gestio* occurred when a landowner was absent for a period of time and his property had fallen into disrepair. In these circumstances, another person was allowed to enter and make the necessary repairs. Ordinarily, a person was legally permitted to step in and take charge of another's affairs only: 1) if the owner could not manage his own affairs—due to certain obstacles; 2) if no other person was authorized by the owner to manage his affairs; and, 3) if immediate measures were not employed, the owner would have suffered more substantial damage than he would otherwise. In such circumstances, although there was no agreement, an *obligatio quasi ex contractu* was created, and the owner was legally required to pay a reasonable fee to the person who performed the services (the *gestor*).

§ 18.09 Real Security

Very early in their history, the Romans practiced the custom of taking collateral (real security) for loans. *Fiducia* was probably the first type of real security legally recognized in ancient Rome. *Fiducia* was accomplished by an actual transfer of ownership (*dominium*). In other words, the debtor actually transferred ownership of the collateral to his creditor. *Fiducia* was doubly burdensome for a debtor since, because he no longer owned the collateral, he was unable to take out a second mortgage using the same collateral. Obviously, if the collateral were *res mancipi*, the method of transfer was *mancipatio* or *in iure cessio* (for intangible *res mancipi*).[10] For *res nec mancipi,* transfer was usually effected by *in iure cessio.*[11] This was a great deal for creditors, who could simply keep the security if the debtor failed to repay the loan. A creditor could sell the security and pass good title to it, since he was, in fact, the owner. In many instances, however, a creditor allowed his debtor to retain possession (*detentio*) of the collateral during the pendency of the *fiducia.* If, on the other hand, the creditor had possession (*detentio*) of it and refused to return it after the debtor had repaid the debt, the debtor was entitled to a legal action against the creditor, called *actio fiduciae.*

Another truly antique type of real security was *pignus.*[12] The principal distinction between *pignus* and *fiducia* is that in *pignus* the debtor transferred merely possession (*detentio*) of the collateral to his creditor; but unlike the case with *fiducia,* he (*i.e.,* the debtor) retained *dominium,* ownership of it.[13]

The third kind of real security, *hypotheca,* was common by about 150 B.C. *Hypotheca* merely created a right in the creditor to claim the collateral in the event that the debtor defaulted on his loan. Thus, the creditor did not obtain either ownership, *dominium* (as was the case with *fiducia*) or possession, *detentio* (as was the case with *pignus*) of the collateral.

§ 18.10 Business Entities

In modern law, especially with the rise of capitalism in the 19th century A.D., the recognition of legal entities, or juridical "persons" has become important. One aspect of legal entities that is crucial is the fictitious separation

---

10. *See supra* §§ 13.04[A] and 13.04[C].
11. *See supra* § 13.04[C].
12. *See supra* § 18.04.
13. *See supra* § 13.03.

of the entity from the individuals involved in it (*e.g.,* the insulation from liability for capital investors). This separation was actually an ancient Roman concept. In Roman law, there were a number of recognized legal entities. Technically speaking, at least four types of things were characterized as separate legal entities in Roman law: 1) the property of the Roman State (or the *Populus Romanus*); 2) the *Fiscus* (treasury); 3) *municipii* (local governments); and, 4) a *societas* (an entity that arose when two or more people combined their efforts into a joint enterprise, such as building a ship to transport goods).[14] The notion of the separation of corporate responsibility from personal responsibility evolved in dealing with the *societas.*

§ 18.12 Taxes

Romans paid taxes on such diverse things as the sale of slaves, prostitution, urine (gathered from public toilets), importation of goods, and inheritance. Augustus (27 B.C.–14 A.D.) was responsible for a 5% estate tax (with exceptions only for very small estates and only for very close relatives who were heirs). The *siliquae* was a tax on the sale of goods. In order to fund the Roman army, the middle class paid high taxes. By the latter part of the 2nd century A.D., the tax burden had become extreme.

§ 18.13 Chapter Summary

The robust nature of Rome's economic growth influenced development of contract and commercial law. Roman contract law (a sub-part of the law of obligations) did not ripen into a general theory of contract but rather developed as a number of discrete types of individual contracts; each requiring for validity either specific language coupled with specific conduct or a relationship to a specific purpose. Roman contracts may be categorized into five basic types: 1) real; 2) verbal; 3) literal; 4) consensual; and, 5) "innominate".

Verbal contracts, the oldest recognized Roman contracts, required that the promisor and promisee say aloud a scripted formula of words. The earliest verbal contract was the *stipulatio* (also known as *sponsio*) in which the promisee asked the promisor to make his promise using the Latin verb, *Spondesne?* And the promisor responded by making that exact promise, *Spondeo.* Because ob-

---

14. *See supra* § 18.05.

ligations created by contracts formed by *stipulatio* were originally considered unshakable, praetors inevitably excused and provided redress for parties who had entered into such contracts due to extortion or fraud.

The head of a Roman household created a **literal** contract when he recorded a particular kind of memorandum in his ledger.

Several types of **real** contracts could be created when one party delivered an object (usually personal property) to another. Roman law had four of these real contracts, which required the transferee later to return either the thing delivered or its equivalent: 1) *mutuum* (a loan of fungibles); 2) *commodatum* (a temporary loan permitting the bailee merely to use the object); 3) *depositum* (a temporary loan for safekeeping); and, 4) *pignus* (a delivery of collateral as security for a debt).

The law, thanks no doubt to praetors' innovations, permitted four kinds of **consensual** contracts (*i.e.*, contracts that demanded no formalities but merely the good faith agreement of the parties): 1) *emptio venditio* (purchase and sale); 2) *locatio conductio* (renting and hiring); 3) *societas* (partnership); and, 4) *mandatum* (a grant and acceptance of a gratuitous commission).

Among the most important of the **innominate**, or miscellaneous, contracts were *permutatio* (barter), *aestimatum* (conditional sale), and *transactio* (settlement).

Occasionally parties to a written contract included a provision (*sanctio*) stipulating liquidated damages, but if they did not, in the event of breach, the breaching party was ordinarily liable for damage suffered as a consequence of the breach (*damnum emergens*) and/or lost profit (*lucrum cessans*).

The law of *obligationes quasi ex contractu* imposed an obligation to pay for a benefit conferred (*e.g.*, services rendered) or to return money or property in circumstances where the beneficiary would be unjustly enriched if he were permitted to retain the money, property, or benefit without payment.

There were several variations of contractual real security. The contract known as *fiducia* allowed a debtor to transfer ownership (*dominium*) of a collateral to his creditor. But the law also permitted a debtor, through a contract called *pignus*, to transfer merely possession (*detentio*) not ownership of a collateral to his creditor. Beginning about 150 B.C., a third type of real security, *hypotheca*, granted a creditor the right to seize the collateral in the event that the debtor defaulted.

There were at least four legal/business entities recognized: 1) *Populus Romanus* (any property of the Roman State); 2) *fiscus* (treasury); 3) *municipii* (local governments); and, 4) *societas* (partnership/joint venture). The State assessed taxes on the sale of goods, slaves, prostitution, imports, and inheritance.

Law in Literature:
A Unique Combination of Both Greek & Roman Elements of Law: Terence's *Phormio*

Introduction

In addition to side-splitting comedy, Roman playwrights incorporated political commentary, social allegory, and social criticism, into their plays. Terence is certainly no exception. In the *Phormio* Terence used his knowledge of Roman slave law, marriage and family law, contracts and commercial law, and the Roman law of procedure to poke fun at law and the legal profession.

The *Phormio* is based on a Greek play, *The Claimant*, written by the Athenian Apollodorus. Of that play virtually nothing is known, but we can be fairly certain its plot and that of *Phormio* are essentially the same.

I. Plot Summary

A thorough understanding of the complex plot of the *Phormio* can cause even the most savvy of observers to suffer headaches. Much of the key plot points have already taken place before the live action of the play begins.

The two main characters are Demipho and Chremes, wealthy Athenian brothers. The latter, unbeknownst to all except his brother, has had a long term affair (also referred to as a "marriage") on the island of Lemnos, which has produced a daughter. Chremes has been able to conceal this marriage because he routinely traveled to Lemnos on business.

On one fateful voyage, Chremes was traveling to Lemnos at the same time that his daughter, Phanium, was traveling to Athens with her sick mother and her nurse in search of her father. When they arrive in Athens, Phanium's mother dies. Chremes' nephew, Antipho (Demipho's son), passes Phanium, who is in mourning, develops a swooning crush on her, and wishes to marry her. Ordinarily a Greek marriage requires a father's permission, and the father is, of course, out of town. Phormio, the play's protagonist and namesake, suggests to them that they go to the courts and claim that Phanium is an *epikleros*. As an *epikleros*, through the legal doctrine of *epidikasia*, Phanium would be required to marry her nearest male relative. Phormio suggests that they couple "pretend" that Antipho is her closest male relative and thus they will be required to marry, and that's exactly what they do.

In the meantime Phaedria, Chremes' legitimate son, has fallen in love with a slave girl. He wishes to purchase her from the slave dealer, Dorio, but he does not have enough money. All of this has occurred before the opening curtain. The action actually begins on the day that both Chremes and Demipho return to Athens from separate voyages.

Demipho learns of his son's marriage and threatens to annul it. He demands to know how the marriage is legal and by whom the two are related. The newlyweds enlist the help of Phormio again and he concocts a scheme to save the marriage. He tells Demipho that the relative's name is "Stilpo," which happens (by luck or otherwise) to be the pseudonym that Chremes used on Lemnos. Demipho is still outraged and offers Phormio money to marry the girl himself after Demipho gets the marriage annulled. He responds that Demipho really does not have standing to contest the marriage since the court was not dealing with him, but rather with his son, when it ordered the marriage.

Meanwhile, Phaedria argues with the slave-dealer, Dorio, about the contract for his slave-girl love interest. Eventually they agree to a unilateral contract, whereby the first person to pay the slave-dealer, as between Phaedria and another "customer" of the slave-dealer, will get her.

Phormio, after learning of the dire nature of Chremes' situation (*i.e.*, he may have to reveal to the world his affair on Lemnos in order to get his daughter's marriage annulled) offers to marry her himself, as Demipho had offered, but for a large sum of money (3,000 drachmas). This is precisely (not coincidentally) the amount of money needed by Phaedria to marry the slave-girl. Phormio did not actually intend to marry the girl but made this promise to secure the money for Phaedria. Eventually Chremes becomes aware of what has happened; that his daughter has married Antipho, his nephew, which is what he wanted all along. Chremes learns this secret far too late, however, because by then Phormio has already been paid his 3,000 drachmas.

Demipho's slave informs Phormio of the situation, and Phormio designs a plan to keep his 3,000 drachmas. Phormio plans to claim that he must keep the 3,000 drachmas as compensation for the loss of a previous engagement. In truth, of course, he intends to give Dorio the money to pay for Phaedria's love interest. When Demipho and Chremes confront him about the money in the last scene of the play, by shear luck Chremes' Athenian wife, Nausistrata, appears and Phormio tells her all about her husband's bigamy. She is enraged and, essentially, "hires" Phormio to help her deal with her husband's treachery.

II. Legal Procedure

A. Overview

Phormio gives modern audiences a glimpse into Ancient Greek and Roman legal procedure. Through a careful reading of the play, it is possible to hypothethesize which aspects of the play are based on Greek law and which are based in Roman law. Additionally, *Phormio* gives modern audiences an idea of Roman and Athenian views on lawyers and the law as a tool in their day-to-day lives.

B. Greek and Roman Legal Procedure Generally

Differences between Greek and Roman legal procedure are especially evident in *Phormio* when one character threatens another with a lawsuit. An example of this is Phormio's threat to sue Demipho and Chremes on Phanium's behalf should they throw her out of Demipho's home. Phormio's threat is a product of Greek law since Roman law generally did not permit one person to bring a lawsuit on behalf of a third party. Under Solon, by a procedure which later was known as *graphe*, individuals were allowed to bring lawsuits on behalf of a third party, allowing private parties greater access to the law. The ancient Athenian courts, however did not permit the use of advocates during a trial. Advocates wrote speeches for claimants but parties were expected to argue on their own behalf. In this way, those scholars who have asserted that Phormio is a lawyer may be right, in the Greek sense, given that he advises many other characters regarding their legal rights.

C. Manipulation of the Law

In addition to serving as a window into Greek and Roman law, the *Phormio* also offers modern audiences a glimpse of how citizens perceived the role of the law in their lives. The *Phormio*'s characters manipulate the law to achieve personal gain. Antipho's marriage to Phanium, the main conflict of the play, is achieved through manipulation of the law. Phormio convinces Antipho to allow him to argue, in court, that Antipho must be allowed to marry Phanium without his father's blessing, generally a requirement in Athenian law, because Phanium is an *epikleros*. Similarly, throughout the play, various characters threaten to use the law for personal advantage. Phormio, Demipho and Chremes all threaten others with lawsuits in an attempt to get what they want, seemingly regardless of whether their claim has any real merit or basis in law.

Characters also blame the law for their own indiscretions. For example, the slave Geta advises Antipho to tell his father that the law forced him to marry Phanium. Characters use the law as an excuse so frequently that Antipho's father, Demipho, is able to guess his son's alibi: "Perhaps he'll say, 'I didn't want to do it' The law compelled me." The frequency with which characters manipulate law illustrates the Athenians' excessive use of the courts, and their willingness to use the courts on their own. The actual lawyers in the play give no useful counsel whatsoever.

III. Slave Law

In the play male slaves have greater freedom than female slaves. One example of this is the way that Dorio and Phaedria discuss Pamphila. Throughout the negotiations for her sale, she is referred to as an item to the transaction. Additionally, when Dorio is renegotiating his deal with Phaedria, there is never any consideration of her feelings or autonomy.

Under Athenian law, slaves had no rights whatsoever. They could not own property and they were not permitted to sue in Athenian courts. Athenian slaves did manage to work outside of their masters' households, but in those situations the law required that they give a percentage of their earnings to the masters. Similar to Athenian law, Roman law treated slaves as property. In both Rome and Athens masters were allowed to beat their slaves.

Roman slaves were allowed to hold positions with a certain amount of responsibility. Many Roman slaves were given these types of positions, and such a slave had the right to act on behalf of his master (similar to agency law today). In exchange many received a stipend or property. Thus one way in which Roman law differed from Athenian law was that Roman slaves were treated with more dignity than Greek slaves.

The play suggests that there were probably limitations to a slave's authority in conducting business on behalf of his master. The slave Geta presents Phormio's idea to marry Phanium in exchange for 3,000 drachmas, to Demipho. As a result, Demipho challenges Geta's authority to say such a thing.

Athenian law permitted owners to free slaves through a rather informal process. This could have allowed Phaedria to free Pamphila once he purchased her from Dorio. However, an Athenian citizen could not marry a slave. Roman law required that both husband and wife be Roman citizens, or that one had to be a citizen of a state that had a right of intermarriage with Rome.

IV. Family Law

A. *Family Law Generally*

The *Phormio* contains many references to Athenian marriage laws but at the same time mocks Roman sensibilities to humor the Roman audience. Much of the play is based on the Greek marriage law of *epidikasia*, a law that required an orphaned female with no brothers to marry her nearest male relative. The theory that animates *epidikasia* lies in the importance of having a male heir. The Greeks believed that male heirs to continue a family line were so important that, if a man died with no male heir, his daughter should marry a relative and try to produce a male child. The *epikleros* was so important that the nearest male relative could force the female orphan to divorce her husband in the name of marrying him. And under Solon's laws the *epikleros'* husband was required to have sexual intercourse with her at least three times a month to increases the chances of eventually producing a male heir.

The *Phormio* contrasts this strict policy with the complete lack of respect that the sons pay their fathers in the play. In Roman law the father was the *paterfamilias*, the head of the household who held each family member's life in his hands. The *paterfamilias* gave permission for a family member to have any kind of legal relationship, had to give his blessing for a child to get married and, before Antoninus Pius (Emperor 138–161 A.D.) changed the law, could even break up a son's marriage without the son's permission. The characters' actions in the *Phormio* completely differ from those expected of Roman children towards their *paterfamilias*. In the *Phormio*, Antipho marries Phanium and Phaedria contracts to buy a wife from Dorio, each knowing full well that his father will disapprove. Terrence's Roman audience certainly would have laughed at these children contracting and marrying, and, in fact, disregarding the authority of their fathers entirely. And even when Chremes and Demipho do react to their children's disobedience and attempt to put things right, they fail miserably. Demipho tries to annul his son's marriage and is told that he lacks the power to do so. While this may have been the case in Athenian *epidikasia* law, in Roman law it is likely that he could have cancelled the marriage. When Chremes and Demipho try to stop payment for Phormio to marry Phanium, they look all the more like foolish old men. Phormio takes advantage of them with a complete and utter lack of respect.

B. Epikleros *and Questions of Athenian Law*

The *Phormio* exemplifies the importance of the *epikleros* in Greek society, but apparently, they play misinterprets the law. In order for a woman to be an *epikleros*, she must be an orphan. Although Antipho and Phormio lie and claim that Phanium is an *epikleros*, Chremes certainly knows that he is alive. Thus, Chremes, who works throughout the play to try to get his illegitimate daughter married, should know that Phanium is no *epikleros* at all. Further, Chremes has a male heir, Phaedria. So even if he did die he would have a male heir. Thus, there is no possible way, technically speaking, that Phanium could be an *epikleros*. Why then would Chremes try to marry Phanium to Antipho? Perhaps because Chremes was, rightfully we find out later, fearful that his wife would find out about his illegitimate affair, and that's why he was trying to claim that Phanium's "father" had died. Still, neither the characters in the play nor subsequent commentators have discussed this misreading. Perhaps the whole of the *Phormio* merely mocks the institution of marriage. Despite the sometimes complicated marriage laws of Athens and Rome, ultimately the play involves a bigamist father and two sons very much willing literally to beg, buy, or steal a wife. Lastly, the play illustrates the realities of many typical marriages. Nausistrata berates and embarrasses her husband; perhaps making a point to highlight some of the more unfortunate aspects of marriage and marital relations.

V. Contracts & Commercial Law

There are two very important contracts in the play. The first is the contract between Dorio and Phaedria for the sale of Pamphila. The other is the agreement that Chremes and Demipho make with Phormio whereby Phormio promises to marry Phanium. Although the two contracts are different, we learn as the play progresses that they are intertwined.

Initially when Dorio had agreed to sell Pamphila to Phaedria, they had set a date for the sale to occur. Dorio breaks his agreement and contracts instead to sell Pamphila to another person, a captain, even though the date agreed-upon for the sale to Phaedria has not yet passed. Phaedria then succeeds in negotiating another deal with Dorio whereby Dorio agrees again to sell Pamphila to Phaedria, provided that he brings 3,000 drachmas to him before the captain.

Even though there is technically an agreement in place between Dorio and Phaedria, there is at the same time, realistically speaking, no agreement at all. Dorio guarantees nothing to Phaedria. Dorio only looks out for himself. Dorio does not feel constrained by the law. Although Dorio had promised to sell Pamphila to Phaedria, he, nevertheless, does not hesitate to breach when the captain is willing pay first. Dorio's principal concern is to get money for the sale of Pamphila as soon as possible.

To advance his position, Dorio treats all of his contracts with buyers as unilateral contracts, whereby the only valid means of acceptance is by actual payment. There is no discussion in the play as to individual rights when a seller breaches a contract.

This could be a comedic commentary on the attitude of slave traders in the ancient world. Average citizens probably believed that slave dealers were simply out to make a profit with few ethical limitations. Slave traders were probably viewed in a light similar to modern-day used car salesmen.

That the other would-be purchaser, the captain, could arrive at any moment and buy Pamphila adds a sense of urgency to the plot. This sense of urgency intersects with the other principal contract in the play. Chremes and Demipho have agreed to give Phormio 3,000 drachmas to marry Phanium. Phormio plans to give the 3,000 drachmas to Phaedria to buy Pamphila. Thus, Phormio has to act fast in convincing Chremes and Demipho that his deal is a good idea, and that they should transfer the 3,000 drachmas to him as soon as possible.

The contract between Chremes, Demipho and Phormio for the 3,000 drachmas is structured in such a way that Phormio is paid first, and then later he is to perform his end of the bargain. Curiously, however, Phormio's feigned willingness to marry Phanium would not solve the problem. The marriage between Antipho and Phanium first would need to be annulled.

Of course when Chremes and Demipho learn that Antipho has in fact married Phanium, they try to call off the deal. At this point in the play, Phormio relies on his smooth talking to argue that he should be allowed to keep the 3,000 drachmas. Phormio uses various arguments to try to convince Chremes and Demipho that he is entitled to keep the money. His reasoning strikes modern day lawyers as being based on theories of liquidated damages, reliance damages, or consequential damages. For example, he argues that he has relied on their agreement in calling off a marriage with another girl that he alleges he had promised to marry.

Conclusion

Terence's *Phormio* illustrates a variety of principles of Roman and Athenian slave, marriage and family, contract, and procedural law, intertwined in a humorously constructed plot line. Many readers will, correctly or otherwise, associate the scheming and backhandedness of Phormio with the modern lawyer, or at least with the caricature of the modern lawyer that has been developed over the years through a combination of various negative stereotypes. However, despite what Terence may or may not have believed about lawyers, Phormio's scheming did not prevent the eventual outcome of the play. Phaedria and Antipho each won their love interests and Chremes was punished for his adultery. Indeed, justice prevailed. Of course, since this is after all a comedy, perhaps justice prevailed *in spite of* Phormio's questionable and deceptive antics.

INDEX